P9-DYO-449

Planting *the* *Landscape*

Planting the Landscape

A PROFESSIONAL APPROACH TO GARDEN DESIGN

Nancy A. Leszczynski

JOHN WILEY & SONS, INC.

New York • Chichester • Weinheim • Brisbane • Singapore • Toronto

Library of Congress Cataloging-in-Publication Data:

Leszczynski, Nancy A.
    Planting the Landscape / Nancy A. Leszczynski
       p.   cm.
    Includes bibliographical references and index.
    ISBN 0-471-29215-X
    1. Planting design.   I. Title
SB472.L47   1997   97-17966
712'.2—dc21

Printed in the United States of America.

10 9 8 7 6 5 4 3 2 1

This is dedicated to the ones I love.

Contents

Preface vii

Introduction xi

CHAPTER 1 *Examination of Historical Precedent 1*

CHAPTER 2 *Analyzing the Environment 41*

CHAPTER 3 *Exploring Design Ideas 55*

CHAPTER 4 *Creating a Design Vocabulary:
Elements of the Garden 81*

CHAPTER 5 *Composing the Planting Design 111*

CHAPTER 6 *Developing a Plant Palette 141*

CHAPTER 7 *Planting the Garden 171*

CHAPTER 8 *Maintaining the Garden 181*

Glossary 189

Bibliography 193

Index 197

Preface

My experience, both in designing gardens and teaching students, has taught me the importance of the art and science of planting design. When I was an undergraduate student studying at a large midwestern agricultural university, I loved to talk to my professors about the beauty of a calla lily or the form of a redbud tree. One day a professor said to me, "Leszczynski, are you here for the art or for the science?" I knew the "correct" answer was science—after all, I was going to receive a bachelor of science degree. But instead I answered, "I would like to think I could be here for both." "Preposterous!" he exclaimed. "Horticulture is a science."

Years later, when I returned to school to study landscape architecture, I hoped to combine the art and science of plants in design. As I entered my second year of study, a professor tried to encourage me by saying, "Nancy, your work is improving and we [the faculty] finally got you to quit talking about plants." "Just for now," I thought secretly.

In 1994 I began to teach two courses at the University of California at Berkeley: Planting Design and Plant Identification. I tried to inspire my students to not just "round up the usual suspects" when designing with plants but to expand their concept of plants as key design elements. I searched for a text that combined design principles with horticultural practicalities and found none. This book, *Planting the Landscape,* is a result of my effort to bridge that educational gap, not just at the university level but in the professional realm as well.

Anne Spirn, a landscape architect at the University of Pennsylvania, accurately describes the challenge facing the landscape profession:

> The fundamental challenges of the discipline of landscape architecture are the complexity of the medium itself and the fact of its abiding change. The landscape is at once a natural phenomenon and a cultural artifact, a dynamic entity shaped by the processes of both nature and culture. The landscape is composed of air, earth, water, and living organisms (and recently of plastic, glass, and metal as well). Some of these elements are invisible or ephemeral; most are dynamic and interacting. Plants grow, reproduce, and shape the landscape over time, as do people and other animals who inhabit the landscape.[1]

The ephemeral nature of plants is only one of the reasons for the lack of proficiency in planting design. There are numerous others. Many landscape architecture programs, graduate and undergraduate, across the country no longer teach planting design. It is possible at some universities for a graduate student to obtain a master of landscape architecture degree without learning the name of one plant. Because of the complexities of planting design, it is often poorly executed in design offices. Practical knowledge of plants and their use in the landscape is a weakness for many professional landscape architects. Today, many landscape architects work on large, multidisciplinary projects located all over the country or world that afford them little time to concentrate on planting design. The role of plant selection is often delegated to horticultural consultants, specialists in the growing of plants, who lack design expertise. In addition, the nursery industry makes decisions about what to grow, responding to a low level of taste and horticultural interest. "Safe" plant choices are made on projects, creating mediocre, mundane, or repetitive landscapes. In addition, many landscape architects reject residential work as too insignificant or not profitable enough and favor larger, more commercial projects with ample design fees. They miss an opportunity to experiment with plants in design and affect change at a grassroots level. Residential work is a lab for planting creativity and experimentation. As a result, less work has been done to push the envelope in planting design.

This book is written for students, professionals, and gardeners interested in learning to design with plants. Its purpose is to present design principles applied to plant composition in combination with sound environmental practices. The method it presents provides a tangible starting place in a step-by-step format. In the process, special emphasis is placed on historic precedent as a source of inspiration and information. Historic precedence introduces the designer to a vocabulary of garden elements that is invaluable for becoming an adept plantsperson. Though older generations of landscape architects remain cognizant of these terms and history, they are often misused or unused by today's students.

In addition, I think it is essential to include planting and maintenance as key elements of the planting design process. An awareness of some of the issues that develop during installation and maintenance will enable the reader to become a better designer.

Throughout the book I use the terms *landscape* and *garden* both. I employ the term *garden* in a broad sense: to quote the landscape scholar John Beardsley, "in the most humble and most exalted of senses: to refer to the patch of earth from which we coax our food and to our prevailing metaphor for paradise."[2] I apply the term *landscape* to the great outdoors in all its splendor and majesty. *Landscape architect* and *designer* are used interchangeably in the text.

I wish to acknowledge the work of Florence Bell Robinson in her book *Planting Design*. It is a valuable resource and serves as a constant source of inspiration in both teaching and writing. Her concise approach to the subject, her knowledge of color theory, and her sketch problems illuminated my path.

I want to thank the Department of Landscape Architecture at the University of California at Berkeley for the opportunity to teach and for their enduring support of this project. A special thankyou to my mother and father, Arcadia, Melanie Austin, Russ Beatty, Carol Bornstein, Winn Ellis and David Mahoney, Dr. and Mrs. John Ewell, Terry Gamble, Ray and Barbara Graham, Barbara Giuffreda, Lawrence Halprin, Peggy

Knickerbocker, Sarah Kuehl, George Laskowicz, Dennis Leszczynski, Robyn Menigoz, Kirsten Miller, Marjorie Newman, Jenny Stein, Marc Treib, Leo Wong, and my editors, Jane Degenhardt, Carla Nessler, Beth Harrison, Madeline Gutin Perri, and the teams at Van Nostrand Reinhold and John Wiley & Sons, Inc. More specifically, I wish to thank my colleague and dear friend Chip Sullivan for reviewing the text and whose drawings, encouragement, help, and advice have been invaluable. I am also grateful to Michael Laurie for his wisdom and support. I am deeply indebted to Jeff Charlesworth for reviewing the text and for his constant encouragement and intelligent suggestions. I am tremendously grateful for being able to work with Laura Weatherall, whose beautiful drawings are such an asset to the text. Lastly, to the one person whose love, patience, and faith in me were unfailing, my husband, Charles Ewell.

ENDNOTES

1. Anne Spirn, Martha Schwartz and Diane Balmori, "Perspectives," *Progressive Architecture* (August 1991), 92.

2. John Beardsley, *Gardens of Revelation* (New York: Abbeville Press, 1995), 8.

Introduction

A landscape is the state of the soul!

Aristotle

Planting design is a process, an art, and a science. In order for it to achieve the distinction of fine art the principles of design must be combined with the rigors of science. The process is one of planning before planting; the two go hand in hand and cannot be separated. It requires skill, vision, and patience. When planning a garden as a landscape architect, horticulturist, or landscape designer, the use of a systematic procedure brings ideas to reality. One should become familiar with this procedure in order to work with plants as a limitless design resource.

Planting design entails devising a concept in the abstract and combining this abstraction with the environmental demands of the site to produce a planting plan that is beautiful, functional, and appropriate. But the work does not stop there. Good design must be followed by proper installation and quality maintenance.

(photo on previous page)
Almond orchard

How can such a task be accomplished? The principle aim of this book is to establish a step-by-step process of planting design. Aspects of this process can be utilized in the overall design of a garden as well; however, garden design envelops more concepts of spatial design, manipulation of landform, and hardscape construction. This book clarifies the design process, focuses on design techniques, and applies them to designing with plants. This process builds a good foundation from which you can eventually improvise.

THE PLANTING DESIGN PROCESS

The planting design process is divided into the following eight steps:

1. *Examination of Historical Precedent:* Examining gardens from earlier times and other places allows us to understand the evolution of specific design forms, to learn the names and origins of plants, and to comprehend their adaptations to other environments.

2. *Analyzing the Environment:* This aspect of the design process, done in conjunction with the design exploration, is the analysis of the environmental relationships of plants. An *environmental relationship* is a plant's natural affinities that evolve from interaction with the physical characteristics of the site—light, soil, moisture, and wind.

3. *Exploring Design Ideas:* The exploration consists of three aspects of landscape design that influence the form of the plan:
   - *Design Concept* is the idea that inspires the form of the garden.
   - *Design Program* is the different ways the garden can be used.
   - *Design Analysis* is the study of the opportunities and constraints of the site as they affect the design concept and program.

4. *Creating a Design Vocabulary:* In this step of the design process physical, three-dimensional form is given to our design concepts by introducing garden elements into the design.

5. *Composing the Planting Design:* A thorough command of composition is necessary to combine abstract concepts of design with the horticultural requirements of plants.

6. *Developing a Plant Palette:* A landscape architect chooses a range of plants to create a landscape in the same way that an artist creates a range of colors to use in a painting. This process is called developing a plant palette.

7. *Planting the Garden:* Planting a garden brings the design into reality. It is the rewarding culmination of all the prior stages of the design process.

8. *Maintaining the Garden:* The final step in the planting design process is to ensure proper maintenance of the new garden. Maintenance is the key to the success of any planting design.

Each of these steps is addressed in a separate chapter of this book.

Plants are fun! They are fascinating gifts from nature to enjoy. Their artistic combinations are endless; they provide amusement, solace, and wonder for everyone. For me, planting design is an outward expression of an inner love of plants. As planting designers you must acquire vision, patience, and skill as you learn to read the landscape in all its myriad forms to create meaningful and lasting environments.

Examination of Historical Precedent

Just outside the entrance to the courtyard, surrounded

by a wall, lies a large orchard of four acres—pears and

pomegranates, apple trees with glossy fruit, sweet figs

and luxuriant olives.

HOMER, *The Odyssey*[1]

Thus we are not the slaves of history but its heir. History

is the body of tradition from which we start. The purpose

of creative design in any field is to continue the life and

vitality of the tradition by developing it and expanding it.

GARRETT ECKBO, *Landscape for Living*[2]

Historic precedence is a significant aspect of planting design. Landscape architectural history is a design tool and many landscape designers look to the past in order to understand how to proceed in the present. The landscape represents a culture's relationship to nature, whether embodied in an orchard or an elaborate *parterre.* Garden design concepts evolved from history and the use of plants influenced developments in design. The history of plant introductions parallels the evolution of garden styles. Understanding plant origins is beneficial when creating a planting design because it enables you to consider how plants reinforce cultural design philosophies and to use plants in a meaningful way with appropriate climatic associations.

Typical modes of design characterize different cultures. These motifs develop over time into categories of style. A garden is often described as "in the Renaissance style" or "Japanese in style." Style is the design philosophy of a culture manifested in physical form. The landscape architect Sylvia Crowe explains the term *style* in her book *Garden Design* as "the moment in history when the spirit of a nation is translated into a garden, a new and distinct garden style is born—a style which will be the perfect expression of its own place and age and which will never again be seen at its best in other lands or future times."[3]

Garden forms evolved as cultures evolved. They were often the result of a combination of three cultural factors:

1. *Physical environment:* the topography, climate, vegetation, and materials of construction.

2. *People:* the designer, client, and craftspeople who combined traditions, training, and social conditions of specific nationalities.

3. *Function:* the purpose for which the gardens were made, such as fruit and flower production, pleasure, or a sanctuary from the outside world.[4]

By examining historical plant uses, you become aware of a vocabulary of planting design elements and develop an understanding of a plant's cultural requirements. (Design vocabulary is explained in detail in Chapter 4.) Design terminology—*allée, courtyard, palisade*—is a result of cultural adaptations of form. Plant cultivation reflects cultural and climatic requirements varying from the date palms of Ancient Egypt to the linden trees of central Europe. In planting design, art creates form and the environment gives life to the form.

REFLECTIONS OF A CULTURE

Gardens mean something different to every culture. "The creation of gardens is determined by intellectual, social, economical, political, and artistic forces, which in their turn are mirrored in gardens."[5] These words, written by garden historian John Dixon Hunt, express the diverse forces that affect the design of gardens. By briefly examining historic design concepts, forms, and the plants utilized to enhance them, you can begin to use plants as a design tool. The following discussion of historic cultures is accompanied by a brief description of their design philosophy, the vocabulary (noted in italics) that developed as a result of this philosophy, and, lastly, a list of significant plants.

The Ancient Egyptians had one of the earliest gardening cultures. Their country was protected by formidable desert barriers and confined to a narrow river valley. In an almost rainless country, the annual flooding of the Nile River provided the renewal of life with each deluge. This benign flooding produced two Egyptian characteristics. First, it influenced architecture by leading to an early mastery of geometry and development of an affinity for right angles. The Nile represented a great axis running north and south along the valley with Egyptian settlements organized at right angles to the river. Consequently, orthogonal planning came naturally to the Egyptians. Mirroring this narrow stretch of land, the Ancient Egyptian concept of design was a series of linear episodes along a predetermined path.

Second, the certainty of the yearly flood gave the Egyptians a sense of stability and permanence, perhaps suggesting that life after death would continue in the same way. This belief necessitated the creation of elaborate tombs. Because of the Egyptian obsession with immortality and the hereafter, life was recreated in their tombs and in funerary art. In death one was surrounded by images necessary for an abundant afterlife. According to the architectural historian Spiro Kostoff, "One's tomb was like one's house, but built to last for eternity."[6] The preservation of tomb architecture provides much of what is known today about Ancient Egyptian attitudes toward gardens and plants.

The Egyptian garden was primarily a refuge from the harsh, searing heat and winds of the desert. It provided people with shade trees, cool water channels, and fruit to refresh and restore the spirit. Figure 1–1 is an axonometric drawing of a garden from a tomb painting. The design is organized around a main axis upon which garden elements are symmetrically arranged. This reflects the Egyptian sense of order. Landscape forms—allées of trees, vine-covered trellises, and pools are repeated on each side of the garden. Walls enclose the garden to protect it from hot, dry winds, trees provide shade or fruit, and water irrigates the whole.

1-1 *Egyptian garden; axonometric interpretation of a tomb painting from the court of Amenhotep III. (Rosellini, Monument dell' Egitto, II, plate 69. Perrot and Chipiez History of Art, II, 31.)*

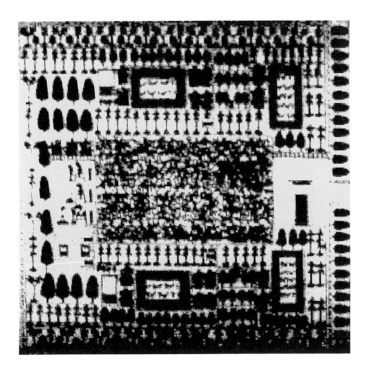

Specific plants possess both a utilitarian and symbolic purpose in Egyptian culture. The date palm, *Phoenix dactylifera,* supplies food and is a symbol of fertility. Papyrus plants, *Cyperus papyrus,* symbolize the resurrection; its form appears in numerous architectural motifs (Figure 1–2). Pomegranates, *Punica granatum,* were a symbol of fertility. Fig trees, *Ficus carica,* carob, *Ceratonia siliqua,* the horseradish tree, *Moringa aptera* syn. *M. peregina,* and grapes supplied essential fruits as well as shade. Although Egypt is not rich in native flowers, field poppies, *Paparer rhoes,* opium poppies, *P. somniferum,* and the blue annual cornflower, *Centaurea depressa,* were grown.[7]

The following list contains plants thought to be commonly used in Egyptian gardens:

Botanical Name	Common Name
Chamaerops humilis	palmetto
Cyperus papyrus	papyrus
Ficus sycamorus	sycamore fig
Nymphaea caerulea	lotus
Phoenix dactylifera	date palm
Punica granatum	pomegranate

ANCIENT GREEK GARDENS (480–146 BC)

Many original aspects of Western culture, history, and design are derived from the civilizations of ancient Greece and Rome. Through the heritage of the ancient world it is possible to follow the connecting thread of a large part of our own mentality, sentiments, and design concepts. Aspects of ancient history are part of our lives. The Greeks were pioneers in the fields of philosophy, drama, town planning, painting, sculpture, and architecture. They influenced our spiritual life through plays and poems on human morality, inspired forms of our entertainment from theater performances to the Olympic games, and laid the foundation for later political achievements in our governmental processes.

1-3 *(left) A Greek temple at Adelphi. (PHOTO: GEORGE LASKOWICZ)*

1-4 *(right) Corinthian column at the site of Corinth. (PHOTO: GEORGE LASKOWICZ)*

The Greeks lived in a world of tension and violence; their consequent search for reason and order explains their immense and varied output. The central principle of the Greek classical ideal was that existence could be ordered and controlled. This meant that human ability could triumph over the apparent chaos of the natural world and create a balanced society. The Ancient Greek spiritual doctrine combined belief in the gods with belief in the individual and in human potential.[8] They felt that people were the symbol and measure of harmony and order reconciling two opposite tendencies of nature—namely, imagination and spontaneity versus rationality and order. These founding principles dominated both the philosophical and physical life of the ancient world for centuries.

Imagination and mathematical order permeated Ancient Greek architecture and site planning. The Greeks possessed a tremendous empathy for their natural land form, enabling them to merge nature and geometry. The siting of their cities on hilltops, *acropolis,* not only glorified the gods but also honored human achievement. Temples were sensitively situated with awe-inspiring, panoramic views that "seem to draw down and establish upon the earth the eternal rhythms of the heavens"[9] (Figure 1–3). Theaters nestled artfully into hillsides exemplified their builders' skill at manipulating topography. The distant landscape became an integral part of the theater scene because it freed the imagination to be transported beyond the visible picture into a landscape of one's making.[10] By contrast, the design and execution of the classical orders of architecture exhibited the highest possible tribute of their search for order.

For the Ancient Greeks, plants personified mystery and imagination, playing an important role in architecture, landscape, and myths. Trees and flowers were incorporated as architectural elements in Greek architecture and decorative arts. According to the Roman architect Vitruvius (late first century BC–early first century AD), the architectural motif of acanthus leaves, *Acanthus spinosa,* on the capitals of Corinthian columns was created when a fifth-century Greek sculptor, Callimachus, adapted the leaf design after seeing it growing on a Corinthian girl's grave.[11] Fig.1–4 shows a temple at the site of Corinth which displays the acanthus leave motif.

"Trees have always been regarded as the first temples of the gods and *sacred groves* as their first place of worship."[12] The plane or sycamore tree, *Platanus orientalis,* was thought

1-5 *A sculpture of the Greek myth of Apollo and Daphine illustrates Daphne turning into a laurel tree. Sculpture by G. Bernini.* (PHOTO: ALINARI/ART RESOURCE, NY)

to be sacred because of its size and delightful shade; also, its presence often indicated the location of a nearby spring. In Plato's time, (428–348 BC) the plane tree shaded the pathways of his academy and created a comfortable setting for philosophical discussions. On tree-lined walkways of the Lyceum the philosopher Aristotle paced to and fro while teaching his students. This method of teaching by walking or strolling about is described as *peripatetic* and is commonly associated with Aristotle to this day.[13]

Plant symbolism permeated Greek myths. For example, Daphne, daughter of the river god Ladon, was a nymph loved by Apollo. She was a beautiful, shy young girl and when Apollo's desire became too aggressive she, according to one version, fled to her mother, Gaia, who changed her into a laurel tree, *Laurus nobilis* (Figure 1–5). From then on the laurel was sacred to Apollo; he used its strong, aromatic scent as a means of purification and as a symbol of peace and victory. The fruit of the pomegranate, *Punica granatum*, was commonly associated with Persephone, queen of the underworld, as a symbol of eternal life represented by the rebirth of the deciduous plant each spring. Ancient Greece also left as part of our common heritage a series of mythical figures often utilized in garden design—sculptures of Herakles, Artemis, Poseidon, and Apollo often adorn our landscapes, bestowing iconographic significance on the design concept.

The following plants were significant in Greek culture:

Botanical Name	Common Name
Acanthus spinosa	acanthus
Crocus sativus	saffron crocus
Hedera helix	ivy
Laurus nobilis	bay laurel
Myrtus communis	myrtle
Olea europaea	olive
Platanus orientalis	sycamore
Punica granatum	pomegranate
Taxus baccata	yew

ANCIENT ROMAN GARDENS (27 BC–476 AD)

The Romans were masters of assimilating influences from other cultures, adapting and adopting what suited them and going on to create from them something new and uniquely Roman. The Roman Empire encompassed an enormous territory from England to North Africa and from Spain to the Tigris and Euphrates rivers in the east, permitting the spread of ideas the Romans had drawn from other peoples.[14] Evidence of this is seen in their architecture, gardens, and in the plants they collected—and propagated—from conquered nations.

Roman art, architecture, and representations of nature demonstrate Greek influences on Roman forms. One of the best examples may be found in the houses and gardens of the city of Pompeii.[15] Houses were inward-looking sanctuaries of peace and privacy. Early Pompeian houses consisted of rooms arranged around an *atrium*, or inner courtyard, which provided light and air (Figure 1–6). Atria generally featured an *impluvium* or catch basin submerged in the pavement and often connected to a cistern below. The *tablinum*, or reception room for guests, often connected the atrium to a

I-6 *An atrium in Pompeii.*

I-7 *A peristyle on the right at the house of Venus in Pompeii.*

I-8 *A wall painting at the house of Venus in Pompeii depicting images of flowers, fountains, and birds.*

back garden. This axial room arrangement created alternate light and dark spaces throughout the house.

In later houses the tablinum opened on to a colonnaded *peristyle* surrounding a courtyard (Figure 1–7). This form, which originated with the Greeks and was refined by the Romans, was located along the central axis behind the tablinium. With a fountain in the middle, this courtyard became a garden or colorful oasis in the depth of the house. The garden was further extended into the house through the use of wall murals painted with garden scenes complete with plants, trellises, and fountains (Figure 1–8).

The increasing amount of space devoted to gardens throughout Roman history reflects their love of nature. A garden provided greenery and coolness. It was planted with fruit trees, hedges, and *topiaries* in whimsical designs. According to the classical archaeologist Wilhelmina Jashemski, "the major plants were evergreen, producing beautiful gardens the year round. There were formal beds, their edges outlined, perhaps, with clipped box, *Buxus* spp. Among the greenery, in season, would be the profusion of the dainty white flowers of myrtle, *Myrtus communis*, the greenish-yellow blossoms of ivy, *Hedera helix*, and the white clusters of the viburnum, *Viburnum tinus*, the daisy chrysanthemum, *Chrysanthemum sege-tum*, the stately Madonna lily, *Lilium candidum*, and accents of color when the rose, violet, the poppy, and the iris were in bloom."[16] The heart and center of the house was the peristyle garden. Figure 1–9 is a garden reconstruction of the Roman villa of Oplontis near Naples. From archaeological research conducted by Jashemski, the plants have been identified and replanted with hedges of boxwood, *Buxus*, evergreen Oleander, *Nerium oleander*, and laurel trees, *Laurus nobilis*.

Another Roman development, the rural estate, called the *villa suburbana*, was created as a result of burgeoning urban populations and the increased wealth of the middle classes.[17] In his *Georgics,* Virgil exalted and idealized agricultural pursuits as an expression of pure *otium,* or the optimum in rural life.[18] These estates were often part-time country residences and held the comforts of the town rather than of the country. It was thought that in the country air, surrounded by nature, people could become masters of their own destiny. Design criteria were elaborate and well thought out. The first and most important design principle was the siting of the house. Views were as important as health and comfort. A hillside location facing southeast was most highly recommended. This allowed for the low winter sun to shine into the *loggias,* which in summer provided cool shelter from the sun. Trees such as the plane, or sycamore, and the cypress, brought from Greece, and perhaps the Italian stone pine from Egypt decorated the villa. The estate contained a *hortus* or vegetable garden for practical food provision along with hunting parks, fish ponds, and sculpture.

Plants cultivated in Ancient Roman gardens included:

Botanical Name	Common Name
Acanthus spinosa	acanthus
Buxus spp.	boxwood
Citrus spp.	lemon
Cupressus sempervirens	cypress
Hedera helix	ivy
Laurus nobilis	bay laurel
Lavandula spp.	lavender
Mentha spp.	mint
Myrtus communis	myrtle
Olea europaea	olive
Pinus pinea	stone pine
Platanus orientalis	sycamore or plane tree
Prunus spp.	apricot, cherry, plum
Thymus spp.	thyme

ANCIENT CHINESE GARDENS (1600 BC–1279 AD)

The Chinese culture has one of the oldest continuous traditions of garden design. In China, two cultural philosophies produce a duality of design concepts. The Confucian approach to a regulated society led to the strict geometry of Chinese houses and cities; straight lines and rectangles typify artifacts that concern people's relationship to one another. The Taoist principle of harmony with nature, in contrast, governed garden design. It was felt that through meditation on the unity of creation, real order and harmony would be revealed. Chinese gardens sought to display in symbolic form the essence of this harmony. The Chinese found both Confucian and Taoist philosophies valuable and applied them side by side in design.

Taoist beliefs and ideals influenced garden forms through an intimate association with nature, a striving for movement, a representation of permanence, and a unity of ethical and philosophical ideals. Unlike the Western use of precise geometries in formal plans, Chinese gardens embodied organic forms that revealed the mystery and wonder of nature with people as a subordinate element to the whole. China's inherently dramatic

1-10 *Guilin River area in Southern China.* (PHOTO: LEO WONG)

1-11 *Summer Palace near Beijing, China.* (PHOTO: LEO WONG)

1-12 *Pavilion on West Lake in Hangzhou, China.* (PHOTO: LEO WONG)

Planting the Landscape

landscape of mountain peaks and lakes (Figure 1–10) provided the image and inspiration for their pleasure gardens. For example, according to garden historian Christopher Thacker, "The sacred groves leading to the tomb of the philosopher Confucius are today old, gnarled, and knotted and held together by iron rings. To the Chinese the writhed, contorted appearance of these old and almost lifeless trunks is worthy of lengthy contemplation revealing qualities of fortitude and grandeur."[19]

For centuries the use of rocks, pools, and plants has been a design device. Natural materials such as stone suggest the permanence and continuance of the greater universe. From a single stone to a large collection, stones were revered for their form and endurance, which represented the stability and strength of the mountains. *Grottoes* built of rocks were developed as sanctuaries for poets and as places to contemplate the universe. Grottoes often comprised part of an artificial mountain used in a garden design. Water in the form of an irregular lake or gardens located on an existing lake were considered special places of serenity (Figure 1–11).

Movement or circulation occurred on irregular pathways diversified the journey through the garden, bringing the viewer in close contact with plant materials. Experiences of scent and sound mixed with the visual enjoyment of the natural world. For example, the pleasure of admiring the moon's progress over the garden was enjoyed from *moon viewing pavilions,* structures built and located specifically for this purpose. Figure 1–12 shows a pavilion located at the Summer Palace outside Beijing; the lake is filled with lotus blossoms.

Plants were carefully chosen for their form and appreciated for their accumulated symbolic and literary associations. A typical garden would include the flowering plum tree, *Prunus mume,* which was much loved and often written about. Its flower signaled the end of winter and its delicate blossoms were often a tremendous contrast to its gnarled bark and branches. Bamboo and pine were also significant garden trees. Bamboo, because it is sturdy yet elegant, suggested strength, and its evergreen quality resilience. Pine trees combined with rocks in design represented silence and solitude. Together the plum, bamboo, and pine were referred to as "the three friends of winter" due to their combination of evergreen characteristics, early flowering, and pleasing forms.

Significant flowers in the Chinese garden were the chrysanthemum, tree peony, and lotus. The chrysanthemums, one of the earliest-cultivated flowers, symbolized longevity due to its autumn and winter blooming. The tree peony, *Paeonia suffruticosa,* was thought of as the "king of flowers" because of its perfect form and size (Figure 1–13). And almost every lake in a Chinese garden contained lotus blossoms, *Nelumbo nucifera.* Lotus represented the ideas of perfection, purity, and integrity as it rose majestically from the water with erect leaves and fragrant pink blossoms.[20]

Plants commonly used in Chinese gardens include:

1-13 *Tree peony, Paeonia suffruticosa.*

Botanical Name	Common Name	Botanical Name	Common Name
Azalea spp.	azalea	*Morus alba*	mulberry
Bambusa spp.	bamboo	*Nelumbo nucifera*	lotus
Camellia spp.	camellia	*Nymphae* spp.	water lily
Chrysanthemum spp.	chrysanthemum	*Orchid*	orchid
Ginkgo biloba	ginkgo	*Paeonia suffruticosa*	peony

JAPANESE GARDENS (575–1600 AD)

The Japanese garden evolved from the Chinese garden but developed its own unique design philosophy. Japan's gardens were a distillation of the natural landscape that symbolized and reproduced the processes and appreciation of nature through the manipulation of stone, plants, and water. The garden often appeared as a stage set. For example, the enjoyment of moonlight, similar to the Chinese sensibility, evolved further in Japanese garden design. Not only could one enjoy the movement of the moon through the night sky but the placement of white flowering plants, white sand, and light-colored rocks in the garden enhanced the moon's effects—and the experience.

Because Japan is an island country, it was able to greatly restrict input and influences from other cultures, allowing an isolated evolution of cultural significance in garden design that does not exist in the West. Throughout its history Japan has effectively used the garden to manifest artistic expression. From the eighth to the eleventh centuries AD, the aristocracy of Japan produced gardens that contained islands, waterfalls, and naturalistic plantings that incorporated the scenery beyond the garden into the *borrowed view* or *shakkei*. The austere attitudes of Zen Buddhism in the sixteenth and seventeenth centuries reduced the scale of gardens. Flowers, considered frivolous, were banished and replaced with evergreen trees and shrubs thought to represent eternal, not transient, beauty. Waterfalls and lakes were represented by gravel, stone, and the *dry garden* (Figure 1–14). These changes created a garden suitable for the importance of the Buddhist tea ceremony. One of the results was admiration for the form of the plant itself more than its flower or fruiting capabilities (Figure 1–15). For example, azaleas may be pruned for their overall form in the design, the effect of their blossoms becoming a sporadic display and secondary design consideration.

Throughout history a specific set of rules evolved that continues to govern Japanese garden design today. Plants, views, stones, circulation, and water—these elements are integral to the composition but each subordinate to the total effect. There are traditional guidelines for the proper placement of rock groupings and stepping-stones, and the raking of gravel gardens. Plants are chosen for their symbolism and seasonal changes. There is no single vista but many different views as one moves throughout the garden. Water movement is studied and many different forms are recommended, including proper directional flow—east.

Japanese planting design strives to combine plants found together in nature. Mixing plants from sea coasts and mountains and creating plant combinations from very different climates are avoided. Simplicity, restraint, and constancy are displayed in planting schemes through use of evergreens that produce a subtle gradation of color and form. Asymmetry and odd-numbered groupings are favored (Figure 1–16).

Plants are not crowded together, but allowed to have plenty of room for growth. A garden is often framed in evegreens; Japanese Black Pine, *Pinus thunbergiana,* Japanese Red Pine, *Pinus densiflora,* azaleas, and camellias. Numerous species of bamboo add textural contrast to the garden. Ferns and moss are associated with water and used appropriately. Because color is treated so subtly, plants are selected for their properties in different seasons. Consequently, flowering cherries, crabapples or plums, *Prunus spp.,* quince, *Chaenomeles japonica,* Japanese maple, *Acer palmatum,* and Iris, *Iris ensata,* are planted sparingly with much thought given to creating plant relationships of serenity and repose.

1-14 *Dry garden at Nanzen-ji in Kyoto, Japan.* (Photo: Jeff Charlesworth)

1-15 *Plant forms in the garden at Katsura, Kyoto, Japan.* (Photo: Jeff Charlesworth)

1-16 *Garden composition, Arashiyama, Kyoto.* (Photo: Jeff Charlesworth)

Plants used in Japanese gardens include:

Botanical Name	Common Name
Acer palmatum	Japanese maple
Azalea spp.	azalea
Bambusa spp.	bamboo
Camellia japonica	camellia
Cercidiphyllum japonica	Katsura tree
Iris ensata	Japanese iris
Pinus densiflora	Japanese red pine
Pinus thunbergiana	Japanese black pine
Prunus spp.	flowering cherry

MEDIEVAL EUROPEAN GARDENS (AD 500–1200)

Religious devotion, mysticism, intuition, and belief rather than rational science guided the medieval concept of the garden. The horticultural expertise of the Romans was lost after the fall of the Empire in AD 476, and through centuries of war. People looked inward rather than embrace new scientific or mechanical ideas. Man's outlook on the world, civilized in Roman times, became more primitive; fear of the wild, fear of the unknown, and fear of one's fellow man became standard guides for European behavior. Medieval culture created a defensive civilization manifested in fortressed castles and walled communities, towns, and villages.

The concept of the garden changed greatly from the sixth to the thirteenth century. In Roman gardens people saw themselves as one with nature as they reached out into the countryside. During medieval times, this idea disappeared. Gardens existed primarily as adjuncts to cloisters and monasteries. "Since medieval monasteries survived good times and bad, famine and plague, we can conclude that monastic gardeners must have been successful, on the whole, in their efforts to provide enough food to sustain life, even for large communities with many mouths to feed."[21] A cloister consisted of a grouping of monks' separate cubicles with a covered walkway uniting them around a central common space. The covered walkway or arcade surrounded an open court that varied in design from place to place and with the passage of years. Sometimes it was paved, sometimes used as a garden for growing medicinal herbs; almost always there was a well in the center of the cloister (Figure 1–17). The laboriously hand-copied herbal manuscripts and records of seed- and cutting-exchange networks that existed between the monastic houses during the twelfth and thirteenth centuries spread knowledge of medicinal, fragrant, and flowering plants.

As a result of their endurance, monastic libraries and manuscripts provide much of our information concerning the medieval environment at this time. Another source of medieval horticulture is the plan of an ideal monastery proposed in the ninth century for a Benedictine cloister at St. Gall, Switzerland. In the Plan of St. Gall (Figure 1–18), 830 AD, the church is at the center of the cloister complex. There are areas for animals, textile manufacturing, and a garden; the entire complex is surrounded by walls. The vegetable garden is laid out in a series of eighteen rectangular plots containing vegetables such as onion, leek, and parsnip, and herbs including dill, coriander, and thyme.

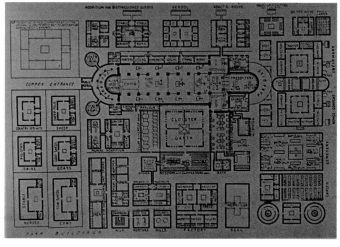

1-17 *(left) Cloister garden at the church of Santissima Annunziata, known as Chiostro dei Morti, located in Florence, Italy*

1-18 *(right) Plan of St. Gall. (HGSD slide, Newton's Design on the Land, 19.)*

Although much of our knowledge of medieval gardens involves monastic life, private pleasure gardens were also common in the later Middle Ages. A typical medieval pleasure garden consisted of a variety of design elements. Enriched by walls or thick hedges, often referred to as a *hortus conclusus*, the garden was often square or rectangular in shape and contained wooden trellises, pergolas, and arbors. Within the enclosed space would be a small area of grass in the form of a meadow known as the *flowery mead.* Along the walls or near the grass would be raised seats made of turf. In later gardens there might be a *mount* or small hill, square or round in form, either in the middle of the garden, or more often to one side against a wall as a vantage point from which the attractions of the garden might be seen.[22]

Similar to the monastic garden, plants cultivated in the pleasure garden included many herbs, such as rue, *Ruta graveolens;* sage, *Salvia;* mint, *Mentha;* catmint, *Nepeta;* and basil, *Ocimum basilicum.* Vegetables were also grown "and sometimes the garden was divided into groups, such as *for potage, for sauce,* or *for coppe, for salad.*"[23] Although the growing of herbs and vegetables was main concern, fruit trees were valued and the practice of propagating numerous fruits on a single tree (through grafting) was a popular medieval activity. Scented flowers were planted and the aroma of the Madonna lily, *Lillium caudidum;* roses, *Rosa;* and violets, *Viola;* often permeated the air.[24]

Plants grown in medieval European gardens included:

Botanical Name	Common Name
Artemisia abrotanum	southernwood
Foeniculum vulgare	fennel
Helleborus niger	Lenten rose
Lillium caudidum	Madonna lily
Morus alba	mulberry
Prunus persica	peach
Quercus spp.	oak
Rosa spp.	rose
Ruta graveolens	rue
Salvia spp.	sage

MOORISH GARDENS

1-19 *A Persian garden carpet depicting the four-river motif surrounded by trees and flowers. (RONALD PRESS CO.)*

While the Western world progressed slowly in the darkness of the Middle Ages, the followers of Mohammed swept across North Africa from Egypt to Morocco and eventually spread to Spain in AD 712. Consequently, the gardens of Persia, Syria, and Ancient Rome were direct prototypes for the Moorish gardens of Spain. The first Moorish gardens in Cordoba may well have been laid out by people who remembered the gardens of Islam, and some of the fruits and flowers that to us are typical of Spain were introduced from the East by Muslim invaders. In the hot, dry Spanish climate the Moors had no need to change their inherited way of life. An appreciation for the outdoors together with a mathematical genius in architecture created a rich tradition of landscape design.

Moorish tradition furthered the evolution of the Roman peristyle garden into the *patio* or courtyard garden. The patio was a large space open to the sky but enclosed by walls or buildings for protection. Irrigation features remaining from the Roman occupation included the *rill,* which evolved from a simple irrigation ditch to an idealized design form. The rill cooled the air on a warm day, and the sound of its running water was soothing to the ear.

Moorish gardens were arranged geometrically and developed according to Koranic teaching. They represented a sensual experience, a terrestrial paradise—the Garden of Eden, a foretaste of heaven. The garden was a calm place for contemplating the afterlife, in contrast to the noisy, dusty world outside. Most often the design was a rectangle divided into four sections by water channels, or rills, the center being occupied by a circle in the form of a fountain or pool. The square represented nature's manifestations and the circle depicted heaven, while the four water channels represented purity, the source of life, and a means of refreshing body and spirit. This design motif is represented in the Persian garden carpet (Figure 1–19).

Water, trees, flowers, and fruit were the primary elements of the Moorish garden. Water suggested coolness and, precious in quantity, took the form of fountains, rills, or pools. The water features were either deep, dark, tranquil, and restrained in design, or swiftly flowing and scintillating (Figure 1–20). Because of the great expanse of the Islamic world, plants from the Eastern Mediterranean, Persia, and the Far East were often cultivated in the Moorish flower gardens of Spain. The original plantings of the Mughal gardens are largely unknown. It is thought by scholars that plants such as cit-

1-20 (left) Water was an essential element in Moorish gardens. The Alhambra. (PHOTO: MARC TREIB)

1-21 (right) Annuals planted in the form of an oriental carpet, Kensington, California.

rus trees—orange and lemons—perfumed the courtyards along with hedges of myrtle, *Myrtus communis*. Large date palms, *Phoenix dactylifera;* sycamores, *Platanus orientalis;* and cypress trees, *Cupressus sempervirens* provided shade. The quadrangle planting beds, which were sunken and filled with flowers, created the illusion of walking on a rich woven oriental carpet (Figure 1–21). These flowers were most likely drought tolerant plant species due to the preciousness of water.

Numerous plants were cultivated by the Moorish people in Spanish gardens. Some of the favorites were:

	Botanical Name	Common Name
Fruits	*Citrus* spp.	orange, lemon trees
	Ficus carica	fig tree
Ornamentals	*Cinnamomum camphora*	camphor tree
	Cupressus sempervirens	cypress
	Rosa spp.	roses—white and yellow
Herbs	*Coriandrum sativum*	coriander
	Cuminum cyminum	cumin

GARDENS IN RENAISSANCE ITALY

The birth of the Italian Renaissance in the mid-fourteenth century brought about great changes in art, architecture, and gardens as the focus of thinking shifted from the medieval obsession with the afterlife to the Renaissance appreciation of this life. The term *renaissance* denotes the revival of the classical humanist ideals from the ancient Greek and Roman cultures. Humanism sought to recapture the spirit of the classical world and its ideals of beauty and nature described through philosophy, poetry, music, architecture,

1-22 *Villa Medici in Fiesole: view from the house to the terrace.*

1-23 *Villa Medici in Fiesole: view from terrace back to the house.*

1-24 *Villa Medici in Fiesole: second terrace; note retaining wall and pergola.*

1-25 *Original fifteenth-century parterre at the Villa Ruspoli, north of Rome.*

1-26 *Labyrinth at the Villa Uzzano, Greve-in-Chianti.*

1-27 *River gods, Villa Farnese in Caprarola.*

and gardens. For Renaissance artists the idea was not to just imitate the achievements of antiquity but to surpass them. To this end, many Renaissance design concepts originated in Greek and Roman tradition but appeared in refined and expanded forms.

The Renaissance world was hierarchical, with God at the top and man and nature below. To know the natural world was to know God; this idea was expressed through the paired concepts of art and nature and was especially relevant in garden design. "There the raw materials provided by nature—the terrain, trees, plants, flowers, stones, and water, with their infinite variety of forms, colors, textures, and scents—were selected, cut, shaped, and organized by art."[25] In fifteenth-century Florence the architect Leon Battista Alberti (1404–1472) formulated the mathematical interpretation of nature as an artistic concept. Alberti's treatise on architecture used numbers, dimension, and the classical orders to convey an ideal proportional system by which to display the relationship between man and nature. In architecture, concepts of scale, symmetry, and proportion were cultivated. These ideals were thought to be eternal, natural laws and were accepted as fact by Renaissance artists and architects and used as tools of design. The relationship between man and nature and the house and the landscape could reveal itself in a formal system of dimensions and proportions.

The design of the *villa* embodied these artistic ideals. It combined the relationship of house, garden, and the natural environment into a single architectural element. The Villa Medici in Fiesole is a good example of the use of *terraces, loggias,* and *pergolas* linking the house to the garden (Figures 1–22, 1–23, 1–24). Plants in geometric forms of topiary, parterres, and labyrinths articulate the garden (Figures 1–25, 1–26). A *bosco,* a small woodland planted in regimented rows, or a *barco,* grounds for hunting, in addition to organized vineyards and orchards in the form of a *quincunx,* brought order to the natural environment of the villa. References to antiquity were made by the use of Greek and Roman garden elements: tree houses, grottoes, fountains, and sculpture. Villas belonging to the wealthy and powerful were often overlaid with iconography of Greek and Roman myths as part of the design (Figure 1–27). These stories added a level of sophistication to the garden and illustrated the owner's link to the classical world.

Plants filled a significant role in the Renaissance villa garden. Climbing plants such as honeysuckle, *Lonicera caprifolium,* or Grapes, *Vitis vinifera* trailed along walls and pergolas; hedges of Laurustinus, *Viburnum tinus* or myrtle, *Myrtus communis* outlined garden rooms and pathways; and herbs and flowers filled the planting beds. Common herbs and flowers were the daisy, *Bellis perrenis;* Lavender, *Lavandula angustifolia;* mallow, *Malva sylvestris;* and rosemary, *Rosmarinus officinalis.* In the late sixteenth century, parterre beds were often decorated with complex geometric motifs, as in the parterre garden at the Villa Ruspoli (see Figure 1–25). Numerous plants from Greek and Roman gardens were planted—the strawberry tree, *Arbutus unedo,* evergreen oak, *Quercus ilex,* sycamore, *Platanus orientalis,* along with the pomegranate tree, *Punicum granatum.* Evergreen plants sustained the design throughout the year while herbs and flowers added seasonal accents of color.

It was thought by Renaissance scholars that villas should not only contain plants from antiquity but also a collection of plants then known to the scientific world. Because of trading and exploration in the Middle East and the discovery of America, an explosive arrival of foreign plants created a new science—botany. From these discoveries villa owners amassed plant collections of rare and exotic specimens as sym-

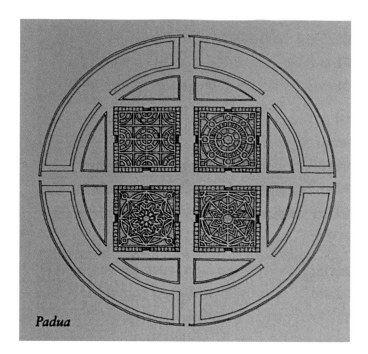

bols of their wealth and prestige. At first plants were traded by physicians and botanists; consequently, the first botanical gardens were founded in conjunction with universities—the universities of Padua and Pisa in Italy, and of Oxford and Cambridge in England. The concept of the botanical garden developed from the vain search for the Garden of Eden. When it could not be found, scholars began to think in terms of bringing the scattered pieces of creation together into a new Garden of Eden. The botanical garden represented an encyclopedic collection of plants offering a complete guide to the many faces of the Creator. Each plant family was thought to represent a specific act of the creation.[26] This same inspirational theme influenced the plant collections of the Renaissance nobility.

Figures 1–28 and 1–29 depict the Padua Botanical Garden as it was originally laid out and the way it looks today. Founded in 1545, the garden is designed in a four-square, each bed representing one of the four continents—Africa, Asia, Europe, and America. This simple pattern has been repeated in botanical gardens, arboretums, public parks, and private estates, throughout history. One enters the Botanical Garden in quest of a restful place and shuts the door on the outside world to recover one's innocence and learn about the world of plants.

Significant plants of the Italian Renaissance include:

Botanical name	Common Name	Botanical name	Common Name
Arbutus unedo	strawberry tree	*Pinus pinea*	Italian stone pine
Castanea sativa	chestnut	*Platanus orientalis*	plane
Citrus spp.	lemon, orange	*Punicum granatum*	pomegranate
Cupressus sempervirens	cypress	*Quercus ilex*	evergreen oak
Lavandula spp.	lavender	*Rosmarinus officinalis*	rosemary
Olea europaea	olive	*Viburnum tinus*	laurustinus

THE FORMAL FRENCH GARDEN

Landscape architecture in seventeenth-century France was an important art form rivaling architecture, sculpture, and painting. The French dominated nature, in contrast to the Renaissance concept of interaction with nature. It was an age in which the power of wealth, of intellect, and of man's ascendancy over nature were glorified.[27] This powerful design concept later spread throughout Europe and America.

When the French no longer needed the defensive sitings of the Middle Ages, they began to site châteaux on broad expanses of land that created an admirable backdrop for displaying the spectacle of a large court. Ruled by a rich and powerful aristocracy, society was grouped round the king and court. The garden was not for meditation or escape but a stage for the display of magnificence. There was no better way of expressing grandeur than by the effect of an almost unlimited extent of landscape (Figure 1–30).

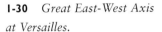

1-30 *Great East-West Axis at Versailles.*

1-31 *(top left) Newly planted allée through the woods at Versailles.*

1-32 *(top right) Versailles,* parterre en broderie.

1-33 *(bottom left) The Fountain of Spring, Versailles.*

1-34 *(bottom right) Orangery at Versailles.*

Inspired by the flat landscape of northern Italy, which resembled French topography, the French concept of landscape architecture further expanded axial vistas and extended symmetry to distant horizons. French gardens were in their formality and symmetry the outdoor counterparts of the structures they embellished.

Paramount in this achievement was the work of the landscape architect André Le Nôtre. While architect to Louis XIV, Le Nôtre designed the garden at the Palace at Versailles, expanding the Italian Renaissance theory of perspective and proportion by using an ingenious series of design devices in his gardens. One device was the use of grand allées or rows of trees on either side of a pathway through a wood. The immensity and rigidity of the planting extended the power of the linear perspective (Figure 1–31). Allées connected points of interest along the axis, creating a succession of vistas. This is significant because landscape design of this magnitude had never been seen before.

The great *parterre* was another device designed as a setting for architecture and the display of decorative designs. The design of the *parterre en broderie,* as it was called, mimicked the fine embroidered clothing worn by patrons of the garden, through the use of low shrubs, flowers, and sand (Figure 1–32). Designed to be viewed from the house, parterres added color and texture to a flat topography.

Le Nôtre incorporated water elements as a device to enhance and expand the drama of the sky. At Versailles he created tremendous water mirrors along the upper terrace, designed the mile-long canal that reinforced the axial vista, and devised fountains that are almost as impressive when silent as when flowing[28] (Figure 1–33).

A slight change in grade is another technical device used by Le Nôtre. Changes in grade offset the fundamentally flat countryside that might otherwise have seemed monotonous. The combination of these design techniques created a commanding scale that gives the sense of being in a heroic landscape of the gods. This suited the ideals of Louis XIV, who considered the palace and gardens at Versailles the visible symbols of the French monarchy. With the sun as his emblem he declared himself Apollo, the sun god, and this classical mythological figure provided the iconography that overlaid the entire design.

Le Nôtre utilized plants in a variety of ways. He abstracted forms of green architecture according to specific rules. Green-on-green plants dominated the design, with very few flowers. To strengthen the main axis he applied a *tapis vert,* a swath of lawn rectilinear in shape, which added depth to the ground plane. Le Nôtre used topiary more than any other designer in history. He planted trees close together and clipped them to form solid walls of greenery. Woods, called *bosquets,* were laid out on a regulated, tight grid that gave the illusion of control and organization. Formal geometric woods with tall hedges flanking open pathways of grass and sand created a sense of wilderness.

Plant collecting was an avid pastime. At Versailles an assortment of tender plants were sheltered during the winter in an *orangery,* originally a structure for cultivating oranges that were placed outside in the warm months (Figure 1–34). Hardy new and exotic plants were cultivated in the royal fruit and vegetable garden.

Versailles exercised an enormous influence over garden design throughout Europe and America. The grandeur and scale of the French garden was imitated in gardens all over England, Holland, Germany, and Italy.

Plants in French formal gardens included:

Botanical Name	Common Name
Acer pseudoplatanus	Sycamore maple
Anenome ssp.	windflower
Aquilegia vulgaris	columbine
Buxus sempervirens	boxwood
Carpinus betulus	hornbeam
Fritillaria imperialis	crown imperial
Lillium spp	lily
Polianthes tuberosa	tuberose
Taxus baccata	yew
Tilia platyphyllos	linden

THE ENGLISH LANDSCAPE GARDEN (1715–1820)

England's rejection of the French formal garden ushered in the English landscape garden movement. England's wish to develop an indigenous garden style suitable to the climate, topography, and spirit of the people, just as Italian and French gardens reflected their cultures, came about in a very dramatic way. Italian gardens were built on concepts from antiquity and the French landscape furthered this tradition, but the English pastoral garden was unlike anything that had been done before. It emerged at a time in history when forces moved from all directions toward a common objective and manifested themselves in every art. In England artists, philosophers, gardeners, and especially writers began to respond negatively to the French philosophy of landscaping that had permeated the English countryside.[29] The English began to think of nature as something simple, beautiful, true, and good, and found the French garden too rigid, pompous, and unnatural. Beauty was redefined by scholars who, challenging earlier views of nature, believed that objects have an inherent or intrinsic beauty that was found in the untouched landscape. Nature was no longer thought to be something to be tamed and organized, but rather the natural environment was embraced in all its wildness. Designing a garden in the pastoral style was considered a sign of true morality. Horace Walpole wrote in his book *History of the Modern Taste in Gardening*, "Poetry, painting, and gardening, or the science of the landscape, will forever by men of taste be deemed the three new graces who dress and adorn nature."[30]

England's land and climate were perfectly suited for this new design concept. The rolling, green hills, misty, gray skies, and abundance of water enabled the landscape to appear seamless. One did not perceive where the garden ended and nature began.

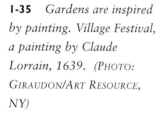

1-35 *Gardens are inspired by painting. Village Festival, a painting by Claude Lorrain, 1639. (PHOTO: GIRAUDON/ART RESOURCE, NY)*

Another tradition, the grand tour, contributed to the new design aesthetic. Men and women of privilege and taste traveled to Europe to see the great works of art and architecture and brought back to England their own ideals of paradise. Many of these architectural masterpieces were often recreated on their estates as a reflection of the owner's refinement and knowledge of classical art.

Three men, William Kent, Lancelot "Capability" Brown, and Humphey Repton, are closely associated with garden design from this period. Using land form, trees, water, and architecture, they substituted symmetry and the dominance of the central axis with a painter's subtlety for balance, organic form, and, most importantly, the *genius loci*. To consult "the genius of the place" was to seek an understanding of the potential natural perfection of a site and to assist in its artistic emergence, where necessary, by discrete intervention.

As a result of a combination of the new concept of beauty, the climate, the experience of the grand tour, and the spirit of the genius loci, the ideal English landscape became an Arcadian paradise echoing scenes of the Roman countryside. The goal was to compose a garden like those in the landscape paintings of Claude Lorrain (1600–1682) and Gaspard Poussin (1615–1675) (Figure 1–35).

Consequently, numerous elements of the natural landscape were combined with classical architectural features to create a design viewed as a series of paintings. Stourhead in Wiltshire is a model of this garden concept (Figure 1–36). The scenes of the garden are meant to be visited in a specific sequence. They are punctuated at intervals with classical replicas of the Pantheon in Rome, a grotto, the Temple of Flora, and various urns and statues recalling episodes in Virgil's *Aeneid*. Overlaid on the sequence of Virgilian scenes is a collection of medieval buildings as references to England's glori-

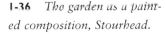

1-36 *The garden as a painted composition, Stourhead.*

ous past. The result is a bucolic landscape that tells a story as one walks along admiring the picturesque views.[31]

Water, topography, planting, and the borrowed view were manipulated to achieve this landscape effect. Undulating forms of rivers and lakes created the illusion of vast expanses of water. Plants arranged in carefully manipulated masses were located on hilltops to enhance the extensive grading of the natural terrain. Plant massings were grouped into organic forms that led the eye along the terrain and pulled the viewer into the landscape. Planting schemes were dominated by large coniferous and hardwood trees underplanted with ornamental shrubs to balance large greenswards and meadows. The approach to an estate was often designed along a graceful curve providing sweeping views of the carefully crafted landscape, animated by deer or cows (Figure 1–37). The *ha-ha*, a ditch wide and deep enough to serve as a barrier to animals, is often cited by historians as the design device that allowed people to fully embrace nature. It was designed to be as invisible as possible to create the illusion that the garden and surrounding countryside were one.

This new philosophy of nature was also reflected in the English attitude toward plants. Rather than being clipped, pruned, and forced into a desired shape, they were appreciated for their intrinsic form. Vegetation was thought of in terms of massing and grouping as part of the bigger picture. Little attention was given to flowering plants. In contrast, trees were chosen to stand alone in all their natural glory and splendor as *specimen plants*. All these ideas were supported by the arrival of plants in greater and greater numbers from foreign explorations. Plant explorers brought back pine trees from Canada, New England, and Georgia; fir and spruce trees from Scandinavia; linden, sycamore, walnut, and cedars of Lebanon from the Middle East; and tea trees from Australia, expanding the plant palette and adding diversity to the English landscape.

The natural landscape style manifested in English park and garden design had an impact on gardens all over the world—especially in America, from the work of Thomas Jefferson at Monticello to Frederick Law Olmsted's numerous park designs.

1-37 *Entrance to Wakehurst Place.*

Planting the Landscape

A concise list of plant introductions is impossible due to the explosion in plant species brought to England at this time. Some of those used most frequently are:

Botanical Name	Common Name
Cedrus deodora	Cedar of Lebanon
Leptospermum scoparium	Australian tea tree
Liriodendron tulipifera	tulip tree
Magnolia grandiflora	evergreen magnolia
Philadelphus coronarius	mock orange
Syringa vulgaris	lilac
Ulmus americana	American elm

THE ENGLISH VICTORIAN GARDEN (1820–1880)

"By the 1820s and 30s gardens were no longer idealizations of nature where artistry was disguised but plots in which as many plants as possible should be grown."[32] The garden of the Victorian era, 1820–1880, was a melting pot of Italian, French, English, and Chinese design concepts. The overall design philosophy embraced a rich profusion of styles. Gardens became exotic plant collections of trees, shrubs, and herbaceous plants arriving from abroad. Garden design was eclectic; it revealed a combination of parterres, winding paths, picturesque imagery, and a lack of competence in any single design form. Flowers as individual design elements had been in eclipse since medieval times, but all through the nineteenth century the flood of herbaceous plants returned, especially the use of annuals, often grown in greenhouse settings and moved outdoors. *Carpet bedding* was a prevalent design element in many gardens. This design technique, still seen today, combines annuals planted to make carpet-like patterns (Figure 1–38). Plant collecting was sometimes carried to an extreme and gardens were designed for botanical display, mean-

1-38 *Contemporary version of carpet bedding: plants arranged to form a star.*

ing plants were appreciated individually and the bigger picture ignored. Tropical plants collected and grown in a *conservatory* became popular. New plants, cultivars, and commercial nurseries in combination with skilled gardeners, horticulturists, and botanists disseminating information enabled the greater public to become plant enthusiasts.

Plants of English Victorian gardens included:[33]

Botanical Name	Common Name
Albizzia julibrissim	silk tree
Ageratum houstonianum	NCN*
Antirrhinum majus	snapdragon
Begonia spp.	NCN*
Callistephus chinensis	China aster
Centaurea cyanus	bachelor's button, cornflower
Chamaecyparis pisifera	false cypress
Chrysanthemum maximum	shasta daisy
Dianthus chinensis	pinks
Euonymus japonica	euonymus
Iberis umbellata	candytuft
Impatiens balsamina	impatiens
Tagetes erecta	marigold
Tsuga heterophylla	western hemlock
Zinnia elegans	zinnia

*NCN—No common name

THE EDWARDIAN GARDEN (1880–1914)

I-39   *A drift of poppies.*

The Edwardian era in England is defined by the work of two plantspersons—William Robinson and Gertrude Jekyll. Robinson is often referred to as "the father of the English flower garden." He aimed to abolish the idea of the flower garden as a set piece (usually geometrically placed on one side of the house) and to eliminate carpet bedding. In his book *The Wild Garden*, he promoted the virtues of naturalistic plantings in almost every kind of garden—in woods and copses and along margins of shrubbery, streambeds, and meadows. These plantings featured perennials or shrubs found growing in the wild, then cultivated in great irregular masses called *drifts* (Figure 1–39). The emphasis was on plant form in broad, sweeping masses to define garden spaces.

Robinson's idea of naturalistic planting began a debate with the architect Reginald Blomfield about the relative merits of the geometric formal garden versus the naturalistic garden. Blomfield, in his book, *The Formal Garden in England*, reacted against both the mindless geometry of Victorian bedding-out and the naturalism of Robinson. He wrote, "The formal treatment of gardens ought, perhaps, to be called the architectural treatment of gardens, for it consists in the extension of the principles of design which govern the house to the grounds which surround it."[34]

Although each garden theory has its value, they are both contrived forms. Edith Wharton commented on this controversy in her book *Italian Villas and Their Gardens*, and she has perhaps the best last word on the subject: "The quarrel then begun still goes on, and sympathies are divided between the artificial-natural and the frankly conventional. The time has come, however, when it is recognized that both these *are* manners, the one as artificial as the other, and each to be judged, not by any ethical standard of 'sincerity' but on its own aesthetic merits."[35]

As a result, the Edwardian garden, 1880–1914, is distinguished in garden history by its combination of formal layout and exuberant natural plantings (Figure 1–40). Many of these gardens were designed by the architect Sir Edwin Lutyens in conjunction with the unsurpassed plantswoman Gertrude Jekyll. Jekyll's work showcased plants in a method never seen before. With her painterly eye, the result of her earlier career as an artist, she combined colors and forms in large drifts and emphasized the perennial as a viable design tool. Vibrant plantings were paired with the classical design elements of axes and vistas, and classical structures, such as pergolas, loggias, and statuary, reappeared in the landscape.

The formal characteristics of Edwardian gardens were the projection of the lines of the house outward along routes and vistas; the repetition of forms and materials of the house increasing the apparent size of house and garden; and the subsequent softening of these forms with luxuriant plantings (Figure 1–41). The harmony of materials emphasized the garden as a series of related outdoor rooms.[36] Jekyll often softened the geome-

1-40 *Planting design by Gertrude Jekyll at Hestercombe, Taunton, Somerset is a combination of architectural spaces softened by plants.*

1-41 *Exuberant planting soften pergola structure at Hestercombe.*

try of rooms and forms by using a *perennial border,* (Figure 1–42), a long, narrow bed planted with perennials that articulates the line but loosens the form.

There was a clientele eager for these gardens. Because a love of nature had always been an important national characteristic of England, and in reaction to Victorian industrialization, many of the urban middle class now became inspired by the Arcadian dream of rural life. Surburban villas were constructed as a counterpoint to life in the city.[36] The garden was seen less as a spectacle to be viewed from the house and more as a series of outdoor rooms for tea parties, recreation, or reading.

Renewed interest in the work of Gertrude Jekyll and William Robinson developed in both England and America in the late 1970s and 1980s and continues to this day.

The creation of the border enabled the use of numerous woody and herbaceous plants. Some Edwardian favorites were:

Botanical Name	Common Name
Alchemilla mollis	Lady's mantle
Anenome japonica	Japanese anenome
Artemisia absinthium	wormwood
Azaleas spp.	azalea
Campanula persicifolia	peach bluebell
Ceanothus 'Gloire de Versailles'	wild lilac
Dianthus spp.	carnations, pinks
Euphorbia wulfenii	spurge
Heuchera sanguinea	coral bells
Hosta spp.	plantain lily
Iris spp.	iris
Laburnum watereri	goldenchain tree
Lavandula spp.	lavender
Rhododendron spp.	rhododendron
Rosa spp.	shrub rose
Santolina chaemacyparis	grey cotton
Sedum spectabile	stonecrop
Stachys olympica	lamb's ears
Verbascum orientale	mullein

THE AMERICAN GARDEN (1840–1920)

The nationalistic ideal of America as the melting pot of numerous cultures is reflected in its gardens. Because settlers in a new country try to recreate what is familiar to them, the design of gardens in America is often a collection of concepts from other cultures. The variety of cultures combined with diverse climatic conditions and topography has produced a panoply of landscapes. The results are found in gardens and town planning throughout the United States. From New England to the South and to the West, the adaptation of garden styles can be seen in both public and private landscapes (Figures 1–43, 1–44).

1-43 *Japanese style Zen Garden at Bloedel Reserve, designed by Dr. Koichi Kawana, Bainbridge Island, Washington.*

1-44 *An Italian style garden at Val Verde, designed by Lockwood de Forest, Santa Barbara, California.*

Although landscape gardening had been practiced in America for generations, it was with the 1841 publication of Andrew Jackson Downing's *A Treatise on the Theory and Practice of Landscape Gardening Adapted to North America* that the first major American book of landscape design appeared. Downing's landscapes were characterized by undulating lines and the picturesque imitation of nature popularized by Humphrey Repton and John Claudius Loudon in England. Partially due to Downing's early death, Frederick Law Olmsted became the next prominent landscape architect in America. Olmsted adapted the English pastoral garden as an engine of social reform in many great urban parks including Central and Prospect parks in New York City. He believed that changing the physical landscape could alleviate social tensions, create a space for exercise, and raise the standard of American culture (Figure 1–45). His beliefs reflected the utilitarian-transcendentalist currents of the mid-nineteenth century and he saw his work as quintessentially American and democratic.[38] Working with his partner, Calvert Vaux, Olmsted focused on moral and social issues by such means as including a dairy in the design of Central Park in order for poor mothers to feed their children sanitary milk. In the design of Mountain View Cemetery in California, he integrated the layout of internment plots so that people of various faiths could grieve together.

However, late in Olmsted's career a new trend developed. A change in public taste was occurring, fostered by a perceived need to improve society. As a tremendous influx of immigrants swelled the population of America, living conditions for many worsened and the notion of saving the country through culture and architecture arose. This new perception changed the direction of both architecture and landscape architecture. Architects, landscape architects, and artists felt that if these arts were practiced as fine arts in the classical style, they would alleviate the problems of urban congestion and

1-46 *The Italian Garden at Dumbarton Oaks, designed by Beatrix Farrand is an example of European influence on American gardens.*

unplanned development. They believed that the discipline of historic precedent and the use of principles of proportion and symmetry could raise the standards of intelligence and morals and dignify and refine the national style. By heightening public awareness of the visual quality of the environment, focus on the American landscape would enable it to become a well-ordered work of art.

Seeking symbols to raise the aesthetic consciousness of the young country, architects fastened on classical forms. The choice of styles available to them was an element of individual preference and they began to design French châteaux, Tudor mansions, and Italian villas, each with their appropriate gardens (Figure 1–46). This change created a new orientation in landscape design; formal compositions of symmetrical axes and cross-axes and imagery specifically derived from classical sources appeared. The change created a conflict in the profession. For some practitioners, the seemingly incompatible formal and picturesque philosophies were firmly establishing themselves as separate entities. The debate was similar to that occurring in England at this time between Reginald Blomfield and William Robinson. One faction of the profession, following the philosophy of Downing, felt that natural landscape scenery addressed the simpler and nobler part of nature; these designers emphasized pastoral and picturesque scenery. Other practitioners championed a landscape of formally organized compositions—one that could be considered a "true art form"—combined with a pastoral landscape. Geometric gardens organized around a central axis with symmetrical plantings accompanied classical architecture.

Professionals working in America in the late nineteenth and early twentieth centuries were quite knowledgeable about plants. The tendency was strong among numerous landscape architects to use native plants. Planting design at this time combined the use of natives and plants ecologically suited to their growing environment. For example, at

Naumkeag in Massachusetts, Fletcher Steele designed the now famous Blue Steps among a planted grove of native birch trees, *Betula papyrifera* (Figure 1–47); Beatrix Farrand used her home, Reef Point in Bar Harbor, Maine, as a laboratory for experimenting with and collecting plants; and in southern California, Lockwood de Forest initiated the use of native-and drought-tolerant plants. Frederick Law Olmsted's environmental sensitivity pioneered the preservation of the American wilderness at Yosemite and Yellowstone national parks and shortly before his death in 1903, he was planning a school of Forestry at the Biltmore estate in North Carolina. Olmsted's numerous park designs, created all over America, showcased native plants and were models for parks everywhere. As a result, in the East and Midwest hardwood trees such as oaks, elms, and maples, and conifers such as pines, hemlocks, and spruce trees permeated the landscape in the form of grove and *glade.*

In contrast, estate plantings necessitated a rich variety of vegetation in addition to native plants. Herbaceous perennials were combined with annuals and ornamental shrubs filled out the design picture. Plant explorations to China and Japan added numerous plant species such as Japanese maples, rare rhododendrons, peonies, and camellias to garden collections. As the designs of parks, campuses, and country estates grew more elaborate, a network of nurseries, gardeners, and horticulturists emerged to meet the planting demands. But because these were the days before engineering intervention, the diversion of natural water systems, and the use of irrigation tactics, care was taken to understand a plant's natural environment and to cultivate it under similar conditions.

The Beaux-Arts design tradition popularized plant forms such as topiary, mazes, and parterres.[39] The geometric garden designs with central axes and cross axes were typical of the Beaux Arts tradition but the plantings softened the overall effect. The focus was on the flowers, not the patterns they formed. Around 1918, Gertrude Jekyll's theories on color and planting became popular in America; consequently English perennial borders began to appear in estate gardens. This period, often described as the Golden Age of Landscape Architecture, or the Country Place Era, lasted until approximately 1929, ending with the Great Depression and the advent of the income tax (Figure 1–48)

Plants both native and exotic popularized in American gardens, 1820–1930, included:

Botanical Name	Common name
Acer palmatum	Japanese maple
Camellia japonica	Japanese camellia
Coreopsis grandiflora	coreopsis
Cornus florida	American dogwood
Fagus sylvatica 'Atropunicea'	purple beech
Liriodendron tulipifera	tulip tree
Platanus acerifolia	American sycamore
Quercus spp.	evergreen and deciduous oaks
Tsuga canadensis	Canadian hemlock
Tsuga heterophylla	Western hemlock
Ulmus americana	American elm

I-47 *Native birch trees at Naumkeag, in Stockbridge Massachusetts, designed by Fletcher Steele.*

I-48 *Watercolor of the flower garden at Crosswicks, Jenkintown, Pennsylvania, designed by Beatrix Farrand 1893.* (COURTESY OF DOCUMENTS COLLECTION, UNIVERSITY OF CALIFORNIA AT BERKELEY)

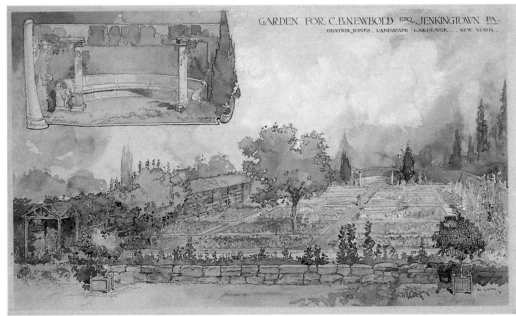

MODERN LANDSCAPE ARCHITECTURE IN AMERICA (1940–1970)

The classical ideals of America's Golden Age were later rejected by three young landscape architecture students—Garrett Eckbo, Dan Kiley, and James Rose.[40] In the 1930s, these Harvard students wanted to explore ideas prevalent in modern art, especially painting. In addition, they believed that landscape architecture should be adapted to the site, speak to client needs, and address social and environmental problems.[41] The work of the California-based landscape architect Thomas Church, an earlier Harvard graduate, was also influential. Church's designs combined classical ideals with new theories of modern space. Together these four landscape architects have been described by the architect Marc Treib "as the model for, and a yardstick against which, modern American landscape design could be judged."[42]

In order to fully embrace modernism, landscape architects wanted to develop a new design vocabulary based on emerging concepts of space and form inspired by modern art. They shunned the vocabulary of the symmetrical plan, the axis, and the simple geometric forms of the Beaux-Arts style because these represented copies of earlier garden traditions. The new vocabulary embodied notions of modern space and form as the building blocks of modern landscape architecture. Space was thought of as a three-dimensional continuum expressing movement and rhythm. Form, inspired by modern painting, took on an organic shape. The free-form, kidney, and amoeba shapes appeared in swimming pools, planting beds, and on the ground plane, constructed of turf or hardscape materials. The Donnell garden in Sonoma, California, is perhaps one of the best-known designs of this era incorporating the elements of modern design (Figures 1–49, 1–50). The modern forms, the zipzap and piano curve, were incorporated first in residential design and later into the corporate campus.[43]

Planting design became a scientific process that interfered as little as possible with nature. Plantings emphasized plants as specimens, locating them in a modern space as botanic entities. Here a plant would "inevitably express itself."[44] Little emphasis was

1-49 *(left) Plan of Donnell Garden, Sonoma, California, designed by Thomas Church.*
1-50 *(right) Donnell Garden, Sonoma, California.*

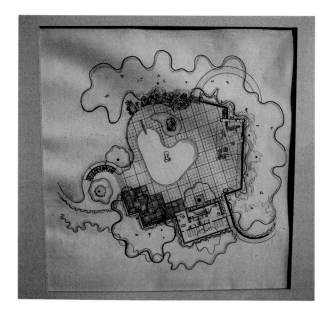

placed on color. A plant is either a sculptural entity unto itself or it is part of the bigger picture.

Christopher Tunnard in his book, *Gardens in the Modern Landscape*, suggests a plant list for the modern garden entitled "Architect's Plants" which he describes as "useful structural material and (which) have not been chosen especially for their interest when in flower."[45] For an exotic effect he suggests, Adam's needle, *Yucca gloriosa;* New Zealand Flax, *Phormium tenax;* and Windmill Palm, *Trachycarpus fortunei.* The use of variegated plants especially those "with bright, well-defined variegation" are encouraged, such as Golden oleaster, *Eleagnus pungens aureo-variegata* (now referred to as simply "Variegata") and variegated periwinkle, *Vinca major elegantissima.*[46] Unusual conifers, like Monkey Puzzle tree, *Araucaria imbricata;* and weeping European Spruce, *Picea excelsa pendula* are recommended for their shape as well as the winter form of Chinese Witch hazel, *Hamamelis mollis.*

As a result of the abstract treatment of plants, the modern movement left very few memorable planting designs in its wake because a collection of sculpural plants does not create a design. What characterized this period of landscape architecture was sensitivity to the site, awareness of the climate, the development of new design materials, and an organic form and movement in the landscape.

Plants recommended for creating a Modern American Garden include:[47]

Botanical Name	Common name
Elaeagnus pungens aureo-variegata	golden oleaster
Hamemelis mollis	Chinese witch hazel
Hosta fortunei	plantain lily
Juniperus chinensis Pfitzeriana	spreading Chinese juniper
Phormium tenax	New Zealand flax
Yucca gloriosa	Adam's needle

THE ENVIRONMENTAL MOVEMENT (1970–PRESENT)

Modernism in the landscape labored along until the 1970s, when it was eclipsed by the birth of the environmental movement. Through the influence of the book *Design with Nature,*[48] by landscape architect Ian McHarg, landscape design began to embrace the larger concepts of environmental planning, the conservation of open space, and the preservation of *ecosystems.* The field of environmental science was born and, concurrently, an ecological view of nature was espoused in design. McHarg felt the environment, defined in terms of preserved ecosystems, should determine locations for specific land uses. This concept encourages stewardship of the land as a viable prerequisite for design. By integrating art and environmental science in the landscape, "equanimity, health, and introspection" could be preserved.[49]

Environmentalism advocates the preservation and use of native plants in an artistic way. Through an understanding of the fragile interdependencies of natural systems, comprehension of the *microclimate,* and the ramifications of plant placement, a pattern emerges that guides the design. The significant plants are natives that display contextual regionalism—plants of the region, which vary in different parts of the country.

A good example of this design concept is the Crosby Arboretum, located in Picayune, Mississippi, designed by the Philadelphia firm Andropogon Associates working with the Mississippi landscape architect, Edward Blake. The flat site of the Crosby Arboretum, often referred to as Pinecote, displays the ecosystems of the region.[50] A pine savanna landscape is ecologically controlled by fire (Figure 1–51). The newly constructed pond surrounded by cypress, beech, and tupelo trees mimics the water fluctuations of a typical beaver pond; its form creates a picturesque stroll garden that introduces and isolates different plant communities and offers views of the Pinecote Pavilion (Figure 1–52). The pavilion, designed by architect Fay Jones, is an inspiring wooden structure nestled in the landscape. The Crosby Arboretum promotes ecologically sound design by understanding local ecosystems, utilizing native plant species, and preserving the naturally evolving processes in the landscape. (A list of typical plants is not possible due to the regional nature of this design movement.)

1-51 *Crosby Arboretum, Picayune, Mississippi, designed by Andropogon Associates and landscape architect Edward Blake.*

1-52 *Pinecote Pavilion at Crosby Arboretum, designed by architect Fay Jones.*

SUMMARY

This brief overview of significant historic developments in landscape architecture is presented as an inspiration for planting design. These concepts are not to be copied or inserted as a "style" into a planting plan but are offered to increase the reader's awareness of historic precedent and to serve as a point of departure for expressing today's design ideals.

ENDNOTES

1   Homer, *The Odyssey*, trans. E.V. Rieu (London: Penguin, 1946), 98.

2   Garrett Eckbo, *Landscape for Living* (New York: F.W. Dodge, 1950), 10.

3   Sylvia Crowe, *Garden Design* (Woodbridge U.K.: Garden Art Press, 1958), 36.

4   Henry V. Hubbard and Theodora Kimball, *An Introduction to the Study of Landscape Design* (New York: MacMillan, 1927), 29–30.

5   John Dixon Hunt and Peter Willis, *The Genius of the Place: The English Landscape Garden, 1620–1820.* (Cambridge: MIT Press, 1975), 2.

6   Spiro Kostoff, *A History of Architecture* (New York: Oxford University Press, 1955), 70.

7   Penelope Hobhouse, *Gardening Through the Ages,* (New York: Simon and Schuster, 1992) 12–14.

8   Lawrence Cunningham and John Reich, *Culture and Values: A Survey of Western Humanities,* Vol. 1 (Orlando: Harcourt Brace, 1994), 75–78.

9   G.A. Jellicoe, *Studies in Landscape Design* (London: Oxford University Press, 1960), 31.

10   Ibid., 48.

11   Helmut Baumann. *The Greek Plant World in Myth, Art, and Literature* trans. William T. Stearn and Eldwyth Ruth Stearn (Portland OR: Timber Press, 1993), 185–187.

12   Ibid., 47.

13   *Peripatetic* is derived from the Greek word *peri* (around) *patein* (to tread).

14   Cunningham and Reich, *Culture and Values,* 148.

15   Pompeii was a city near Naples, Italy, that was destroyed in August, AD 79, by the volcanic eruption of Mount Vesuvius. Lava preserved a great deal of the remains, which provide knowledge of ancient Roman life.

16   Wilhelmina F. Jashemski, "The Campanian Peristyle Garden," *Ancient Roman Gardens* (Washington, D.C.: Dumbarton Oaks, Vol. 7, 1981), 46–47.

17   The term *villa* refers to not just the house or garden but the entire estate or complex of main building, garden, farmland, and outbuildings.

18   Hobhouse, *Gardening Through the Ages,* 18.

19   Christopher Thacker, *The History of Gardens* (Berkeley: University of California Press, 1979), 44.

20   Much of the information on plants utilized in Chinese gardens is derived from Thacker, *History of Gardens,* 56–58.

21   Paul Meyvaert, "The Medieval Monastic Garden," *Medieval Gardens,* Elizabeth MacDougal (Washington, D.C.: Dumbarton Oaks, Vol. 9, 1983), 31.

22   Thacker, *The History of Gardens,* 1979, 84–85.

23   Ibid., 86.

24   Ibid., 86.

25   Claudia Lazzaro, *The Italian Renaissance Garden,* (New Haven: Yale University Press, 1990), 8.

26   John Prest, *The Garden of Eden: The Botanic Garden and the Re-Creation of Paradise* (New Haven: Yale University Press, 1981), 9–10.

27   Crowe, *Garden Design,* 38–39.

28   Hubbard and Kimball, *An Introduction to the Study of Landscape Design,* 43–44.

29   Crowe, *Garden Design,* 52.

30   Horace Walpole, quoted by Hunt and Willis in *The Genius of the Place,* 11.

31   Charles Moore, William J. Mitchell, and William Turnbull Jr., *The Poetics of the Garden* (Cambridge: MIT Press, 1988), 136–144.

32   Hobhouse, *Gardening Through the Ages,* 222.

33   This list is compiled from John Highstone, *Victorian Gardens* (San Francisco: Harper & Row, 1982).

34   Reginald Blomfield and F. Inigo Thomas, *The Formal Garden in England* (London: Waterstone, 1892), 2.

35   Edith Wharton, *Italian Villas and Their Gardens,* (New York: Century, 1904), 205.

36   David Ottewill, *The Edwardian Garden* (New Haven: Yale University Press, 1989), 71.

37   Ibid., 2.

38   Richard Guy Wilson, "The Great Civilization," *The American Renaissance: 1876–1917* (New York: Brooklyn Museum, 1979), 82.

39   The École des Beaux-Arts was an architecture school in Paris (1819–1968) whose doctrine was characterized by by the revival of classical design principles of antiquity and the Renaissance. This method of teaching dominated architecture schools in America during the late nineteenth century and through the middle of the twentieth century.

40   In architecture schools today, the Golden Age is often referred to as the Beaux-Arts Tradition.

41   Frederick Law Olmsted was very concerned with preserving the environment and incorporating the idea of "communitiveness"—community—in his projects. Eckbo, Rose, and Kiley were not the first designers to be concerned with societal issues.

42   Marc Treib, ed, *Modern Landscape Architecture: A Critical Review.* (Cambridge: MIT Press, 1993), x.

43   Treib's *Modern Landscape Architecture: A Critical Review* was an invaluable source of information for this portion of chapter 1.

44   James Rose, "Plants Dictate Garden Forms," *Pencil Points* (November 1939), 695.

45   Christopher Tunnard, *Gardens in the Modern Landscape,* (London: Architectural Press, 1938), 118.

46   Ibid., 120.

47   This list is adapted from plants recommended by Christopher Tunnard in *Gardens in the Modern Landscape,* (London: Architectural Press, 1938), 118–125. He describes the plants listed as "examples of useful structural materials that have not been chosen for their interest when in flower . . . which in various ways can be employed to contribute to the shape of the atmosphere of certain familiar settings."

48   Ian McHarg, *Design with Nature,* (Garden City, NY: Doubleday/Natural History Press, 1967).

49   Ibid., 5.

50   "Pinecote" was the name given to the Intrepretive Center's pavilion by architect Fay Jones. Since 'cote' is a shelter for birds; it became linked in Jones' mind with the natural shelter provided by the nearby pine trees. The name was later extended to the entire sixty-four-acre site. This is described in Felice Frankel and Jory Johnson's book, *Modern Landscape Architecture: Redefining the Garden.* (New York: Abbeville Press Publisher, 1991) 237.

Analyzing the Environment

Plants are not jumbled together in chance assortments by nature but are grouped in very definite associations depending on the five conditions of ecology—soil, moisture, temperature, light, and wind.

FLORENCE BELL ROBINSON, *Planting Design*[1]

THE ENVIRONMENT: CLIMATE AND SOIL

Planting design is complex because it incorporates design concepts with intricate technical requirements. We must combine horticultural knowledge with artistic sensibility if the plants are to live. This aspect of the design process, done in conjunction with the design exploration in Chapter 3, is the analysis of the environmental relationships of plants. An *environmental relationship* is a plant's natural affinities that evolve from interaction with the physical characteristics of the site—light, soil, moisture, and wind. We can think of this as "nature's principles of composition."[2] Numerous factors influence these plant alliances; the most important are climate and soil. Climate is the combined effect of temperature, moisture, light, and wind that directly affects a plant's vitality and adaptability. Soil composition, a combination of mineral elements, chemical compounds, organic matter, and living organisms nourishes and anchors plants.

The relationships among the physical environment (climate and soil) and the plants and animals that inhabit it produce *ecosystems* in nature. Bob Perry discusses ecosystems in his book *Landscape Plants for Western Regions*. He states that the success of native plant species and natural landscapes is a result of the complex process of evolution. By studying how plants and animals interact in their environment, natural landscape patterns emerge like an intricate tapestry upon the land. These relationships are all interconnected and collectively work as a whole system.

Perry cites the California native oak as a good example of an ecosystem:

The structure and function of a native oak reflects an entire ecosystem from soil nutrients and moisture to sunlight and topography. During its evolution, associated species of squirrels and birds have come to depend upon it for food and shelter that are necessary for their survival. At the same time, they often bury acorns in places where new trees can become established. The shade and leaf litter produced by such a tree provides microclimate conditions and a source of nutrients for understory plants. This increased diversity of plants provides additional sources of food, shelter, and habitat for animals and plants.[3]

In each different ecosystem, a specific interdependent community of plants and animals form. It is essential to study plants as members of an ecological community rather than just for their individual merits, because this tells us which plants are similarly adapted to a local climate and soil type and consequently grow together successfully as a group.

A maple and birch forest, located in northern Michigan, is a plant community named for the predominant plant species (Figure 2–1); so is an oak savanna landscape (Figure 2–2), located in northern California. Plant communities are exemplary vegetative models to be studied as design tools. By examining plants that characteristically grow together in their native habitat, you begin to observe climate and soil conditions conducive to their existence.

Understanding these environmental relationships is a fundamental step to many planning and design decisions because the proliferation of these relationships, benefits the environment, increases sustainability, and directly influences a plant's ability to grow, develop, and, ultimately, survive. In addition, sound environmental decisions contribute to the appropriateness of the design. You will be able to combine native plants with plants from all over the world that suit your environmental conditions.[4] Then ask yourself, does the design look believable? or inevitable? or does it appear out of context? That

2-1 *(left) Plant community: maple/birch forest, Houghton Lake, Michigan.*

2-2 *(right) Plant community: oak/savanna landscape, California. (PHOTO: CAROL BORNSTEIN)*

is, does the design flow and appear as an outgrowth of the climate the project is located in? A planting design that is out of context is one that tries to create a tropical rain forest in the desert or a coniferous forest in the tropics. Possible, perhaps, but probable, no. A good designer needs to learn to read the landscape. Looking at these relationships provides clues that will help you to determine the best plants to use.

CLIMATE

Temperature

A keen understanding of climate is a key factor in proper plant selection. When beginning a new project or exploring a new site, start by obtaining regional weather data for the project location. Typical high and low temperature ranges begin to define your plant palette selections. Effects of temperature vary with plant species, stage of plant growth, soil type, and plant hardiness.

The hardiness of a plant is its ability to grow in the expected minimum or lowest temperature of a region. These regions are referred to as plant hardiness zones. The Agricultural Research Service of the United States Department of Agriculture (USDA) studied this issue and created eleven zones in the United States, each with a common set of temperatures ranges (Figure 2–3). However, humidity patterns, rainfall distribution, and evening temperatures may vary region to region and one must use caution when interpreting this information. For example, zone 8 in Athens, Georgia, is very different from zone 8 in central California.[5] The western United States was studied in detail and broken down into a system of twenty-four climatic zones.[6] Hardiness zones are for general reference and serve as a broad classification of climatic factors.

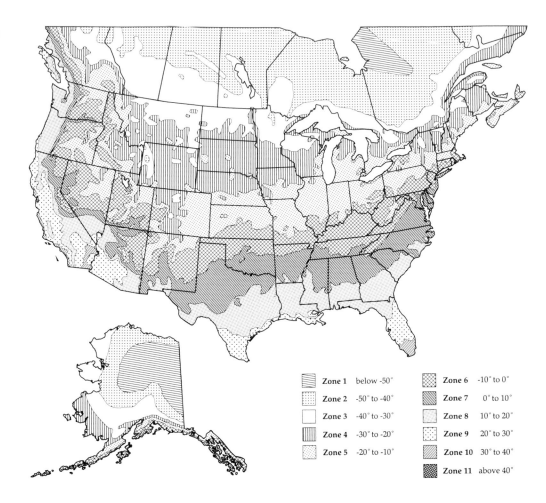

Zone 1 below -50°			**Zone 6** -10° to 0°	
Zone 2 -50° to -40°			**Zone 7** 0° to 10°	
Zone 3 -40° to -30°			**Zone 8** 10° to 20°	
Zone 4 -30° to -20°			**Zone 9** 20° to 30°	
Zone 5 -20° to -10°			**Zone 10** 30° to 40°	
			Zone 11 above 40°	

It is the local climate that inevitably directs our design decisions. The intimate interaction between site and local climatic factors—slopes, valleys, proximity to large bodies of water, wind, and altitude—directly affects our plant choices and their placement (Figure 2–4). When visiting a site, make careful observations of microclimate and local weather conditions. Visit botanical gardens and arboretums in the region where you can talk to horticulturists who can advise you on specifics of the locale. Retail nursery people are also a good source of climate information and a link between what can be grown in a region and what is available for sale. Obtaining lists of native plant species, indigenous soils, and peculiar weather conditions can inform plant choices.

Moisture Conditions

Moisture is the environmental factor referring to the amount of rainfall, snow, fog, and other forms of water a region receives. The average annual rainfall and the season it falls in are important to plant growth. Available moisture influences the growing season. The growing season of a region is typically determined by the number of days that occur between the last frost of winter and the first frost of autumn. Temperate regions such as the Northeast, Southeast, and Midwest combine increasing temperatures (frost-free days) with spring and summer rains and lengthening daylight for active spring and summer growing seasons and a dormant winter period. In contrast, Mediterranean climates, such as California, experience very few frost days and the growing season depends more upon

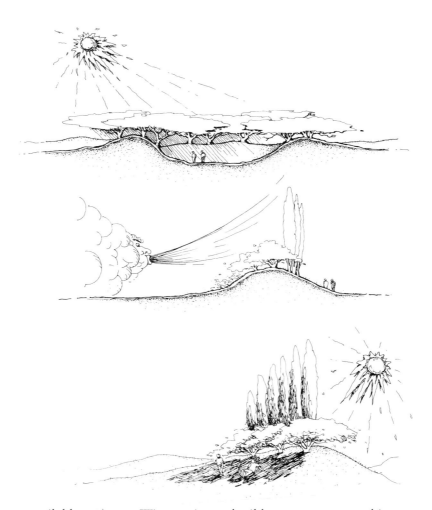

available moisture. Winter rains and mild temperatures combine to create a midwinter to late-spring growing season. Mediterranean plants often experience a summer dormancy when little moisture is available and temperatures are extremely high.

In addition to rainfall, humidity, dew, and fog are important sources of moisture. High humidity over extended periods of time fosters a rich and luxurious vegetation. The Pacific Northwest, Florida, England, and the tropics are examples of areas with high humidity producing lush plant growth.

Dew as an available source of moisture is a common result of clear nights, rapid radiation loss, and moist air mass. In desert regions dew accumulation is significant, one to two inches per year, as an added form of moisture essential to some desert plant species.[7]

Fog can be an important source of moisture for plant growth, particularly if it occurs during the growing season. Not only does it add to the actual soil moisture supply but it also adds moisture to leaf surfaces and delays increases in temperature. For example, in the San Francisco Bay area the fog cover can add approximately eight inches of moisture *annually* to the coastal region.[8]

Light

Sunlight in varying degrees is a necessity for plant growth. The ingredients and method for the basic process of capturing and storing the sun's energy are known as *photosynthesis*. The energy in sunlight is trapped by plant leaves and used in photosynthesis to convert carbon dioxide from the air, and water transported by plant roots, into sugars, which feed the plant. Oxygen is released as a by-product of the process. Chlorophyll, the green pigment in plants, is the agent for the transaction. Sugar, the principal product of photosynthesis, sustains all plants and in turn, all animal life as well.

Light Duration and Intensity.   The characteristics of light that are most important for plant growth are intensity and duration. The strength, angle, and number of hours of sunlight directly affect plant growth. In most areas of the world these characteristics of sunlight vary from sunrise to sunset and from season to season. As the earth revolves around the sun, the Northern Hemisphere tilts toward the sun part of the year and away from it for part of the year. As a result, the sun is strong in the summer and weak in the winter, and areas shaded most of the day in one season may be in full sunlight in another. Light intensity also varies from north to south. The sun in the south is stronger than in the north. Furthermore, sunlight is greater at high elevations and in dry climates than at low elevations in moist climates because it passes through less atmosphere and moisture. Light intensity can be reduced by smoke, pollution, and dust—all are detrimental to plant growth. The sun controls daily, seasonal, and latitudinal variations in light intensity.

Vegetation also changes light intensity. Forests and woods create varying degrees of intensity. Plants at the top of the forest canopy have a different vigor than plants growing on the forest floor. Over time the intensity alters as some plants die and understory or younger plants receive more direct sunlight. Plant species are adapted to specific degrees of sunlight and are classified accordingly as shade-tolerant, sun-loving, or tolerant of partial shade. (This is explained in detail in Chapter 6.)

Duration of sunlight controls the following processes in certain plant species: leaf abscission (leaf fall), dormancy, hardiness, leaf size, pigment, and germination. In tropical regions where there is little variation in light intensity the effect of light duration is barely noticeable; plants grow, flower, and fruit virtually year round. In climates where the quantity of daylight fluctuates with the seasons, plants respond differently to the light they receive. Plants must grow, flower, and fruit within a limited time period because there are more hours of daylight in the summer and fewer hours in the winter as one moves further north from the equator.

Wind

Wind, or the circulation of air over the earth's surface, affects the growth and persistence of plant communities. Circulating air increases evaporation from plant foliage and the ground surface. More wind increases transpiration which is the evaporation of water from plants. Weak or brittle plants do not grow well in windy areas. Many plant communities evolve according to the ability of the plant species to survive wind.

Topography affects climate by its orientation to the sun as well as influencing air movement. Wind speeds on the crest of a hill may be 20 percent greater than those on flat ground, and the wind is generally quieter on the lee side of a hill than on its weather side.

Wind can be significantly modified by structures and plants. It may be intercepted, diverted, or lessened by obstructions such as buildings, walls, fences, earth forms, and plants. Plants control wind by obstruction, guidance, or deflection. This can be achieved not only

2-5 *A windbreak. (Photo: Marc Treib)*

by the form and texture of the plant itself but also by its placement. Plants may be used in conjunction with land forms and architectural materials to alter airflow over the landscape and around or through buildings. Plant forms such as *windbreaks, shelterbelts,* and *hedgerows* manipulate wind conditions (Figure 2–5).

The Environmental Analysis Drawing: Climate

Record significant sunlight, wind, and moisture variations on a site survey or measured drawing of the site to initiate the analysis. A measured drawing entails the accurately surveyed project site boundaries including contours and important structures and plantings within the site (Figures 2–6 and 2–7). This drawing is referred to as a base plan and provides the basis for the environmental analysis. The drawing is most usefully rendered at 1 inch = 20 feet for residential projects and 1 inch = 100 feet or 1 inch = 200 feet, depending on the site size, for larger projects. (The survey drawing is useful for the design exploration described in Chapter 3.)

Using a compass, orient yourself due north in order to identify the direction of the sun at noon. Note the movement of the sun throughout the day and throughout the seasons. Label areas that are extremely sunny or shady (Figure 2–8). This is also the stage in your analysis at which to indicate significant slopes that occur on the site or any unusual land masses. The degree of existing slope provides information that can be used in conjunction with plant choice, soil amendment, or potential erosion and drainage problems. Check the directions of the prevailing winds. Indicate radical temperature changes on the site as well as areas that appear unusually moist or dry.

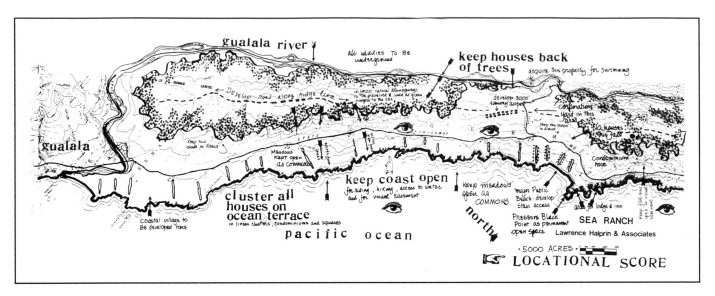

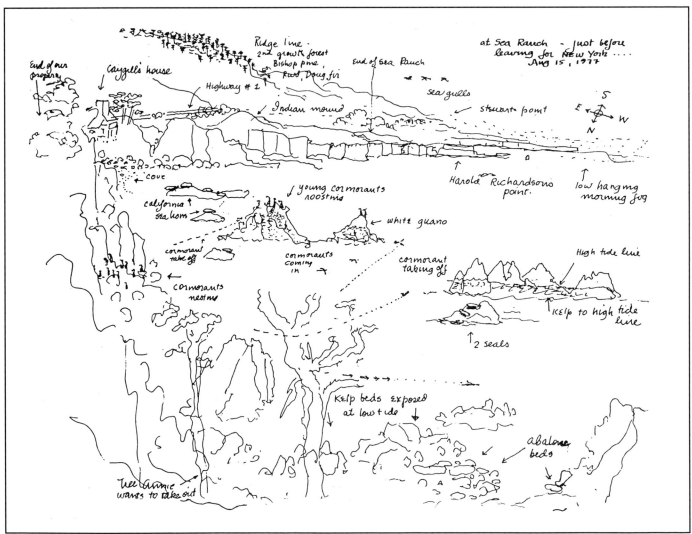

2-6 and 2-7 *A site analysis containing climatic and design information relevant to the project.* (Drawings: Lawrence Halprin & Associates)

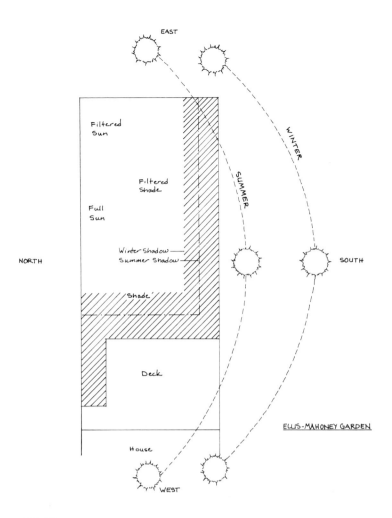

Figure labels: EAST, WINTER, SUMMER, NORTH, SOUTH, Filtered Sun, Filtered Shade, Full Sun, Winter Shadow, Summer Shadow, Shade, Deck, ELLIS-MAHONEY GARDEN, House, WEST

SOIL

Physical and Chemical Structure, Moisture, Aeration

Soil anchors a plant and is its foundation for survival because it provides food and water. Therefore, it is necessary for the designer to understand the chemical and physical composition of the soil before an attempt is made to grow plants in it. The chemical properties of the soil indicate its source and its physical properties reveal the weather conditions that have acted upon it. Rocks of many kinds break down to form the basis of soil. The size of the soil particles, their color, and their hardness are related to the parent rock and these affect the permeability, solubility, and temperature of the soil. Heat and cold, freezing and thawing, blasting wind, and the drip and wear of water all act to break down and wear away the physical structure of rocks, thus producing soil. Chemically, soils vary according to the mixture of organic decay and mineral nutrients they contain. For example, granite decomposes to clay, quartz becomes sand, and calcareous soils result from limestone, causing a diversity in available nutrients and consequently the fertility of the soil.

Physical Structure

The physical structure of soil reveals the climatic phenomena that have created it. Florence Bell Robinson explains it succinctly:

A stratified soil shows the action of water; a fine-textured soil of a homogenous nature, the action of wind; a conglomerate mixture with much coarser material intermingled, the grinding of ice. Wind, water, and ice all act to transport and redeposit the residual soils of the earth and the soil when redeposited becomes known respectively as *aeolian, alluvial,* or *glacial,* according to the agent of its deposition. The loess of China is an *aeolian* soil, a fine silt that the wind picks up and drops again; deltas and valleys such as those of the Nile, the Mississippi, and the Rio Grande are *alluvial* soils deposited from the waters of great rivers when the current is slowed from one cause or another; the soil in the region of the Great Lakes is *glacial* soil, ground and carried and dropped in its present location by the action of the great ice cap that once covered northern North America.[9]

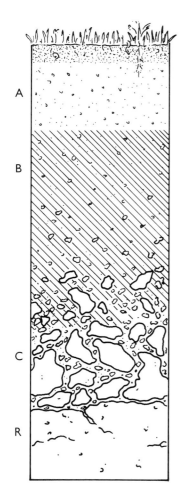

2-9 *Soil profile.*

Soils develop over time into distinctly visible layers; these layers are called *horizons* and their sum makes up a *soil profile* that reflects effects of climate, organic matter, and time. Soil horizons are designated by the letters *A, B, C,* and *R,* moving down from the soil surface. Figure 2–9 is an example of a soil profile typically found under a lawn. The *A* horizon is dark in color as a result of profuse root growth throughout the horizon. It is rarely more than one to two feet deep, often much less, and is most conducive to plant growth because it is high in nutrients from decomposing organic matter. (In a forest, the addition of organic matter to this horizon is from leaves and bark.) This horizon often contains *humus,* the dark brown residue that results from decaying organic matter. Humus is actually a more generic term than a precise one; its qualities reflect its origin and composition. Humus is advantageous because it retains moisture, loosens soil particles, nourishes beneficial microorganisms, and adds nitrogen to the soil.[10] The *B* horizon is often where clay, organic matter, iron, and aluminum accumulate. Parent material or unweathered material composes horizon *C.* Lastly, the *R* horizon is bedrock.[11]

Think about native soil configurations when choosing your plant palette. Be aware of the amount of soil available to the plant for root development, especially for trees and shrubs.

The physical structure of the soil is a composite of its texture, aggregation, density, drainage, and water-holding capacity. Soil texture is an inherent quality. Texture ranges from very fine particles, usually sand, to coarse and gravelly, usually clay. Clay soils hold water and nutrients well but can drain poorly and be difficult to cultivate. Sandy soils are generally easy to work and well drained, but they have poor nutrient profiles and water-holding ability. The ideal soil exists somewhere between sand and clay. It is a soil with a loamy texture that is a balance of fine clay, silt, and sand.

Soil aggregation indicates how well the soil holds together. The ability of soil particles to form stable aggregates, giving it a crumbly, cake-like consistency, determines its structural soundness. Poor soils crumble to dust in your hands or are so dense they do not crumble at all. Structure and aggregation can be improved by increasing humus content. In fact, no matter what soil exists on a site, most of its qualities can be improved by increasing its organic matter and humus content. Earthworms, often present in rich humus, are an additional benefit to the soil. They improve soil quality and leave tunnels that aerate the soil and allow roots to develop.

Soil density is directly related to the availability of moisture and air in soil and is essential for plant growth. A soil may contain all the essential nutrients for a plant and still prohibit plant growth if proper moisture and aeration are not present. Aeration is the amount of air space existing between soil particles. Moisture and aeration are interdependent. A well-structured soil implies that the soil is well aerated because there is plenty of pore space between the soil granules. This pore space enables the soil to conduct moisture toward plant roots. Root growth is necessary for anchoring a plant in the soil.

Pore space affects not only nutrient availability but also soil temperature, drainage, and water-holding capacity, which are important to seed germination and root growth and development. A well-aerated soil is warmer than a wet, compacted soil; good drainage means an increase in soil heat. Dark soil absorbs heat and warms up more quickly than light-colored soil. When a soil is well aerated and the water table is relatively high, plant roots tend to be shallower or near the soil surface. In a heavier soil with little moisture the plant roots extend great depths searching for food. Cultivating the soil provides aeration. Feeding the soil through mulches that add organic matter and organic fertilizers provides nutrients.

Moisture provided to the soil in adequate amounts allows food absorption. A lack of moisture in the form of rain, snow, fog, dew, or irrigation prevents absorption of nutrients. In contrast, too much water can also inhibit plant growth because the plant suffers a loss of oxygen. Pore space in the soil fills with water and roots receive no air. The balance of these two environmental factors, moisture and air, directly relates to the development of a plant community because their combination affects plant distribution. Wet soils sustain bog plants such as the bald cypress, *Taxodium distichum,* seen in Figure 2–10, and *Gunnera manicata,* the large-leafed plant in Figure 2–11. Dry, sandy soils allow the cacti and succulents of the desert to flourish (Figure 2–12).

2-10 *(right) Bald cypress,* Taxodium distichum, *Isola Bella.*

2-11 *(bottom left)* Gunnera manicata. *(NYMAN'S GARDEN, ENGLAND)*

2-12 *(bottom right) Agave,* Agave deserti. *(PHOTO: CAROL BORNSTEIN)*

Chemical Structure

The chemical nature of soil reveals its origin. It is useful to know whether a soil has developed in place or has been transported from a distance. It is important to determine whether or not there has been a prior disturbance to the site.[12] Consequently, the analysis of the soil early on in a project is a necessary component of planting design. Soil can be tested in a laboratory to determine its chemical composition or the pH level of elements available for plant growth. A soil-testing lab can be located in the yellow pages or at a land grant university. A good analysis depends upon careful, accurate, and representative soil samples. For a large-scale project, three to five core samples may be necessary, dug at a depth of twelve to eighteen inches. If in doubt, obtain sampling instructions from the soils laboratory. Soil testing kits can be obtained for independent use at retail nurseries (Figure 2–13). Kits include vials, litmus paper, and nutrient solutions with instructions for determining pH and mineral content.

Determining a soil's pH, the measure of alkalinity or acidity, is essential in plant selection. pH values range from 0 to 14. A pH of less than 7 indicates an acid soil, greater than 7, alkaline, and 7 itself indicates a neutral soil. Soil pH has an visible effect on plant communities. Acid soils support acid-loving plants such as those in the Ericaceae family, which includes rhododendrons, azaleas, camellias, and heathers. Calcareous soils support plants that thrive in alkaline soils, such as hellebores, *Arbutus unedo*, the strawberry tree, and *Viburnum tinus*, laurustinus. Figure 2–14 shows an example of an ericaceous plant community in the Delaware Valley.[13]

Soil analyses also provide a nutrient breakdown. Soils vary in their mineral content as did the rocks from which they came. A soil's mineral nutrients are united in complex chemical combinations, but sixteen elements are considered absolutely essential to plant growth. An imbalance of any one of these nutrients can be detected in a plant. The sixteen essential nutrients are:

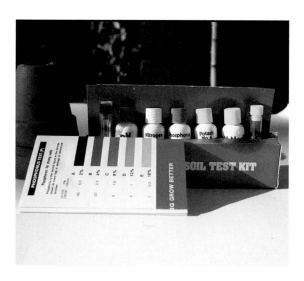

2-13   *(left) Soil testing kit.*
2-14   *(right) Ericaceous plant community, Mount Cuba, Delaware.* (PHOTO: CAROL BORNSTEIN)

	Macronutrients	*Micronutrients*
Available from the soil	calcium	boron
	magnesium	chlorine
	nitrogen	copper
	phosphorous	iodine
	potassium	iron
	sulfur	manganese
		molybdenum
Available from air and water	carbon	
	hydrogen	
	oxygen	

These nutrients exist in plants in a delicate balance. Too much or too little of any one element results in stunted plant growth, lack of flowers and fruits, or leaf discoloration. For example, potassium affects color in flowers and fruit. Lack of it produces stunted growth and browning of leaf margins. Phosphorous deficiency causes poor lateral growth, spindly stems, and poor development of flowers and fruit. Too much or too little iron results in prominent leaf venation and yellow discoloring with leaf drop. An overabundance of nitrogen produces green vegetative growth but very few flowers or fruits.

The Environmental Analysis Drawing: Soil

Determine the existing type or types of soil located on your project site. Note the soil types on the analysis drawing and indicate pH readings (Figure 2–15). Jot down the different plant species growing there, especially plants that seem to be thriving. If you are unable to identify the plants, photograph them and take plant samples that are carefully sealed in plastic bags and labeled according to location. Try to have the plants identified by an expert as soon as possible. Combine this information with your notes on climate.

As you can see, the environmental picture of your landscape begins to emerge. You begin to read the landscape for clues that connect the factors of the environment to the entire ecosystem. Sound design decisions are made by careful analysis of the environment. Through examination of existing vegetation and the prerequisites of plants under consideration for use, one develops the ability to choose plant materials that will succeed and enhance design objectives. As the landscape architect, Beatrix Farrand stated, "We must keep time with Nature and follow her forms of expression in different places while we carry out our own ideas and adaptations."[14]

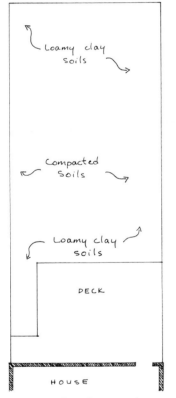

2-15 *Soil analysis can be added to climatic analysis.*

(ELLIS-MAHONEY GARDEN)

ENDNOTES

1   Florence Bell Robinson, *Planting Design* (Champaign, IL: Garrard Press, 1940), 126.

2   Chip Sullivan, *Drawing the Landscape* (New York: Van Nostrand Reinhold, 1995), 14.

3   Bob Perry, *Landscape Plants for Western Regions* (Claremont: Land Design Publishing, 1992), 25.

4   It is important when using plant species from other countries or even other regions of the country to be aware of any invasive characteristics they might have.

5   Allan M. Armitage, *Herbaceous Perennials* (Athens Georgia: Varsity Press, 1989), xii.

6   The Western United States was studied by numerous biologists, climatologists, horticulturists, and the California Agricultural Extension working for the editors of *Sunset Magazine* to develop the 24 climate zones.

7   Bill Mollison, *Permaculture* (Washington, D.C.: Island Press, 1990), 111–112.

8   Richard W. Harris, *Arboriculture: Integrated Management of Landscape Trees, Shrubs, and Vines* (Englewood Cliffs, New Jersey: Prentice Hall, 1992), 110.

9   Robinson, *Planting Design,* 107.

10   Humus is discussed in detail in Chapter 7. Remember, an excess of humus can be disastrous, as it creates excess acid that can be toxic to many plants.

11   F. D. Foth and L. M. Turk, *Fundamentals of Soil Science,* 5th ed., (New York: John Wiley & Sons, 1965), 5–8.

12   Native soils are endemic to the climate and ecosystem, and are constantly evolving, adding organic matter to the soil. Thus, it is best to know what soil is naturally occurring rather than working with an unnatural premix. The added soil will eventually decompose or erode and you are left with native soils that may not agree with the plants you chose for the imported soil.

13   Soil survey maps are available in the United States on a county-by-county basis. Contact the local cooperative extension office in your county.

14   Beatrix Farrand, *"The Garden as a Picture,"* Scribner's 43 (July 1907), 2–8.

Exploring Design Ideas

I believe that architects should design gardens to be used,

as much as the houses they build, to develop a sense of

beauty and the taste and inclination toward the fine arts

and other spiritual values.

LUIS BARRAGAN

In the environmental analysis, Chapter 2, we synthesized the horticultural requirements of the project into a succinct drawing that will eventually guide us in choosing appropriate plants for the site. Now the transition must be made to the artistic aspect of the design. Design exploration is a process that combines investigating or exploring a site (real or imaginary) to determine its parameters and creating from it something new or unique that evolves from one's thought and imagination. Good design creates memorable places. It consists of three design objectives that ultimately form the landscape plan:[1]

1. establishing a design concept

2. determining the design program

3. creating the design

These objectives are not necessarily accomplished in a specific order but rather are refined throughout the exploration. Often when working on one aspect of the design, information is revealed about another. This process is not linear but one that goes back and forth, sometimes repeating steps along the way.

ESTABLISHING A DESIGN CONCEPT

Establishing a design concept begins on the first site visit or when first discussing the project. The design concept is the idea that inspires the form of the garden. Be aware of your initial thoughts, sensations, feelings, and reactions to the project site. There are many potential inspirations for the design—your travels, a painting, gardening, even your dreams can influence the outcome of your work. Maybe the concept is inspired by a piece of music; for example, Antonín Dvořák's *Serenade for Strings* always makes me think of a graceful, sweeping walk through a grove of flowering lilacs. You might feel compelled to tell a story about the client, the environment, or the regional culture through the land-

3-1 *Gateway Garden of New World Plants at Matthei Botanical Garden, Ann Arbor, Michigan.*

3-2 (left) Pavilion in the Garden of Hesperides in southern California. (ARCHITECT: LUTAH MARIE RIGGS, GARDEN DESIGNER: ELIZABETH DE FOREST)

3-3 (right) The borrowed view from the pavilion in the Garden of Hesperides.

scape or landforms. To illustrate, the concept for the Gateway Garden of New World Plants at the Matthaei Botanical Garden in Ann Arbor, Michigan (Figure 3–1), is composed of perennial and annual plants that trace their origins to wild species native to the Americas.

Perhaps the site itself speaks to you in a profound way and your concept reflects the *genius loci,* an environmental phenomena often overlooked or misunderstood but nevertheless one of the most significant aspects of the design process. A site's special qualities or its inherent spiritual character gives a landscape its own intrinsic potential or emotional appeal—its genius loci. This spirit of a place is often so powerful it is an inspiration for the design.

Early American Indians, for example, often selected their settlement patterns and planting traditions through careful study of the environment as revealed through the spirits of trees and rivers. Ancient Romans "read places like faces, as outward revelation of a living inner spirit. Each place had its individual genius."[2] They recognized that certain places had a special character or identity. Consequently, the locations of the great cities of antiquity were a result of a strong spiritual identity with the surroundings. The genius loci was also an inspiration for the English landscape movement of the eighteenth century; to consult the genius of the place was to seek an understanding of the potential natural perfection of a site and to assist in its artistic emergence where necessary by discreet intervention.

A befitting application of genius loci can be seen at a garden in southern California. The design of the mountainside site with sweeping views of the Pacific Ocean was inspired by and named for the Greek myth of the Hesperides—three nymphs who lived in a beautiful garden at the extreme western edge of the world. At the modern-day Hesperides estate, the house was designed by the architect Lutah Marie Riggs and the garden by Elizabeth de Forest (wife of the landscape architect Lockwood de Forest) in 1952. The garden combines classical sculpture, columns and plants reminiscent of Ancient Greece and Rome. Olive trees, acanthus, and lavender re-create a Mediterranean landscape. The design is a series of outdoor rooms, but the most compelling component is the view from the house which pulls you out to the garden pavilion and then to the spectacular view of the Pacific Ocean beyond (Figures 3–2, 3–3).

Discover the genius loci of a site or project. As you walk around the existing landscape, pay close attention to the feelings evoked from shade and sunlight. Be aware of the different fragrances and sounds in the garden. Enhance the genius of the place. In the words of Alexander Pope:

To build, to plant, whatever you intend,
To rear the Column, or the Arch to bend,
To swell the Terras, or to sink the Grot;
In all, let Nature never be forgot,
Consult the Genius of the Place in all
That tells the waters, or to rise or fall.[3]

Whatever the inspiration, the first step is to record and sketch your ideas in both picture and written form. As you walk the grounds or participate in a meeting, keep a small notebook with you at all times to jot down ideas as they occur to you throughout the day (Figure 3–4). Many times these initial thoughts prove to be the catalyst for the entire project. The landscape architect Chip Sullivan stated, "By drawing you experience nuances and subtleties and participate in your surroundings through observation and personal experience. The designer has to learn not only to perceive form, but also to be able to preserve, analyze, and transmit it."[4] Often the concept drawings appear quite abstract. Keep at it. Draw, draw, draw until you begin to see a concept evolve.

3-4 *An assortment of sketchbooks.*

Planting the Landscape

DETERMINING THE DESIGN PROGRAM

In conjunction with the creation of a design concept, the landscape architect must develop a comprehensive design solution that satisfies the needs of a client. This is called determining the design program of the project—the human activities or program uses that a design must accommodate. Contemplate the purpose of the garden. Is it a place for serenity and repose? Does the site need to project a specific corporate image? Or is it a space for recreation and large public gatherings? Is it a community project? Sometimes clients are uncertain of their needs and desires. It is up to you to work with them to determine and achieve the specific goals of the project in an orderly manner. Whether working on a public, corporate, or private project, the necessities and requirements of the program can be outlined. The ultimate form of the garden is influenced by combining the design concept with the project program and the primary requirements of the composition.

CREATING THE DESIGN

The next step of the process is to make a thorough inventory of the site to determine the existing conditions, opportunities, and constraints for your design concept. A schematic design translates the concept into reality. An initial thought, idea, or sketch may lead you to later design solutions. Figure 3–5 is a compilation of four schematic drawings that evolved over time. Figure 3–6 shows the final schematic design. The process of creating the design is one of evolution. Work with the big idea—use a fat pencil and lots of lots of trace paper. Do not be overwhelmed by details at this point. Dream and draw.

Try to think about abstract and concrete aspects of the design. Where is the site located? Is it in the city or in a natural environment? What values or attitudes are revealed in the choice of location? What are the means by which order is imposed on the site? What is the relationship of the building to the landscape? Identify the procession or circulation through the garden, axial conditions, points of transition, thresholds, edges—all these elements must be taken into consideration before a single plant can be chosen. Be imag-

3-5 *Evolution of design concept, trace solutions.* (DRAWING: CHIP SULLIVAN)

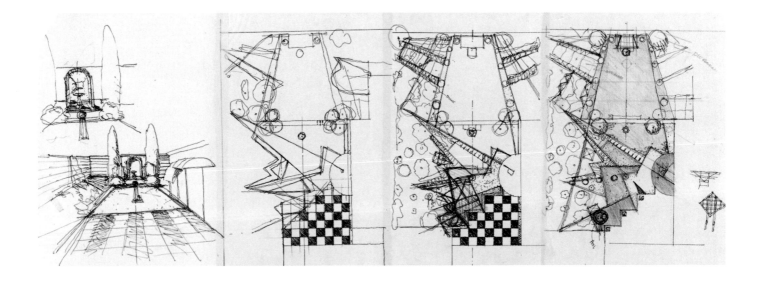

3-6 *Final schematic design drawing.* (DRAWING: CHIP SULLIVAN)

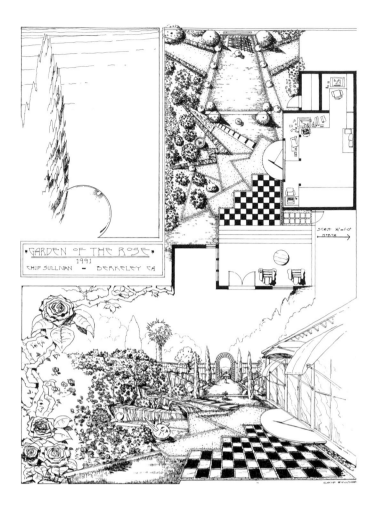

3-7 *Layers of trace paper allow you to examine the effect of various design criteria.*

The method described here is an analytic design tool for translating abstract concepts and ideas into physical form and then examining that form and its spatial characteristics. Ten design criteria were selected to communicate the basic concepts that give physical form to a plan. The criteria offer ways to organize decisions, provide order, and generate form. They are not meant to limit or restrict a designer's thoughts but to serve as catalysts for design. Although there are other criteria, these ten are a good starting place because they convey the essential features needed to develop and illustrate design associations. Each criterion is illustrated in a simple diagram that allows for comparison of different features. The emphasis is on how these concepts create spaces and then how the form of these spaces is reinforced using plants.

1. axial conditions
2. circulation
3. geometry
4. grid
5. hierarchy

6. points of transition
7. structuring elements
8. public versus private space
9. borrowed view
10. figure and ground

Keep in mind that an analysis is a building process and that each step builds upon the other. Begin by placing trace paper over the base plan created in Chapter 2. Outline the boundaries of the site. Transform your design ideas and concepts into drawn form. This process is abstract but the physical act of drawing will put you in touch with your unconscious mind and enable your ideas to flow. Use the design criteria as a way to initiate the process. Axial conditions, circulation, geometry, and grid are all conceptual criteria; these go on the trace paper first (Figure 3–7). Hierarchy refines the conceptual ideas and gives more shape to the form. Structuring elements further define form. Both further define public versus private space. Points of transition applies to all the criteria; it is a subheading of each. The "borrowed view" expands the limits of the design. A figure-and-ground drawing is a test or analysis of what you have designed. Think as you draw. Try to imagine yourself walking through the spaces you create.

inative! Think about elements of surprise, repose, the borrowed view, as well as movement, privacy, and distance. How will plants reinforce these ideas? The exploration begins to expose the necessity of a method of organizing ideas.

DESIGN ANALYSIS OF FOLLY FARM

An analysis of the residential garden at Folly Farm demonstrates how the design criteria have been implemented successfully and displays fundamental and functional relationships central to planting design (Figure 3–8).[5] Folly Farm is located in the village of Sulhamstead in the lush Kennet Valley of southern England. The garden was originally designed between 1906 and 1916 by the architect Sir Edwin Lutyens and the plantswoman Gertrude Jekyll. Folly Farm displays design techniques characteristic of the Edwardian garden. Formal axes and the repetition of geometric forms are softened by exuberant plantings. The planting beds were originally filled with aquilegias, poppies, gypsophilia, irises, and white campanulas amidst a background of cistus, jasmine, clematis, laurustinus, hardy fuchsias, and roses which were typical of Jekyll's designs. Borders were edged with boxwood and the hedges were formed from yews.[6] Although analysis of an existing garden is different from that of a new garden, because all the elements are in place and easy to evaluate, Folly Farm provides a clear, concise study model. Archetypal ideas exist in the design of Folly Farm that transcend time and create architectural form.[7]

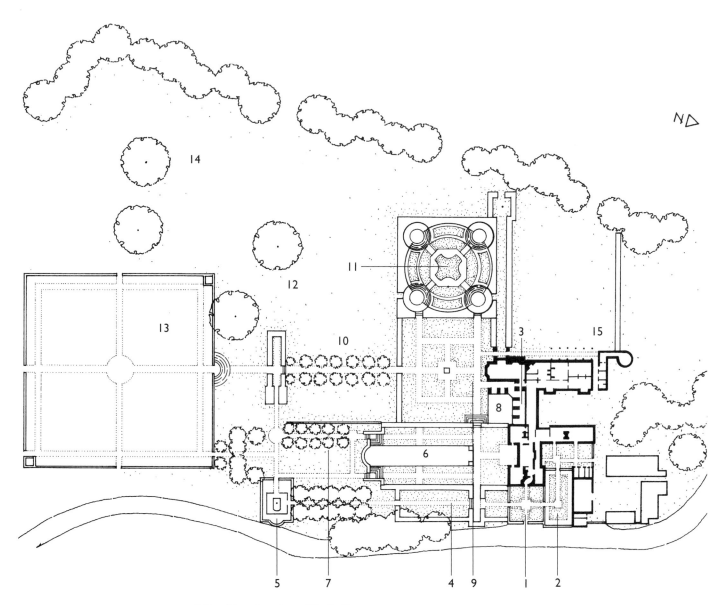

3-8 *Plan drawing of Folly Farm.*

 1. *Entrance Court*
 2. *Barn Court*
 3. *House*
 4. *Walk to White Garden*
 5. *White Garden*
 6. *Canal Garden*
 7. *Laburnum Palisade*
 8. *Loggia and Tank Garden*
 9. *Parterre Garden*
10. *Crabapple Allee*
11. *Rose Garden*
12. *Orchard*
13. *Kitchen Garden*
14. *Rhododendrons and Lawn*
15. *Service Wing*
(Original design, Architect Sir Edwin Lutyens and plantswoman, Gertrude Jekyll)

Axial Conditions

An axis is an imaginary line about which a form, area, or plane is organized. It can impose order on a landscape by focusing or organizing structures. The human need for order and visual clarity is explained by Mark Francis and Randy Hester in the book *The Meaning of Gardens*. "The psychologist or poet might call this the rage for order, a never-ending human quest to grasp the meaning of life within its context. The landscape architect calls this design."[8] An axis is a design tool which provides organization.

In design an axis can have numerous characteristics or forms. It can be a line of vision and/or a line of movement. It can represent an implied direction that unifies a number of elements and relates them to the entire design or it can be a street or walkway connecting two points. As a result, *path* and *axis* are sometimes identical. "Axes reach across space to draw together the important points in a place. . . . At best it is a thing of the mind, not just of the feet."[9] An axis can have horizontal and vertical components. Horizontal axes can be used for linear emphasis to create a direction through a usable space. A vertical axis can organize a volume of space.

In landscape architecture the axis has always been an important means of unifying different areas of a site. It is a statement of power and authority as it extends through the landscape. An axis can terminate with an object—a statue, fountain, art object, building, specimen plant, or a space—a garden room. Sometimes the axis is implied and the viewer can observe a strong visual axis but must proceed along a different path in the garden.

For example, the garden plan at Folly Farm is organized by formal structuring tools of major and minor axes (Figure 3–9). They link different elements of the garden together in a series of hierarchical compositions. There are three north-south axes. One major

3-9 *Axes diagram of Folly Farm.*

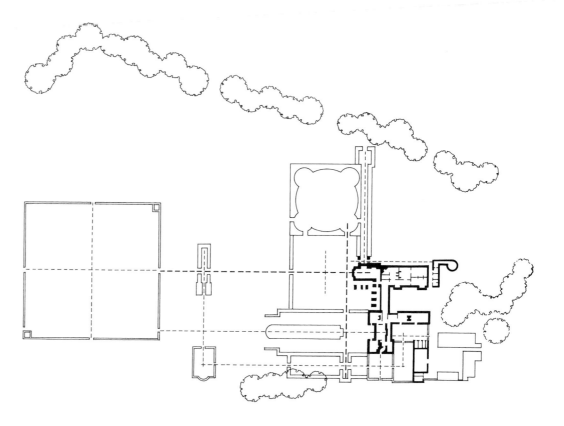

3-10 *Beginning of major north-south axis, Folly Farm.*

3-11 *Major north-south axis, Folly Farm.*

3-12 *Major north-south axis, Folly Farm.*

3-13 *Termination of major north-south axis, Folly Farm.*

3-14 *Secondary north-south axis, Folly Farm.*

3-15 *Secondary north-south axis, Folly Farm.*

north-south axis extends from the dining room of the house to the parterre garden through a crabapple allée (a later addition) and terminates at the gate of the walled kitchen garden (Figures 3–10, 3–11, 3–12, 3–13). A second north-south axis is a visual axis only. It is observed through the library, hall, and sitting room of the house and the small outdoor courtyard (Figure 3–14). It leads the eye out to the canal garden and up to the trees beyond (Figure 3–15). Visitors are immediately engaged by a third north-south axis when they first enter the garden. After walking through a gate on an east-west approach the viewer is pulled left, or south, and up the path by the strong vista that begins at the entrance court and continues through the walled arch, along the lime walk, and terminates with a statue in the white garden (Figures 3–16, 3–17, 3–18).

The major east-west axis in front of the house organizes the sequence of garden rooms (Figure 3–19). It begins at the western edge of the site and terminates in the rose garden. Smaller north-south and east-west axes coordinate views or give direction. Throughout the plan, axes are often terminated by focal points such as a fountain, statue, gate, or outdoor room.

At Folly Farm the planting designs accentuate, define, reinforce, or enclose the axes. Each axis cohesively ties together various elements along its path. In Figure 3–11, an axis integrates the parterre garden accented by the lawn and plantings; in Figure 3–12 the crabapple allée encloses the axis; the canal defines the axis in Figure 3–15; and the length of the axis shown in Figure 3–18 is accentuated by the hedge and trees in the distance.

Additional examples of plantings emphasizing an axis are seen in Figure 3–20, the main axis of the garden at Villa Bozzolo designed in the 17th-century, located in Northern Italy. The axis cuts through a series of terraces, first accented by the green plane of lawn adding width and dimension to the line. The axis changes to steps reinforced by pots of plants and finally slices through an enclosing forest. Each planting changes the appearance and feeling of the axis while still defining it. This grand axial gesture originated during the Italian Renaissance was utilized at Villa Bozzolo to balance the vertical perspective with the horizontal layout or the terraces. Figure 3–21 shows a garden in Virginia; the axis is a solid line of lawn surrounded by plantings that diffuse its power as the eye travels from one side of the garden to the other and eventually to the view beyond.

Circulation

The circulation through a garden represents movement or purpose such as strolling, gathering in a plaza, or bicycling through a park. It produces surprise, repose, or anticipation because the design can create sound or evoke a mood through the choice of materials, width of the pathway, and the planting that surrounds it. Fundamentally, circulation represents design elements of both movement and rest. It determines how a person experiences a garden or landscape—at what speed, revealing what views, creating what sensations, to tell what story. Circulation sets the pace, mood, atmosphere, and experience of a landscape. It is important to grasp the significance of this design element because it directly affects all other design relationships.

Circulation directs the viewers orientation and procession through a garden. When do you want to create a procession that is easy to understand versus one full of surprise and mystery? What is the most important space? The extent of the space, use of materi-

3-16 *Entrance gate in entrance court, Folly Farm.*

3-17 *Entrance court axis, Folly Farm.*

3-19 *Major east-west axis, Folly Farm.*

3-18 *Entrance court axis, Folly Farm.*

3-20 *Axis, Villa Bozzolo, Italy.*

3-21 *Axis, garden in Virginia.*

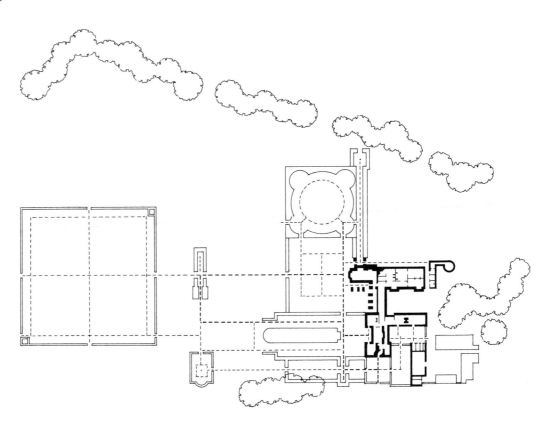

3-22 *Circulation diagram, Folly Farm.*

als, and arrangement of plants give the viewer or visitor the first clues of orientation. Circulation establishes entry, exit, center, terminus, and hierarchy. The choreography or sequence of garden movement directly affects the experience of the viewer. Garden circulation may be designed to lead the viewer to a specific view, smell a specific plant, or hear a particular fountain.

At Folly Farm the circulation diagram designates the primary and secondary circulation routes (Figure 3–22). Figures 3–11 and 3–19 illustrate the primary route—a flagstone-framed brick walkway in a herringbone pattern that flows in both the north-south and east-west directions; it is wide enough to accommodate three to four people walking abreast. The secondary circulation routes are much narrower pathways paved in flag-

3-23 *Gravel pathway, Folly Farm.*

3-24 *Meadow, Folly Farm.*

3-25 *Pathway, Bloedel Reserve.*

3-26 *Open circulation, garden, Newport, Rhode Island.*

3-27 *Circulation at Levi Plaza, San Francisco, California, designed by landscape architect Lawrence Halprin.*

3-28 *Circulation in the rose garden at Naumkeag, designed by Fletcher Steele.*

stone or gravel, designed for the more intimate movement of one or two people strolling along (Figure 3–23).

Planting and hardscape at Folly Farm reinforce the circulation. The wide, durable walkway of the parterre garden expanded in size by panels of lawn is ample enough to accommodate family, guests, and light garden equipment. Gravel pathways produce a pleasant sound as they lead the visitor into the garden. In distant areas of the garden, the pathways shift from paving materials to meadow and then lawn, encouraging the participants to initiate their own route (Figure 3–24).

Planting schemes and paving patterns articulate objectives of circulation in a variety of forms. At Bloedel Reserve (Figure 3–25), the pathway is enticing and mysterious as it pulls the visitor into the garden. In contrast, the open sweep of lawn in Figure 3–26 encourages one to wander alone without real direction or a particular pace. The paving pattern in Levi Plaza (Figure 3–27) suggests movement as it gives numerous choices of direction. Contrast this with the design of the rose garden at Naumkeag in Massachusetts (Figure 3–28), where little thought seems to been given to circulation. After descending the circular steps in the northeast corner, one is uncertain about which path or direction to take.

Geometry

Geometry has been used as a design tool since the beginning of architectural history because its simple forms are easy to understand. It is the single most common organizing tool in gardens. The ability of geometric forms to generate ideas is seen in the size, location, form, and proportion of gardens. The most fundamental geometric forms are the circle, square, rectangle, and triangle. Although geometry may not incorporate every single aspect of the landscape, its presence is frequently dominant and perceptible. Sometimes the forms are combined, contiguous, or within each other. Forms can also be created by using just parts of geometric shapes.[10] Half a circle, square, or rectangle is often seen at all levels of garden design—walls, garden spaces, paving, and planting—perhaps echoing an entire form elsewhere in the garden.

It is also important to realize that site conditions or program requirements can manipulate the pure geometry of a garden. This means that even though a perfect rectangle or circle appeared appropriate for a space, the reality of the site—an existing landform angling one side of the rectangle or a stream slicing across a circle—prevented this occurrence. As you work, ask yourself how the plan responds to the site's shape. What does the use of geometry tell you about the design concept or program?

The space at Folly Farm is organized in classical geometric forms—the square and the *golden section*[11] (Figure 3–29). Both forms create a clear and concise scale and proportion in the garden, organizing it into a series of outdoor rooms.

The garden in Figure 3–30 displays the use of an open circle reinforced by a low hedge and further accented by a half circle of wooden columns topped with cascading vines. In the rose garden at Dumbarton Oaks (Figure 3–31), a large rectangle is divided into circles, square, and triangles.

Grid

A grid is a system of coordinates used in locating the principle elements of a plan while creating an understandable pattern. It consists of a series of parallel lines that perpendicularly intersect at least one other set of parallel lines.[12] Grids surfaced in

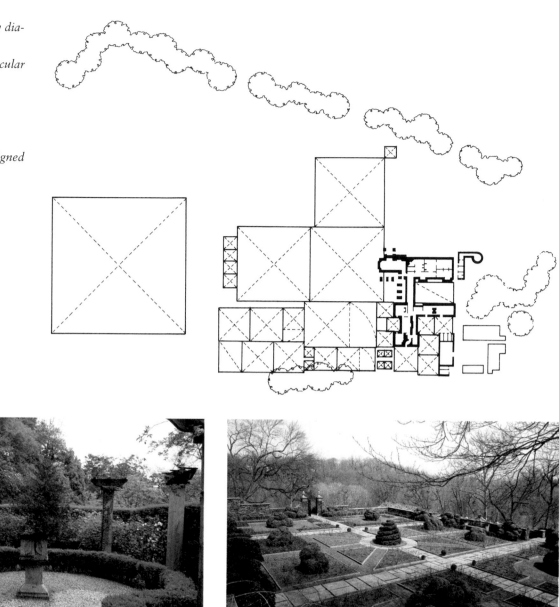

3-29 *(right) Geometry diagram, Folly Farm.*

3-30 *(bottom left) Circular geometry, Millpond, Thomasville, Georgia.*

3-31 *(bottom right) Geometry, rose garden. (Dumbarton Oaks, designed by Beatrix Farrand)*

ancient Egypt and Greece, organized Roman settlements, and Chinese cities. Thomas Jefferson used a north-south, east-west grid to plan the expansion of the United States.

Grids develop from repeating basic geometric forms, usually squares. Because of the equality of its dimensions and its bilateral symmetry, a square grid is essentially neutral, non-hierarchical, and nondirectional. It is an organizational device. Because of its regularity and continuity people can easily orient themselves within a grid plan. It is ideal for extending the boundaries of a garden because the established pattern can be repeated as necessary, creating a seamless boundary between old and new landscape.

A grid of trees in an orchard or a grid of columns in architecture can define a field of space. In an orchard, the space between the trees has a rhythm similar to that of the trees themselves. The absence of a grid element also creates geometric space (Figure 3–32, 3–33).

3-32 *(left) Orchard grid of date palms, Nevis, West Indies.*

3-33 *(right) Grid of trees, orange tree court, Seville, Spain.* (Photo: Marc Treib)

Hierarchy

In garden design, *hierarchy* refers to the physical form of rank ordering of spaces or features. Hierarchy communicates value and importance and adds another element of organization to the plan. It signals a distinction between one condition and another. Which space or garden room is more important than the other? What is public or private space? Combined with circulation, it tells us which gate to walk through or which path to take. Quality of materials, ornateness, and special materials indicate the importance of a change in mood, grade, or experience. Determining the hierarchy of a space and other garden elements is directly related to the design program. Issues of how the space is to be used, by whom, and for what activities influence hierarchy.

Lutyens' plan for Folly Farm establishes a hierarchy of well-defined spaces connecting the house and garden (Figure 3–34). The significance of the rose garden (Figure 3–35) and the courtyard of the canal garden (Figure 3–36) are obvious because of their proximity to the house, their size, design program, and the choice of construction and plant materials.

Plant choices also reflect and reinforce hierarchy. Colorful, elaborate, high-maintenance plantings and specimen plants are located near the house to be enjoyed by both the owner and visitors. Likewise, plantings along a service area are generally simpler and require less maintenance. At Folly Farm the golden chain tree palisade is located along a significant pathway (Figure 3–37). The simplicity of the parterre garden is accented with flowering shrubs and perennials that can be appreciated from the dining room and loggia (Figure 3–38).

Points of Transition

Points of transition are loci of change, thresholds of movement from inside to outside, darkness to light, enclosed space to open space, grade to grade, movement to rest, or places to change direction. This design characteristic is directly related to hierarchy and is based on the design program. How and where are entries and passages defined? Where do they begin and end? Points of transition can be indicated by gates, steps, plantings, or walls. A transition links what is on either side of a space.[13]

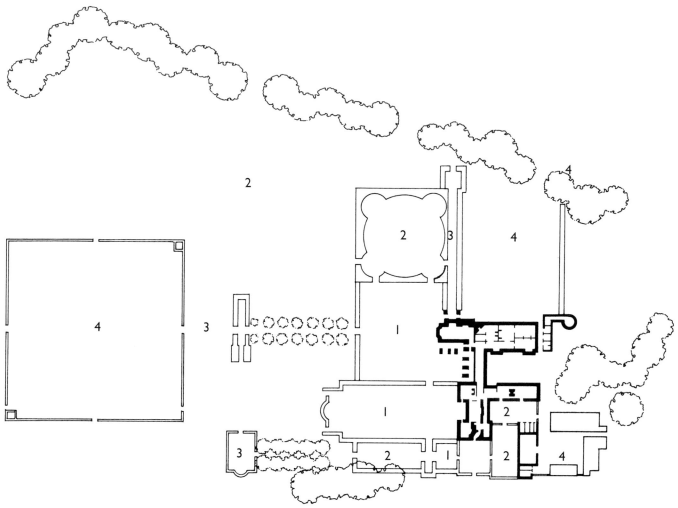

3-34 *Hierarchy and Public-and-Private diagrams, Folly Farm.*

1. Public

2. Semi-Private

3. Private

4. Service

3-35 *The rose garden at Folly Farm. The size of the garden room and materials chosen indicate the significance of the space.*

3-36 *Courtyard in canal garden, Folly Farm is a highly articulated space.*

3-37 *The Golden chain tree palisade at Folly Farm utilizes a sophisticated form and an ornate plant to indicate an important axis and pathway.*

3-38 *The perennial planting in the parterre garden of Folly Farm is an elaborate design for a significant space.*

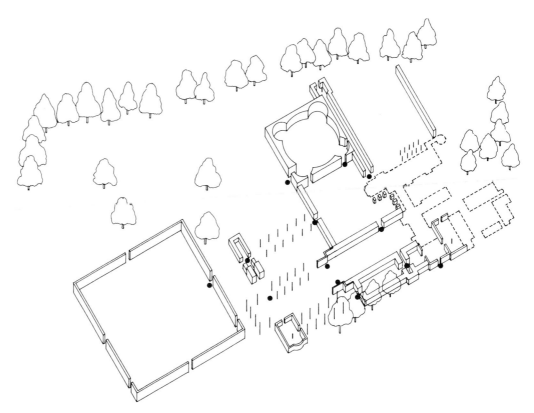

3-39 *Points of transition and Structuring Elements diagram, Folly Farm.*

Points of transition at Folly Farm (Figure 3–39) are simple and straightforward. Movement from one garden room to another is generally made with a change in grade indicated by steps, a wall, a gate, a hedge, or a combination thereof (Figures 3–40, 3–41, 3–42). Movement from open to enclosed space is indicated by a change in plant form.

Designers uses plants to announce transitions by changing the plant form or species. For example (Figure 3–43), two palm trees announce the entrance to a California farmstead; they mark the shift from agricultural field to residential area. A slight increase in plant height subtly indicates a narrow opening or change in

3-40 *Steps in the rose garden, Folly Farm establish a point of transition.*

3-41 *These steps indicate a transition from the pleasure garden to kitchen garden, Folly Farm.*

3-42 *Hedges at Folly Farm establish transition from one garden room to another.*

3-43 *Palms announce this California farmstead.*

3-44 *Hedge form signals point of transition, Sissinghurst.*

direction (Figure 3–44). A dramatic point of transition can be seen from the Moss Garden to the Reflection Garden at the Bloedel Reserve in Bainbridge Island, Washington. The Bloedel family wanted to capture the essence of a Japanese garden—the subtlety, repose, and serenity—but express it in a uniquely American way.[14] Here (Figure 3–45), one moves through the rugged beauty of the forest barely distinguishing the horizontal line in the landscape. This form is a ten-foot-tall yew hedge pruned to enclose the Reflection Garden but left unpruned on the Moss Garden side. The hedge signals a change from darkness to light, enclosed space to open place (Figure 3–46).

Structuring Elements

After establishing the more conceptual elements of a garden, such as grid, circulation, or axis, physical form is added using structural elements such as columns or walls in the form of hedges, trees, or shrub massing. Think of these elements in terms of frequency, pattern, simplicity, and regularity. Structuring elements define space, create units, articulate circulation, suggest movement, or develop a composition. Many of these elements actually become garden architecture; others are articulated by plantings. This device can be used to reinforce geometric patterns, strengthen relationships of circulation, and define symmetry, balance, and hierarchy.[15]

Hedges and trees are the most predominant structuring elements at Folly Farm. In Figure 3–39, observe the form of the hedge plantings; they frame the garden rooms, reinforcing the geometry. The height, length, and density of the hedge reflect the hierarchical level of the space and its extremely private nature. Trees as structuring elements indicate points of transition along pathways. Their stature and form change the mood and movement through the garden.

A similar design device is seen at the Filoli estate in northern California. The house and gardens of Filoli were created over numerous years, beginning in 1909, the height of the Golden Age in American gardens. Plants structure the theater garden, sometimes referred to as the High Place, as seen in Figure 3–47. Here, Irish yews, *Taxus baccata 'Stricta,'* surround columns framing an outdoor theater space. In Figure 3–48, street trees

3-47 *(top left) Structuring elements. (Filoli Garden, Woodside, California)*

3-48 *(top right) Trees as structuring elements. (Portland Building, Portland, Oregon)*

3-49 *(bottom right) Trees as structuring elements, Palo Alto, California.*

mimic the colonnade structure of the building, and weeping cherry trees form a canopy at a park in Palo Alto, California (Figure 3–49).

Public versus Private Space

Good organization and design accommodates the often contradictory designation of public and private use. The program informs the design of the public and private space. Determine the hierarchy of the program requirements by categorizing what happens in the outdoor space. How much space is portioned out for public versus private activities? What space is meant for an individual to experience and what space is used for a group participation? If you want public and private activities to overlap you must prepare the landscape to accommodate them. Decisions made about public and private space directly influence circulation. Plantings respond to these demands. If a space is heavily trafficked, the form and choice of plants must reflect these needs.

In Lutyens' day, public and private activities were segregated and directly related to hierarchy. At Folly Farm, service roads, greenhouses, kitchen gardens, and support build-

3-50 *(left) Borrowed view from vegetable garden to neighboring mountain at Monticello, Charlottesville, Virginia.*

3-51 *(right) Borrowed view of hillside and the Pacific Ocean beyond at Hesperides.*

ings are separated from entrance courts, spaces for entertaining, and recreation (Figure 3–34). The size of the space, its location, and its design program are directly related to its intent for public or private use. The larger garden rooms are public, located close to the house, and used for family, friends, and guests. Private spaces, entrances, or work areas are either smaller and located near private living quarters or located in the vicinity of the service area or servant's quarters.

The Borrowed View

The term *borrowed view* describes scenery or elements beyond the actual design that become an important or integral part of the composition. The distant scene is incorporated into the view. Consequently, the background is described as "borrowed," because it is brought into the garden as part of the composition despite its location far beyond the reach of one's own land or project site. In Chinese gardens it is described as *jie jing,* in Japanese landscapes as *shakkei,* and in Italian design as *integrazione scenica.*

The borrowed view allows the designer to expand the experience of the garden by framing a view through plant massing or focal points that lead the eye to a desired vista. Plantings enhance the visual connection or, in contrast, they block out undesirable views in the middle ground and effect a smooth transition from foreground to background. At Monticello (Figure 3–50), Thomas Jefferson's positioning of his vegetable garden and *folly* borrows the view of the neighboring mountainside. The garden at Hesperides in southern California uses a pavilion to frame the borrowed view of the sky and Pacific Ocean beyond (Figure 3–51).

Figure and Ground

A figure-and-ground diagram enables the designer to measure the success of a design. By darkening in the figures or three-dimensional elements of the design, the form of the ground plane is revealed. It is a different view of geometry, circulation, and hierarchy, or

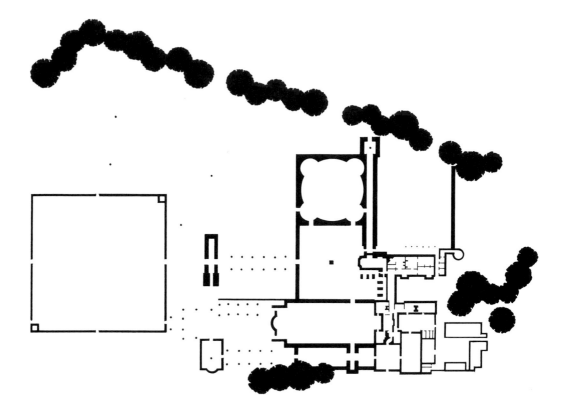

positive and negative space. Figure 3–52 shows a figure-and-ground diagram of Folly Farm. It suggests a geometrical plan of garden rooms. The plan visually and physically connects the rooms of the house to the rooms of the garden. Plant forms mirror the geometry and the ground plane reveals a unity of composition.

SUMMARY

Design exploration is one of the most creative aspects of planting design. You begin to set the stage for plant selection. The concept, program, and design produce the plan. Remember—draw, draw, draw. Use lots of trace paper and a big fat pencil or pen. Overlap the different analyses drawings and observe. What do the drawings tell you? Try combining figure-and-ground drawings with hierarchy sketches. Or perhaps look at axial conditions overlaid with the points of transition. Explore the myriad possibilities.

To summarize the planting design process thus far:

1. Be cognizant of historic precedent in design (Chapter 1).

2. Examine the existing environment of the project site and analyze vegetation, climate, and soil conditions (Chapter 2).

3. Develop a design concept, determine the design program, and complete a design analysis of the site (Chapter 3).

ENDNOTES

1   The plan drawing represents an overhead view of the design, a view rarely seen by the client. In projects where clients need more information to visualize a design, perspective sketches, sections or a model may be beneficial.

2   Charles Moore, William J. Mitchell, and William Turnbull Jr., *The Poetics of the Garden* (Cambridge: MIT Press, 1988), 1.

3   Alexander Pope, "An Epistle to Lord Burlington," 1731, in John Dixon Hunt and Peter Willis, *The Genius of the Place* (Cambridge: MIT Press, 1988), 212.

4   Chip Sullivan, *Drawing the Landscape* (New York: Van Nostrand Reinhold, 1995), 21.

5   The original design has been slightly altered by the present owners. It is in the current form that the garden is analyzed according to both drawings and notes made by Jane Brown in *Gardens of a Golden Afternoon* (Middlesex England: Penguin, 1982), 93–95, and the visitor brochure of Folly Farm.

6   Ibid, Jane Brown, 93–94.

7   By analyzing historic landscapes, design sensibilities that are universal in their application are revealed. Consequently, historic garden strategies are potential models for today's urban, community, or residential design. Through time ideas build upon one another, providing inspiration and knowledge for our new-built environments.

8   Mark Francis and Randolph T. Hester, eds., *The Meaning of Gardens: Idea, Place and Action* (Cambridge: MIT Press, 1990), 12.

9   Donlyn Lyndon and Charles W. Moore, *Chambers for a Memory Palace* (Cambridge: MIT Press, 1994), 5–9.

10   Roger H. Clark and Michael Pause, *Precedents in Architecture* (New York: Van Nostrand Reinhold, 1985), 145–147.

11   The golden section is a rectangle whose sides are proportioned according to a mathematic system that originated with the Pythagorean concept that all is number. The premise is that certain numerical relationships manifest the harmonic structure of the universe. The ratio is approximately 5:8.

12   Ibid., Clark and Pause, 147.

13   Ibid., 151.

14   Felice Frankel and Jory Johnson, *Modern Landscape: Redefining the Garden* (New York: Abbeville Press, 1991), 53

15   Ibid., Clarke and Pause, 3.

Creating a Design Vocabulary:
Elements of the Garden

Aesthetic impressions were considered, and the effect of passing from the sunny fruit garden to the dense grove, thence to the wide reaching view, and again to the sheltered privacy of the pleached walk or the mossy coolness of the grotto—all this was taken into effect by a race of artists who studied the contrast of aesthetic emotions as keenly as they did the juxtaposition of dark cypress and pale lemon tree, of deep shade and level sunlight.

EDITH WHARTON, *ITALIAN VILLAS AND THEIR GARDENS*[1]

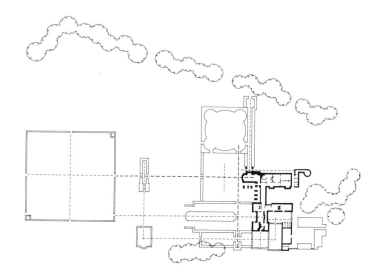

4-1 *Axes diagram, Folly Farm.*

4-2 *Design development drawing, Folly Farm.*
  1. *Kitchen garden*
  2. *White garden room*
  3. *Orchard*
  4. *Allee*
  5. *Palisade*
  6. *Rose garden*
  7. *Parterre*
  8. *Loggia*
  9. *Canal*
  10. *Green room*
  11. *Green walls*

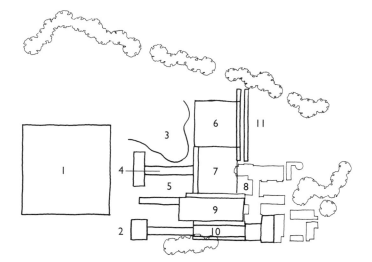

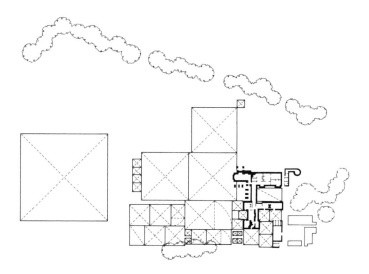

4-3 *Geometry diagram, Folly Farm.*

What is a design vocabulary? Let's hope you have one—if not, it is time to develop one. In Chapter 3 design terms such as *parterre, specimen plant,* and *palisade* were introduced. These terms represent a specific group of forms and devices utilized by design professionals in art, architecture, and landscape architecture, to give physical, three-dimensional form to their design concepts. For landscape architects, design vocabulary may be separated into two general categories: first, forms or elements composed solely of plant materials—for example, *hedge, allée, bosque;* second, structural elements called *garden architecture—folly, pergola, rill.* These elements add richness, meaning, and interest to the landscape.

Various elements are associated with specific cultures or historic garden concepts, as discussed in Chapter 1. Many forms evolved over time. Try to understand both the historic and contemporary usage of the forms. For example, a *meadow* historically was a grassland; today, many people's conception of a meadow is a field full of wildflowers. *Maze* is another example. Originally an intricate, customarily confusing network of twists and turns constructed of stone or vegetation, the historical maze was used for spiritual rituals. Today mazes are usually created solely from plant materials and are intended to entertain.

These elements are design tools, but you must understand their significance in order to properly implement them in the landscape. Some traditional vocabulary has disappeared from use; likewise, new terms have been added. As the landscape architect Sylvia Crowe explains it, "Only by understanding why certain forms were adopted by certain peoples shall we be able to select, eliminate, adapt, and finally evolve for ourselves gardens which will express our ideas, our wants, and the character of our surroundings in a form which will satisfy us as completely as the great gardens of the past satisfied their owners."[2]

From the design exploration and environmental analysis completed thus far, the ideals of the garden begin to combine with the realities and challenges of the site. By shaping and refining space, the design is gradually synthesized into reality. The spatial organization of the concept merges with the physical details of the site. Using the diagrams developed in Chapter 3, locate the circulation, geometry, hierarchical spaces, and points of transitions on the terrain. Spaces and forms emerge, creating a necessity for large-scale gestures to be made in the planting design. For instance, if the schematic design contains an axis, now that axis becomes an allée. Look once again at the design of Folly Farm. The axis diagram in Figure 4–1 becomes an allée in the design development drawing shown in Figure 4–2. The large rectangle from the geometric analysis in Figure 4–3 becomes a parterre or rose garden in Figure 4–2. (Figures 4–4 and 4–5 are photos of these elements.)

Thus we begin to layer the schematic plan with appropriate forms from our design vocabulary. Forms such as meadow and palisade are superimposed on the design (Figure 4–2). These forms are blocked out in a grand scale and combined with landforms, structures, or other vegetation.[3] Let your imagination soar as you begin to flesh out the bones of the garden. The bones are the framework, the larger plants, often evergreen, and structures that anchor the garden or hold the design in place year round. Although the drawing is still quite abstract, it allows you to quickly try out different ideas without worrying about details. You begin to combine form and function.

PLANT FORM AND FUNCTION

Making the transition from concepts to actual forms adds another level of complexity to the landscape plan—function. Plants fulfill a variety of functions in the environment. These seemingly unrelated functional uses of plants, such as their ability to control sound, curtail erosion, articulate space, and block wind have, in themselves, little form or pattern.[4] However, as the planting designer, you can combine these discrete forms and functions into an ecologically sound and artistic design. The art and science of planting design is revealed through form and function. Plants perform four basic functions in the landscape:

1. They create an architectural framework.

2. They produce aesthetic effects.

3. They modify the microclimate.

4. They provide solutions to engineering problems.

As you translate concepts—axes, points of transition, and circulation—into reality, be mindful of plant forms fulfilling numerous requirements simultaneously. To further illustrate this point, look once again at the primary axis at Folly Farm. The axis is reinforced by an allée, an architectural framework that connects spaces in the garden; the allée also creates a shady walkway in the summer and provides a protected walkway in the winter. It produces its own microclimate in the garden.

The following sections examine the four plant functions individually and describe numerous design elements that enable these functions to expand your design vocabulary.

Plants Create an Architectural Framework

Plants furnish an architectural framework for the garden. In this respect the art of the landscape architect is similar to that of the building architect. In planting design, the designer uses plants singly or in groups to form green walls, flowering canopies, lush floors, or fragrant arches in the way that the architect uses brick, stone, or wood to form a house. The architectural treatment of the garden consists of extending the principles of design that govern the house or building to the grounds that surround it. The connection of the building to the landscape can be an integral part of the design. Garden rooms complement circulation and hierarchy.

Plantings have architectural characteristics—floors, ceilings, walls—consequently the garden is a series of outdoor rooms. The arch in Figure 4–6, the lush moss covering the

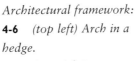

Architectural framework:

4-6 *(top left) Arch in a hedge.*

4-7 *(top right) Groundplane of moss.*

4-8 *(bottom) Walls of green.*

ground in Figure 4–7, and the sheared green walls in Figure 4–8 are examples of outdoor room components. Garden rooms, regardless of their shape or size, integrate form and function. Devise rooms for reading, recreation, walking, eating, concerts, plays, or large gatherings. Because plants are alive and dynamic, the ceiling, walls, and walkways of garden rooms are growing, flowering, fruiting, evergreen, deciduous, and everchanging.

Plants may not define a space as the designer intended until they have reached maturity. This is the challenge of working with plants as design elements, and a way in which landscape architecture is unlike architecture. Patience and vision are required.

The Garden Floor If we think of a garden space as architecture, we can begin with the ground plane or floor as a point of departure.

"The paving material, the size of the path and its relation to other elements combine as key visual signals. Together they tell us not just where to go but whether to rush or linger. They set the mood for the journey. They are the foundation on which any garden is built."[5] The garden floor serves three purposes in the design: (1) a foreground for viewing a composition, (2) a decorated surface that emphasizes form, and (3) an axis or path for circulation (sometimes). The materials available to cover the ground are numerous: stone, wood, grass, gravel, and ground covers. Choices of pattern, texture, and material are determined by the function of the garden. A recreational field requires a different

The garden floor:

4-9 *(left) Carpet bedding.*

4-10 *(top right) Tapis vert.*

4-11 *(middle right)*
Terraces.

4-12 *(bottom right)*
Parterre.

treatment than a residential courtyard. A campus plaza floor is heavily trafficked compared to that of a botanical garden.

The following design terms are associated with the ground plane of the garden:

- *Carpet bedding* is the practice of forming beds of low-growing foliage plants, all of an even height, in patterns that resemble a carpet both in the intricacy of their design and in the uniformity of the surface. Designs can vary from geometrical forms to images and lettered inscriptions (Figure 4–9). Carpet bedding can be used as a focal point of a garden room or outdoor space.

- A *lawn* is a land area covered by grass, usually mown. It creates a green ground plane whose shape and design complements or contrasts with other features. Square, rectangular, round, or irregular in shape, a lawn can be a pathway, reinforce geometry, provide transition, and indicate the hierarchical position of a

space. Lawns form recreational rooms for croquet, volleyball, baseball, lawn tennis, or bocce ball.

- A *meadow* is a richly grassed area for mowing or pasture. It can be composed of open and undulating grasses, wildflowers, or wild prairie plants. It functions as a transitional floor between garden and countryside, provides a setting for specimen trees, and creates the impression of spaciousness.

- *Parterre* is literally translated as "on or along the ground." A parterre is a flat terrace, usually adjacent to or near a building, in which foliage patterns are created from plants, flowers, or gravel. Parterres emphasize the ground plane or serve as a picture for viewing, especially from above. Figure 4–12 shows a boxwood parterre at the Villa Ruspoli in Viterbo, Italy.

- *Pathways* are an ornamental, compositional, and functional component of a garden. Straight, wide, rectilinear pathways give a garden a controlled and orderly character. Curved, meandering paths suggest mystery, discovery, or contemplation. Narrow paths are likely to cause visitors to speed up their pace and bring them closer to the plantings; wide paths allow them to slow down and admire overall views.

- *Tapis vert* literally translates as "green cloth." The tapis vert is a swath of lawn, usually rectilinear in shape, used to strengthen a visual axis or focus attention on an object. It can define an edge, serve as a form of contrast between the smooth texture of the ground plane and the surrounding plant materials, or function as an element of transition between buildings and the natural landscape (Figure 4–10).

- A *terrace* is a raised level of earth, sometimes retained by stone or concrete, with a surface of stone, brick, turf, pea gravel, ground cover, or a combination thereof (Figure 4–11). The geometric structure of a house or building is extended into the landscape primarily by the use of the terrace, which connects the building to the site and establishes the unity of building and garden. At La Foce, shown in Figure 4–13, the proportions of the terrace correspond to the proportions of the building.

The ceiling:

4-14 *(top) Trees.*

4-15 *(bottom left) Arbor.*

4-16 *(bottom right) Pergola.*

The Ceiling   The ceiling of the garden room is usually the sky. However, the mood and scale of a garden can change with an alteration to what is overhead. A tree or group of trees can create a room or shelter, as in Figure 4–14. An arbor, trellis, or pergola provides shelter, shade, and a green ceiling when covered with a vine.

- An *arbor* is a leafy, shady recess formed by tree branches, shrubs, or vines often intertwined on a latticework or other architectural structure. The arbor can announce an entrance, create a change of pace in the garden by providing a resting place, or indicate a transition from one space to another (Figure 4–15).

The garden wall:

4-17 *(left) Green architecture.*

4-18 *(right) Serpentine.*

- A *grove* is a grouping of trees either planted or occurring naturally, usually of the same plant species and can be regular or irregular in form. Groves form an enclosure or connection between earth and sky and were often considered by the ancients to be places of mystical and intellectual power.

- *Pergola* is an Italian term that means arbor, bower, or close wall of boughs. The pergola is a structuring element that extends the house or wall-like enclosures to the garden or provides a place for sitting and enjoying a borrowed view (Figure 4–16). It is a perfect structure for displaying vines or sculpture or for dining alfresco.

Garden Walls   Garden walls articulate the vertical aspect of landscape design. Walls can create boundaries, stand alone as a linear statement, give direction, link different points in the garden, or enclose a space. The form, location, and construction material of walls are determined by the design intention (Figures 4–17, 4–18). Walls can be made of hedges, vines, espaliered trees or shrubs, wood, brick, stone, tile, stucco, or metal.

- *Espalier* is from the Italian word *spalle,* meaning shoulder or to lean on. An espalier is a line of trees whose branches are pruned and trained into formal patterns against a wall, fence or support structure in order to make the most of sunshine and space. Historically, the term *espalier* referred to fruit trees trained in decorative patterns for practical and aesthetic reasons—practical, because the wall protected the plant from the elements, the tree took up less space, and the practice encouraged heavy fruiting, and aesthetic, because the graphic branching patterns are beautiful in winter when they become elegant tracery. Today a variety of plants including apples, pears, apricots, figs, dogwoods, hawthorns, holly, cotoneaster, pyracantha, yew, and viburnum can be trained for espalier (Figure 4–19).

- *Hedges* creates form and line and can be made of vines, shrubs, perennials, or trees. A hedge can form a wall as the backdrop for sculpture or herbaceous plantings, create an edge, or emphasize the outline of a design. The character

4-19 *Espalier.*

4-20 *Pruned hedge.*

4-21 *Unpruned hedge.* (PHOTO: CAROL BORNSTEIN)

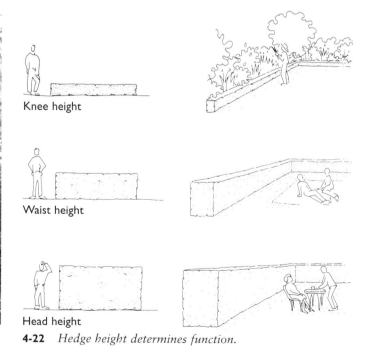

Knee height

Waist height

Head height

4-22 *Hedge height determines function.*

4-23 *(left) Palisade.*

4-24 *(right) Treillage.*

and mood of the hedge depends on whether it is evergreen or deciduous, flowering or fruiting, clipped or unclipped, and on its depth and overall form. Figure 4–20 shows the effects of a well-clipped boxwood hedge, almost looking like green styrofoam, in contrast to the hedge shown in Figure 4–21, a white-flowering irregular form of a Matilija poppy, *Romneya coulteri*. Tall, short, narrow, wide, angular, or serpentine—hedges are walls. A hedge of knee height gives a sense of direction, is readily seen over, and frames a flowerbed, grass plot, or path. A waist-high hedge separates garden elements but still enables the visitor to see out. Hedges head-high or those of four feet and taller form total enclosure and privacy (Figure 4–22). Spacing of the individual plants in a hedge further communicates the design intention. A single plant may appear as an object on the landscape, while several of the same plant spaced at broad intervals suggest a boundary but permit transparency and many planted closely together create a solid hedge or wall.

- A *palisade* is a row of closely planted trees or shrubs clipped into a green wall. It creates an outdoor architectural feature. Cypress, boxwood, and juniper are plants commonly used for palisades (Figure 4–23).

- *Treillage* is a French term meaning trelliswork, a traditional garden craft featuring latticework construction. The term *trellis* fits under the category of treillage, although *treillage* generally implies a sophisticated lattice that is architecturally significant. Treillage is a structure useful for extending architectural forms into the garden. It is a transitional element that incorporates characteristics of both architecture and garden. It can direct and frame a view, highlight specimen plantings, and provide shade and privacy from the elements (Figure 4–24).

Openings   "Openings and their location determine the pattern of connection between one room and another, between inside and out, between light and dark. . . . [They] narrate the life within either directly through the activities they reveal or by inference."[6] The placement of an entranceway, doorway, or window is strategic. These points of transition are thresholds of movement from inside to out places for taking in the long view or apertures that characterize the garden. In Figure 4–25 the opening beckons you and the view

The garden opening:

4-25 *(top left) A window.*

4-26 *(top right) A view.*

4-27 *(bottom left) A natural window.*

4-28 *(bottom right) A living window.*

reveals the world beyond (Figure 4–26). A doorway provokes expectation and an arch gives a glimmer of an unknown world (Figure 4–27). Openings can be fashioned from plants, as an aperture created in a hedge, shrubbery, or trees.

- An *arbor* announces an entrance and indicates a transition to another space.

- An *arch* is a curved structure generally surmounting and connecting two uprights. Arches can be made of plant material, stone, brick, or wood. They provide an entrance or exit, or a view into another world (Figure 4–28).

- A *gate* is an opening in a wall, fence, or hedge that controls the point of transition from inside to outside. Gates can control not only physical but psychological spaces. They create anticipation and expectation. As an entrance to a space, the scale and materials used for a gate indicate the characteristic of the place inside (Figure 4–29). In the landscape gates often tell the eye where to look and the feet where to walk (Figure 4–30).

- A *trellis* can announce an entrance and provide a window into another realm of the garden.

4-29 (left) A grand gate.

4-30 (right) This gate implies direction.

The Garden Hallway   Hallways designate connection, circulation, and transition. They link spaces, connect garden rooms, or indicate direction. Pathways are means of unifying a design and can physically connect the relationship of every garden feature to the building or house.

- An *allée* is a walk bordered by trees or clipped hedges in a garden, park, or street. The spacing, scale, and choice of plant material control the visitor's experience of the allée. By linking landmarks, entries, or gathering places, allées can control the dynamics of the garden and the pacing of the procession. Plants chosen can create walls, frame a view, or define an edge. The length of an allée is best balanced by the scale and width of mature trees or shrubs chosen (Figure 4–31).

- A *border* is a planting bed, usually linear in form, made up of layers of plant materials that one walks beside. It shapes space, defines an edge, provides direction, or links two or more spaces (Figure 4–32).

- A *hedge* is a row of closely planted shrubs or low-growing trees forming a fence or boundary. As a hallway marker it directs movement through the garden (Figure 4–33).

The garden hallway: **4-31** An allée.

4-33 A hedge.

4-32 A border.

4-34 A pleached walkway.

- A *pergola*, as an architectural element, can connect two rooms of the garden or connect the garden to the house.

- A *pleached walkway* is a row of closely planted trees trained to form a continuous narrow wall or hedge. The effect is accomplished by interlacing the branches of the trees and keeping their sides tightly pruned. A pleached walkway can be used architecturally for circulation, as a boundary to define a garden room, or as a transitional device between garden areas (Figure 4–34).

Plants Produce Aesthetic Effects

Gardens, like painting and sculpture, have an enormous capacity to touch people in many ways—to heal, to entertain, to provide serenity, to tell a story about the owner, to describe a culture, or to display philosophical or political ideals. In this way the landscape architect is similar to the artist. There are numerous points of departure a designer, client, or gardener can take when creating a garden; the aesthetic effect is as important as the architectural, engineering, and climatic results.

The aesthetic possibilities of a planting design are endless. Plants are fun! Their shapes delight, surprise, provoke, or astound viewers. They are exciting—full of mysterious smells, beautiful colors, and tactile textures. Planting design is primarily a visual art but it also draws on the senses of smell, hearing, and touch. Consequently, plants can stimulate people and affect their behavior in profound ways. In Figure 4–35 Maya Lin's Wave Field, located on the University of Michigan campus is a provocative statement in the landscape. Children love looking at plants in the garden gazing ball shown

4-35 *Gardens are provocative: Wave Field at the University of Michigan, designed by Maya Lin.*

4-36 *Gardens are fun: a child views a garden through a gazing ball.*

4-37 *Gardens are delightful. (Ganna Walska Lotusland)*

4-38 *Gardens are amusing. (Garden designed by Marcia Donahue)*

4-39 *Gardens are intriguing: an eyecatcher.*

in Figure 4–36, and look at what happened to the author when confronted by a cactus bed Figure 4–37. Does the juxtaposition of forms in artist Marcia Donahue's garden bring a smile to your lips Figure 4–38? Numerous forms from the design vocabulary create aesthetic effects.

- An *eyecatcher* is a feature placed on a distant, prominent point integral to the overall design of the landscape. It is most commonly found in eighteenth-century English gardens but can take on various forms. The eyecatcher gives direction and focus to a garden and is sometimes a place of destination (Figure 4–39). It can be constructed of vegetation or architectural materials.

- A *folly* is a species of garden structure characterized by a certain excess in terms of eccentricity, cost, or conspicuous inutility.[7] A folly can direct circulation in a garden and give pleasure to or dumbfound the visitor. It can be made of trees, shrubs, or vines in an architectural form.

- *Giardino segreto* literally means *secret garden,* a feature found in many Italian Renaissance gardens of the fifteenth century. The giardino segreto is often a small enclosed garden for private use or a space one comes upon by surprise.

- *Giocchi d'acqua—water game—*is a fountain device conceived of in fifteenth-century Italy that consists of water jets located in strategic places throughout a garden that surprise and, with luck, delight the visitor. The water game is an asset to a planting design—water can emerge from plants, paving, or walls. The giocchi d'acqua at the Villa Lante in Italy still delight the unprepared visitor four centuries after their inception (Figure 4–40).

- A *green theater* is an invention of the Italian Renaissance. A theater constructed of plant material is the setting for plays and concerts, the enactment of rituals, the telling of stories, or the creation of illusions (Figure 4–41).

- A *maze* is an intricate, usually confusing network of walled or hedged pathways. The maze is a very ancient form that has appeared in many shapes and sizes, but all mazes have a deliberate design containing twists and turns.

4-40 *(left) Gardens are full of surprises! A water game.*
4-41 *(right) Gardens are a place for green theater.*

- A *rill* is a small channel through which water flows to a garden. Rills evolved from simple irrigation ditches, as design elements they are often associated with dry climates and the corresponding need for irrigation. Acknowledging their respect for water as a sacred element in a garden, many designers implement rills in contemporary landscapes. At Hestercombe (Figure 4–42) the rill moves the eye over the landscape to the view beyond. A rill serves as an axis or a line in the landscape that extends the geometry of the house into the garden and the garden into the landscape.

- *Sculpture* is a multifaceted and diverse three-dimensional art form that has been used to adorn gardens since the time of the Ancient Egyptians. It can take myriad forms in the landscape and in some instances landforms—plants or earth—themselves become sculptures. The sculptural buffalo in a field of prairie grass at the Shaw Arboretum in Saint Louis is designed to evoke memories of the prairie Figure 4–43. Figure 4–44 shows a provocative sculpture at Chesterwood, the sculptor Daniel Chester French's home in western Massachusetts. Maya Lin's wavefield is a sculptural landform (Figure 4–35).

- A *specimen plant* is an individual tree or shrub that is significant enough in its form, color, or size to stand alone as a design device—to emphasize a point of transition, or as a focal point. A specimen plant possesses enough interesting characteristics to attract attention. The plant appears almost sculptural; its size and scale vary according to the location in the landscape. In a garden it dominates a space, draws attention to the place where it is located, and can be a compelling element of the design (Figure 4–45).

- *Topiary* is the art of clipping, trimming, and training trees or shrubs into specific shapes. Topiary can form architecturally clipped hedges that define an edge or playful green living sculptures that decorate and amuse. Topiary can link built forms and the natural landscape or it can be a foil to a more organic treatment of plants. The topiary pandas in Figure 4–46, located on the shores of West Lake in central Hagzhou, China, are created from sculpted boxwood and privet. A topiary rabbit in the children's garden at Longwood Gardens elicits an amused response from both children and adults (Figure 4–47). Yew, juniper, ivy, holly, and laurel are species often used for topiary.

Plants Modify the Microclimate

Plants function extrinsically to modify climate. Landscape architects must rely on their environmental skills to evaluate human requirements for comfort, assess existing climatic conditions, and select correct plants for climate modification. As its name implies, a microclimate is the characteristic weather of a very small area, which can be quite different from the climate of the larger area of which it is a part. The term refers to the scope of the area studied and not necessarily to the size of the climatic differences. An adequate environmental analysis (described in Chapter 2) provides a basis for an initial identification of existing microclimates. Before attempting to alter the site or microclimates you must have a thorough understanding of the ramifications of your plant placement.

4-42 *Gardens tell a story: a rill.*

4-43 *Gardens are a place for sculpture. (PHOTO BY CAROL BORNSTEIN)*

4-44 *Modern sculpture in the garden.*

4-45 *Gardens are nature's gallery for trees.*

4-46 and 4-47 *Gardens are for topiary. (PHOTO 4-46: LEO WONG)*

4-48 *The placement of plants and structures in the landscape can direct wind and alter the microclimate.* (DRAWING: CHIP SULLIVAN)

Plants modify the climate in three ways:

1. wind control

2. modification of sunlight

3. change in moisture

Wind Control Wind can control real or perceived air temperature. Wind may be intercepted, diverted, or lessened by obstructions such as buildings, walls, fences, landforms, and plants (Figure 4–48). Plants can control wind by obstruction, guidance, deflection, and filtration. This is achieved through the form, texture, and height of the plant itself or by its placement. Plants used in conjunction with landforms and architectural structures guide the flow of air over the landscape and/or through buildings.

Plants of varying height, width, species, and composition planted either individually or in rows influence wind deflection. Coniferous evergreens that branch to the ground are generally the most effective year-round plants for wind control; deciduous trees and shrubs, when in leaf, are the most effective in summer.

Modification of Sunlight Trees, shrubs, ground covers, turf, and vines are great devices for controlling sunlight. Plants absorb heat, provide shade, and create insulation. They absorb the sun's heat during the day and release it at night, cooling daytime temperatures and warming evening temperatures. Each plant has its own texture, which determines the density of its shadow. With dense or open foliage, deciduous or evergreen, each plant form has its benefits as a modifier (Figure 4–49). A deciduous tree planted near a building provides cool shade in summer and allows the sun to penetrate in winter. Pleached walkways offer an escape from summer heat and shelter from cold winter winds. An

4-49 *A vine-covered pergola creates its own microclimate.*
(*DRAWING: CHIP SULLIVAN*)

4-50 *Microclimates create unique plant communities.*

evergreen tree casts a year-round shadow that may be more desirable in a tropical than in a temperate landscape. Redwood, beech, and oak trees cast dense shadows that generate a measurable degree of cooler air beneath their canopy. For example, although the weather may be hot and sunny, the microclimate under a redwood tree is extremely cool and moist, supporting plant life such as ferns and wild ginger (Figure 4–50). In contrast, honey locusts, olives, and ash trees create airy, filtered light that does not cause a significant change in the growing conditions beneath them.

Change in Moisture   Moisture in the form of rain, fog, dew, snow, sleet, or hail is intercepted and redirected to some degree by plants. The amount of rainfall that reaches the ground varies according to the ambient plant species, the intensity and duration of the rainfall, and the structure of the tree canopy. Studies show that in light rainfalls conifers retain as much as five times the moisture as broad-leafed trees.[8] Moisture reaching the earth that is intercepted by plants is absorbed better than moisture falling on exposed soil; the plant slows down the rate at which water actually comes into contact with the ground, as precipitation, decreasing surface runoff and soil erosion.

Fog condenses on the needles of conifers and on the upper and lower surfaces of leaves. This water falls to the earth as drip water from various parts of the plant. Fog can be an important source of moisture for plant growth, especially during the growing season. It adds moisture to soil surfaces and delays temperature increases. Plants or groves of trees can effectively protect land areas from incoming fog.

Snow can act as an insulator for plants and protect them from winds, fast thawing, and sunscald. By intercepting snowflakes, directing wind, or controlling snowdrifts, plants redirect snowfall.

Microclimate Elements of the Garden   These forms from the design vocabulary are especially useful in influencing microclimate:

- The *arbor* is one of the most ancient garden forms; it evolved from the bower or tree limbs that intertwined overhead. It provides a shady place to rest and protection from the elements. Arbors are excellent devices for showcasing vines. A deciduous vine gives summer protection and allows winter sun to penetrate; an evergreen vine produces year-round shelter.

- A *bosquet* is a formal grove of trees planted in a geometrical arrangement; often, all the trees are of the same plant species. The bosquet forms a canopy of shade with its own microclimate and ecosystem. In addition to purifying the air, the regularity of the grid and the lack of understory makes a strong design statement in the landscape.

- A *grotto* is a cavelike chamber, often decorated with minerals, shells, or pebbles. It has evolved throughout history as different cultures interpret the space and adapt its use. In contemporary landscapes the grotto's usually subterranean location creates a cool place to sit or a shelter from wind (Figure 4–51).

- *Hedgerows, shelterbelts, and windbreaks* are plant groupings that protect agricultural fields or open space from wind, snow, rain, and erosion. A hedgerow is often composed of a combination of numerous trees and shrubs kept pruned or unpruned; a shelterbelt is a row of trees and shrubs in three distinct layers of tree, small tree, and shrub; a windbreak is a row of trees, generally of the same species. Large-scale hedgerows, shelterbelts, and windbreaks reduce crop damage, decrease evapotranspiration, protect livestock in cold weather, provide shade in summer, and create a diverse habitat in open agricultural areas (Figure 4–52).

- A *loggia* is a roofed porch or gallery with an open colonnade on one or more sides. It provides shade in the summer and allows cool breezes to flow through the structure (Figure 4–53). The loggia is also designed to capture the lower-angled rays of the winter sun, thus heating the space for year-round use in warmer climates.

4-51 *(top left) A grotto is a cool, shady place in summer.*

4-52 *(middle left) A windbreak alters the microclimate.* (PHOTO BY MARC TREIB)

4-53 *(bottom left) A loggia provides protection in summer and winter.*

4-54 *(top right) A palisade is a cool place to sit and admire a view.*

- The *palisade,* in addition to being an architectural element, provides shelter from cold winds during the winter months and a cool, shady retreat from the heat in the summer (Figure 4–54).

- *Pergolas* produce shade. By their very structure, substantial columns supporting cross-beams, they become an architectural feature in the landscape and a place of retreat from hot summer sun or chill winter winds (Figure 4–49).

- *Pleached walkways* provide a cool place for strolling in the summer and a refuge from bitter winds in winter (Figure 4–34).

- *Trelliswork* creates microclimates by directing wind into a structure or away from it. When planted with vines they produce shade and provide an architectural feature to the garden.

Plants Provide Solutions to Engineering Problems

Plants provide solutions to engineering problems such as erosion control and sound mitigation. The right plant in the right place can prevent soil loss, create a view, or improve safety on roadways.

Visual Regulation Plants can screen an unpleasant view or create privacy by visually blocking out an unsightly scene or object with something more harmonious. The size of the object or area combined with the relative distance from the viewer determines the quantity of screening. The speed of the visitor's movement is directly related to his perceived view. If the viewer is in a stationary position the planting may need to be extremely dense; if the view is perceived from an automobile, train, or bicycle the density of the planting may be more transparent.

Erosion Control Soil erosion is the wearing away or loss of soil by action of wind or water. It is usually due to unsuitable ground cover, steep slope, extremely dry soil conditions followed by substantial rains, or a combination of these factors. The degree or severity of soil erosion is determined by the site's exposure to wind and its water, climate, soil character, and the length and degree of its slope on the terrain. Certain plants can reduce or eliminate soil erosion because their root systems form a fibrous network that anchors the soil.

Flowing water causes most common soil erosion. The impact of raindrops dislodges bare soil and carries it away. Plants control water erosion in four ways:

1. Early seeding with erosion-controlling grasses immediately after grading gives roots a chance to develop quickly.

2. Leaves and branches form canopies or blankets that break the force of falling water.

3. Roots form fibrous masses that hold soil in place.

4. Mulch—leaves, pine needles, and other organic matter—aerates soil and increases its water absorption rate.

Sound Mitigation Noise from freeways, airports, and factories can be a problem in urban areas. The effectiveness of plants in controlling sound levels is determined by the sound's characteristics—its type, decibel level, intensity, and origin—and those of the planting—its type, height, density, and location. Plants are more effective at screening sounds of certain frequencies than of others. Trees can reduce the impact of noise by controlling excess attenuated sound. Elements introduced between the sound source and the receiver reduce sound by absorption, deflection, reflection, and defraction of sound waves.[9] Plantings close to the source of the noise are more effective than plantings further away. In addition, climatic factors—wind direction, velocity, temperature, and humidity—contribute to the control of sound.

For example, a better solution to the stark sound walls that line many highways in the United States is to incorporate plants in their design. The horticulturist Richard Harris states in his book *Arboriculture,* "that in order to reduce noise levels appreciably, plantings must be dense, tall, and wide, 25–35m; 80–115 ft."[10] The vibrations of sound waves are absorbed by leaves, branches, and twigs of trees, especially plants with many thick, fleshy leaves. Plants with thin leaf petioles that allow for a high degree of flexibility and vibration also deflect sound. Combining plants with landforms or other structures creates the most effective acoustic control. In addition to absorbing sound, plants sometimes make their own sounds, such as the rustling leaves of aspen trees or the whistling of the wind through pine trees.

Traffic Control   When planning walks, drives, roadways, and parking lots, plants can assist in regulating the traffic. Plant choice, spacing, and width of planting are all important factors in controlling vehicular and pedestrian movement. For pedestrians, determine if the barrier required is physical or psychological; for example, multistemmed plants with thorns are an excellent means of directing foot traffic. Next, the desired height and spacing of the planting is important. If the plant is too low or too sparsely planted it has little effect on foot traffic. Last, the effectiveness of the planting width is dependent on the situation. A narrow planting bed allows people to jump over it. One that is too wide appears frustrating and people may walk through the planting (unless the plant is thorny), creating an unintended pathway.

Controlling vehicular traffic with plants depends on the type of roadway and the speed of traffic (Figure 4–55). Barrier plantings on highways between two-way traffic minimizes nighttime headlight glare and reduces daylight glare and reflection. Parking lot plantings reduce heat and reflection. Street tree plantings psychologically add to the ambiance of the streetscape in addition to reducing glare and providing shade for both pedestrians and parked cars (Figure 4–56).

Pollution Control   The continual dumping of gases and pollutants into the atmosphere—car exhaust, chlorofluorcarbons from air conditioners and refrigerators, and industrial refuse—is destroying our environment. Plants are a natural filter of the atmos-

phere, but if the pollution is too powerful or at a toxic level it will reduce plants' vitality or even kill them. Vegetation improves air quality through its ability to reduce airborne particles. It does so primarily by reducing wind speeds so that heavier particles settle out as smaller particles are absorbed on plant surfaces, primarily leaves.[11]

Many pines and rhododendrons are extremely sensitive to air pollution, whereas ginkgos, oleanders, and pin oaks seem to be very tolerant of it. The exact cause of these conditions is not known, but when planting a street, highway, or city park it is important to keep in mind the pollution tolerance of the plant choices.

Many of the garden terms described in the previous sections also provide engineering controls, including hedgerow, meadow, and tapis vert. The drift is another form which can control erosion, direct traffic, and enhance views (Figure 4–57). A drift is a usually an irregular mass of plants characterized by bold sweeps of mass plantings featuring perennials and ornamental grasses.

SUMMARY: THE ELLIS-MAHONEY GARDEN CONCEPT TO DESIGN DEVELOPMENT

Let us examine a small San Francisco garden that contains a variety of garden elements in an easily comprehensible space. Figures 4–58, 4–59, and 4–60 are schematic drawings for the garden. A final design solution (Figure 4–61) is a compilation of these ideas. The schematic drawing is overlaid with the garden elements (Figure 4–62). A parterre is the main concept of the plan because the garden is in a foggy location and on many days it is viewed only from the house or deck.

4-58, 4-59, and 4-60

Schematic drawings of the Ellis-Mahoney garden.

(DRAWINGS: ARCADIA)

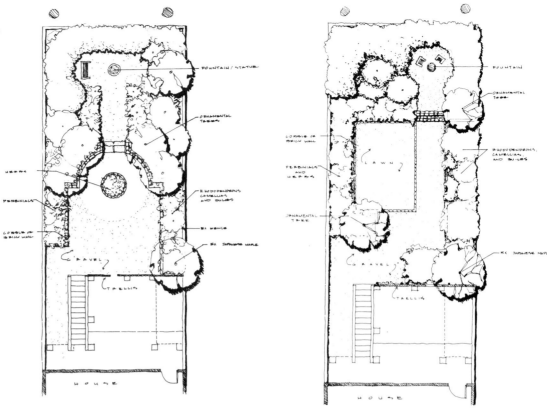

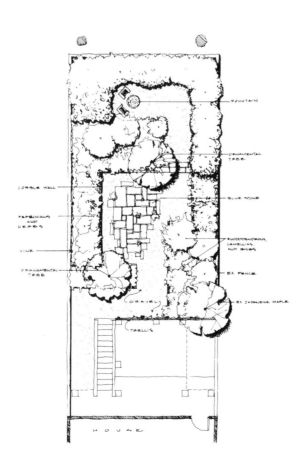

4-61 *Final design solution for the Ellis-Mahoney garden.*

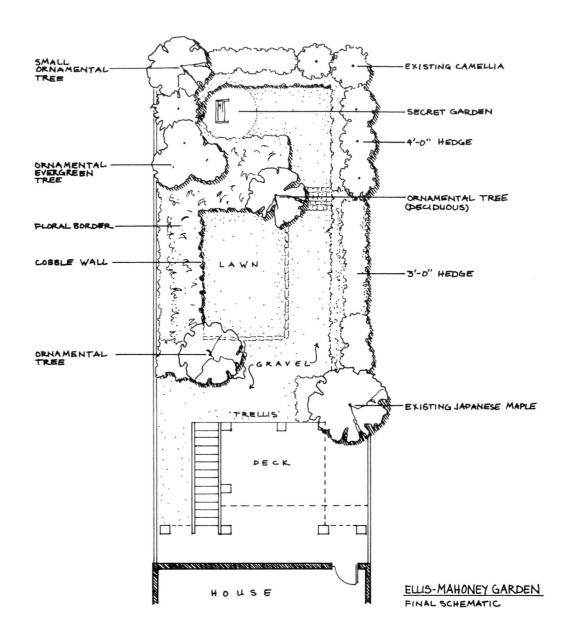

SMALL ORNAMENTAL TREE

EXISTING CAMELLIA

SECRET GARDEN

4'-0" HEDGE

ORNAMENTAL EVERGREEN TREE

ORNAMENTAL TREE (DECIDUOUS)

FLORAL BORDER

COBBLE WALL

LAWN

3'-0" HEDGE

ORNAMENTAL TREE

GRAVEL

EXISTING JAPANESE MAPLE

TRELLIS

DECK

HOUSE

ELLIS-MAHONEY GARDEN
FINAL SCHEMATIC

To fulfill program requirements—space for small children to play, a salvia plant collection display, and a room for reading—the following forms evolved. A lawn or *tapis vert* creates a play space; its shape and location make the garden appear larger. Salvia and other perennial plants grow in the floral border situated in a raised bed; it walls are constructed of cobblestone and double as a seat wall. In the eastern corner, a secret garden room for reading is surrounded by fragrant plants. A specimen tree divides this private space from the more public one and adds a sense of depth to the narrow lot.

Hedges of various heights are planted on the south wall for privacy, enclosure, and wind protection. Treillage screens the utility area under the deck from the garden. A

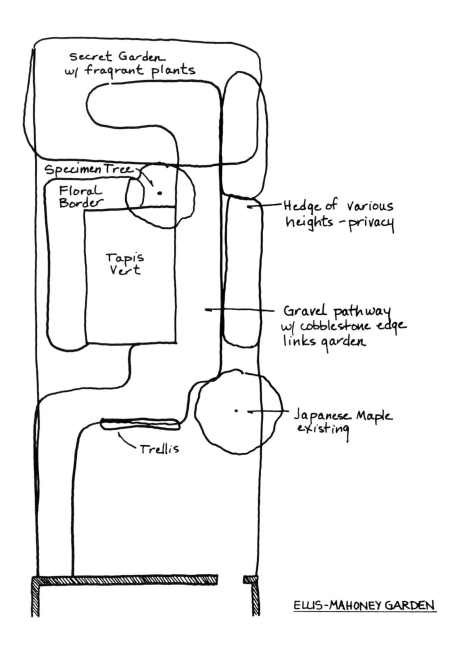

Secret Garden
w/ fragrant plants

Specimen Tree

Floral
Border

Tapis
Vert

Hedge of various
heights - privacy

Gravel pathway
w/ cobblestone edge
links garden

Japanese Maple
existing

Trellis

ELLIS-MAHONEY GARDEN

gravel pathway edged with cobblestones links the garden rooms and provides circulation and drainage. As a result, this small area encompasses an assortment of garden forms that fulfill the design program, solve engineering problems, and create a space for outdoor living.

Take a close look at the functional roles plants play and apply them creatively to planting designs. We begin to see the interweaving of relationships as abstract concepts become built form. Geometry, circulation, and structuring elements translate into a tapis vert, orchard, or windbreak. Each level of exploration adds form and function to the planting design. The success of the planting design is in the skill with which the diverse forms and functions are integrated.

ENDNOTES

[1] Edith Wharton, *Italian Villas and Their Gardens* (New York: Century, 1904), 47.

[2] Sylvia Crowe, *Garden Design* (Woodbridge, U.K.: Garden Art Press, 1994), xii.

[3] Nick Robinson, *The Planting Design Handbook* (London: Gower Publishing, 1992), 189.

[4] I am grateful to G.O. Robinette and his work in the book *Plants/People/Environmental Quality* (Washington, D.C.: Department of the Interior, 1972). Although I disagree with his premise, "the functions of plants being their basis for use in environmental design," the quality of his research and drawings contributed to my work.

[5] Adrian Thomas Higgins, "Off the Beaten Path," *Garden Design* (Autumn 1990).

[6] Donlyn Lyndon and Charles W. Moore, *Chambers of a Memory Palace* (Cambridge: MIT Press, 1994), 104.

[7] Geoffrey Jellicoe, Susan Jellicoe, Patrick Goode, and Michael Lancaster, *The Oxford Companion to Gardens* (Oxford: Oxford University Press, 1986), 192.

[8] Robinette, *Plants/People/Environmental Quality,* 87.

[9] Ibid.

[10] Harris, Richard, *Arboriculture,* 2nd ed., (Englewood Cliffs, NJ: Prentice Hall, 1992), 7.

[11] Ibid., 6–7.

Composing the Planting Design

Proportion is what makes it beautiful. Proportion, scale relationships, texture, light and shade, the material you use and how you use it: all those things . . . have to be correct.

DAN KILEY[1]

Planting composition is the process of combining different plants into a unified whole. Now that the concept is fixed and garden elements are introduced, the next step is to look at plant characteristics individually to determine their effect on the entire design. Before choosing a specific plant, garden elements—shrub massings, allées, drifts, planting beds—are transformed into an arrangement of color, form, texture, line, and mass.

Although planting composition is often compared to other arts—painting, sculpture, weaving, music—it is perhaps, the most dynamic art form because the results are a work of art in three dimensions seen from many points of view, using materials that are constantly changing. The key is arranging these elements into an ordered whole by balancing proportion and scale with texture, form, repetition, and sequence. It is a physical artistic expression of the design concept using plants as the medium. This phase of the process is often referred to as design development.

The work accomplished in Chapters 2, 3, and 4 provides a solid conceptual and physical foundation for composing. Plants enhance and reinforce the design as they fulfill functional requirements. Skill, vision, and patience are required in handling this interweaving of color, form, texture, line, and mass. Skill unites the design and plant material with dexterity. Vision allows you to project the planting design in the future—ten years, fifty years, a hundred years—from the initial design. Patience is a virtue, you cannot rush the growth and maturation of the planting composition.

FIVE FUNDAMENTAL ELEMENTS OF PLANTING COMPOSITION

The five fundamental principles of planting design composition are:

1. Line
2. Form
3. Mass
4. Texture
5. Color

These primary design elements are *physical* aspects of plants. Every plant possesses each of them. *Line* is the essence of plant form (Figure 5–1). Form is the overall outline or silhouette of a plant (Figure 5–2). *Mass* is a three-dimensional grouping of plants (Figure 5–3). The word *texture* is from the Latin verb "to weave" and refers to the surface qualities of plants (Figure 5–4). *Color* is the reflection of the different bands of light on an object. Without light there is no color. The palette of plant colors is almost as varied as plants themselves (Figure 5–5).

Design elements are directly affected by principle design components. A design component is an abstract part of the composition such as balance, emphasis, or repetition—an intangible characteristic. Components are similar to ingredients in a recipe—the presence or absence of one alters the outcome of the final product. Each component varies in significance as it relates to the principles of composition and to the ultimate goal of the design. For example, an emphasis on form is often more dramatic than an emphasis on color; a sequence of texture can be more noticeable than a sequence of line. The following principle components are defined as they relate to planting design:

5-1 *Line.*

5-3 *Massing. (Ganna Walska Lotusland)*

5-4 *Texture. (Ganna Walska Lotusland;* PHOTO: CAROL
BORNSTEIN)

5-2 *Form.*

5-5 *Color;* Grevillea robusta. *(*PHOTO: CAROL BORNSTEIN)

5-6 *Balance.*

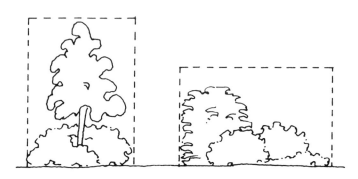

5-7 *Emphasis.*

5-8 *Proportion.*

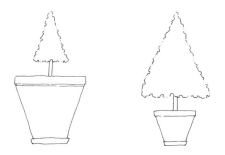

5-9 *Repetition.*

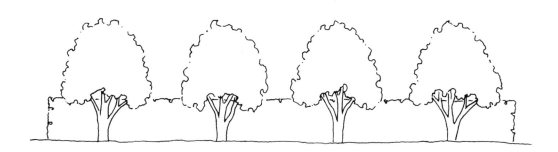

5-10 *Rhythm.*

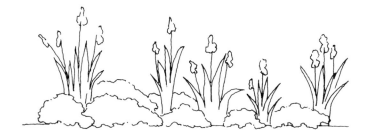

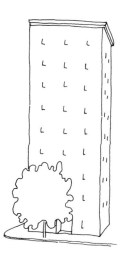

- *Balance* results from the placement of an object (plant) or objects along an imaginary or real axis in a landscape composition. When mass is distributed equally on both sides of the axis, a composition is said to be "in balance." Balance equalizes or adjusts competing forces to obtain stability or repose. A single plant in a plane is a focus; two similar plants in a plane divide interest equally and create balance (Figure 5–6). In planting design, balance reinforces an axis, emphasizes circulation, and accents points of transition.

- *Emphasis* differentiates the more important from the less important. It is created by increasing the dominance of certain elements and the subordination of minor elements (Figure 5 7). A planting composition can emphasize hierarchy, public and private space, and architectural form through the choice of plant species and plant placement.

- *Proportion* refers to the actual size of an object or its size relative to another object (Figure 5–8). Proportion exists the moment two objects are put together. *Absolute proportion* is the size or scale of an object. *Relative proportion* is an object's perceived size in relationship to another object in space.

- *Repetition* is the placement of the same or similar form, texture, or color over and over again. It results from placing like things together, enabling the mind to comprehend a composition (Figure 5–9). There are varying degrees of repetition. It can be complete and absolute or meager and sparing; it can create monotony or stimulate the viewer. Repeating a plant form produces architectural walls, hallways, or floors. Repeating a line creates movement. Repeating a color can make a small space appear larger.

- *Rhythm* is a patterned repetition of a design principle at regular or irregular intervals. As a design tool, it creates a sequence of movement or pattern in the garden. Rhythm of form, color, or texture intensifies the plant composition (Figure 5–10).

- *Scale* is the perception of an object's size based on its relation to the human body or relation to another object (Figure 5–11). Garden design must have both absolute and relative scale. *Absolute* or *human scale* refers to the relationship between the

5-12 *Sequence.*

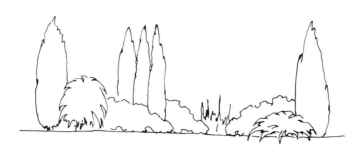

5-13 *Simplicity.*

5-14 *Symmetry.*

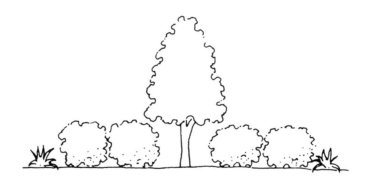

5-15 *Asymmetry.*

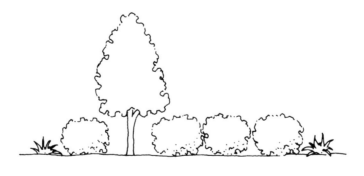

5-16 *Variety.*

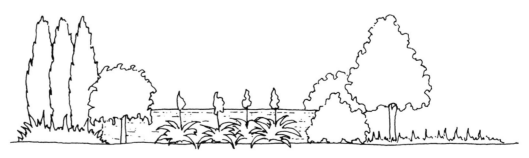

viewer and the landscape. This means the design is compatible in size with the human figure. A well-composed scene allows the viewer to move about freely without pondering the scale, feeling uncomfortable, or lost in the garden. There are exceptions—for example, a children's garden is often arranged for the scale of a child's body, prohibiting an adult from entering. Or, for spectacular effect the scale of objects may be grossly exaggerated to make the viewer feel small and overwhelmed by the scene.

Relative scale establishes the apparent size of an object or space produced by the actual size of its parts. The scale of one part relative to another and each part to the whole is significant. If the scale is discordant, the unity of the composition is destroyed. Constancy of scale creates unity and harmony. If the scale of plant forms and mass is constantly changing the design is scattered and the viewer becomes confused. The height of a tree must be in scale to the size of the garden. A mass of shrubs must be appropriate to the size of the planting bed.

Distance also affects scale. A series of objects of a known size in a landscape serves as a reference point to determine the distance from the observer to various parts of the landscape. The viewer detects greater variety, texture, and detail if the distance is short. Detail is lost from the distant view and the arrangement of mass becomes more significant.

- *Sequence* arranges the design so that the viewer's attention moves in a distinct way. It is a uniform change, movement, or transition of the design leading in some direction or to some desired end (Figure 5–12). It connects design principles because movement from one part of the composition to another can be created through change in form, color, texture, position, or size of plant. Sequence can be created by changing one design component—but not all, or the result is chaos.

  In planting design, sequence focuses on transition or movement from one plant to another. Sequence through repetition links two parts of a design. Sequence through alternation is the repetition of two or more contrasting forms, textures, or colors. The repetition of one feature is broken at regular intervals by the insertion of contrasting features. This alternation continues throughout the composition and is very rhythmic. The success of this sequence relies on the repetition of one feature being broken down at regular intervals by the contrast feature.

- *Simplicity* is restraint, moderation, and fitness in design. These qualities give permanence to the work of great architects and landscape architects. The adage: less is more (Figure 5–13).

- *Symmetry* is the similarity of size, form, and arrangement of parts on opposite sides of a plane, line, or point. Symmetrical design implies order and control and organizes landscape through the use of balance and repetition (Figure 5–14). *Asymmetry* is simply when garden features are not symmetrical or identical on two sides of a plane, line, or point. It is an organizational tool of composition based on balance and the sequence of movement about an imaginary axis (Figure 5–15).

- *Variety* is the diversity of design qualities in a composition. It is the change or contrast in one or two of the design principles—line, form, texture, or color—that holds the observer's attention (Figure 5–16). How much variety is appropriate to a design depends on the complexity of its design principles. Variety is the opposite of repetition. If overdone, it destroys unity. Variety planned with sufficient repetition can maintain unity.

Harmony and unity are the results of the artful application of design principles and components. Composition is subjective. As the landscape designer John Brookes points out, "The appreciation of design is an expression of personal likes and dislikes of a particular composition, for we all react differently to colors, patterns, shapes, and textures,"[2] but there *are* basic guidelines to think about as you begin. The following discussion focuses on individual design principles and their relationship to components in plant composition. Keep in mind that they are means to an end. Design principles are so closely interrelated that examining them separately is purely for study purposes.

LINE, FORM, AND MASS

Line, form, and mass are interrelated. Line creates form, groups of forms create mass. Mass is the grouping of forms in three dimensions. Form and mass are the building blocks on which line, texture, and color are wrapped. Mass is composed of forms, form is built upon line or direction, and both are bounded by silhouette.[3] They are all interconnected.

Line

The trunk and/or branches determine the mass of a tree or plant. Mass and/or the form of a plant can often be simplified to its dominant line, which expresses plant character. Figure 5–17 is a sketch of plant character expressed by simple lines. Understanding the line of a plant entails reducing or abstracting it to its simplest

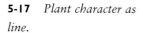
5-17 *Plant character as line.*

5-18 (top left) Flowering dogwood trees display horizontal lines. (PHOTO: CAROL BORNSTEIN)

5-19 (bottom left) Harmonious lines of coastal plant community. (PHOTO: CAROL BORNSTEIN)

5-20 (right) Lines of the Camperdown elm.

form. Careful attention to the natural line, branching habit, or outline of a plant is a valuable design tool enabling you to feel and identify the spirit and mood of trees, shrubs, and flowers.

One of the best ways to become a good planting designer is to sketch plants in the landscape. Simple pencil or ink drawings allow you to explore plant character and begin to know plants—to see the lines that create their form and think about their ultimate stage of growth. In this way you will develop a feeling for plant expression—the different moods and emotions that specific plants evoke.

Think about the plant's framework. Vertical lines tend to move the eye up and down. Horizontal lines move with normal eye movement. Winter is a good time to look at the form of deciduous plants; evergreen plants can be studied year round. Does the plant have a graceful arch or an irregular branching habit? Will the total mass appear dense and heavy or light and airy? Is the growth habit drooping, spreading, or upright? The knowledge to answer these questions directly affects the success of a plant composition.

Begin by looking at plant combinations that are harmonious in nature. The horizontal branching of a flowering dogwood tree is brilliantly displayed against a backdrop of pine trees (Figure 5–18). It would appear chaotic with the weeping lines of a Camperdown elm because branches would be overlapping in all directions (Figure 5–19). One simple way to begin a mass composition is to group plants of similar branching habit or outline. Birch, maple, and beech trees are similar in branching habit, form, and mass. In Figure 5–20, a coastal plant community of lupines and artemesia is harmonious in form, color and texture.

Herbaceous Plants and Ground Covers

foliage mat   spreading   carpet   clumps   spikes

Shrubs

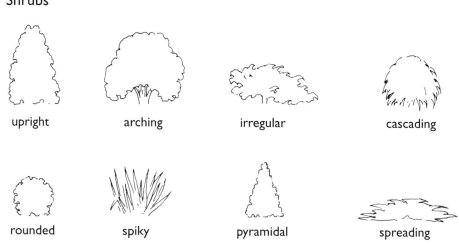

upright   arching   irregular   cascading

rounded   spiky   pyramidal   spreading

Trees

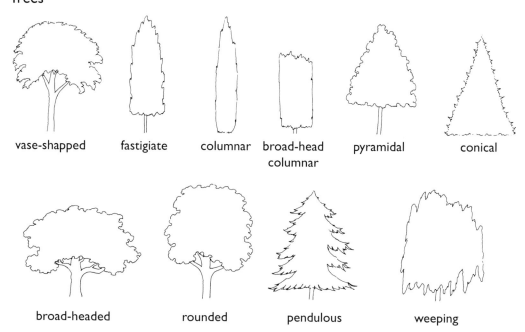

vase-shapped   fastigiate   columnar   broad-head columnar   pyramidal   conical

broad-headed   rounded   pendulous   weeping

5-22 (left) Discordant plant forms.

5-23 (right) Contrasting plant forms.

Form

The form of a plant reduces to a simple diagram. Growth habit determines form. It is the sum of plant parts—branches, trunks, direction of growth. The total mass of a plant is described as form. Tree forms can be vase-shaped, fastigiate, columnar, pyramidal, conical, broadly columnar, broad-headed, rounded, pendulous, or weeping. Shrubs take on upright, arching, irregular, cascading, rounded, spiky, spreading, or pyramidal forms. Ground covers and herbaceous plants form foliage mats, spreading, carpets, clumps, several stems from a crown, or spikes (Figure 5–21). Form varies greatly from a solitary plant to a plant massing.

Plant forms are expressive. A cluster of weeping willows evokes images of water and graceful movement. A statuesque oak, *Quercus* spp., is powerful and majestic in the landscape. Ferns represent lushness and moisture. Coral bells, *Heuchera sanguinea,* dance in a summer breeze. The enormous size of a redwood tree, *Sequoia sempervirens,* the irregularity of germander, *Teucrium fruticans,* and the implied movement of ornamental grasses all affect the composition.

When we are grouping plant forms, once again nature gives us the first clues. The vertical spires of conifers are associated with jagged mountains, round-topped hardwoods are dominant over the glacial moraines of the Midwest, and undulating evergreen oaks roll across the hills of California.

Form can be harmonious or discordant. Sharp peaks and rounded forms, cones and globes, spires and flat-topped plants require caution in their combination. Harsh contrasts and the mixing of numerous forms is discordant. Look at Figure 5–22; there is disparity of form between the spiky potted plants, foliage mat ground covers, and the severity of the hedge. Again, in Figure 5–23 the columnar plant and weeping tree are too dissimilar in form to be engaging when paired.

To achieve harmony of mass, form, and line there must be some repetition in form. Repetition of form at regular intervals creates rhythm in the landscape. It can pull together a design by incorporating the same form or line flowing through a planting scheme such as a single thread running through a textile. Repetition must be proportional to keep the rhythm moving and yet not allow it to get lost or dissipate. If a conical plant is located in a planting of rounded forms, the column has the effect of an exclamation mark. The eye

5-24 *(top left) Form as emphasis.*

5-25 *(top right) Form creates repetition and rhythm.*

5-26 *(bottom) Form suggests variety and asymmetry.*

follows it upward almost to the exclusion of the plants around it. It is a dazzling effect but should be used cautiously in the landscape. Figure 5–24 shows the power of a columnar form in the landscape. This same form, when repeated, as in Figure 5–25, is less emphatic and complements the architecture.

Plant form emphasizes points of transition that signal changes in grade, direction, or mood by creating a sequence of movement. For example, an element may be placed off center or be irregular in shape to provide variety and to keep the scene from becoming static. Look at the photograph of I Tatti, the home of noted art historian Bernard Berenson, in Settignano, Italy (Figure 5–26). If you put your finger over the stone pine in the upper right corner your eye drifts back and forth along the parterre without emphasis or interest; the design becomes static. This stone pine provides a contrast of emphasis that accentuates the formality of the plan. It gives your eye a place to focus and rest, enabling you to comprehend the rest of the design.

Plants emphasize horizontal space when their form or growth habit parallels or echoes the horizon or a flat landscape. Sometimes individual plants have a horizontal habit, such as hawthorn trees on the prairie combined with prairie grasses. Other times the broad expanse of a single type of plant in a large mass or massing underlines horizontal space. An open space shaped by horizontal massing leads your eye toward the horizon line because there is nothing to redirect your line of sight up or down. As your eye follows these forms it moves back and forth or across unless it lights upon something vertical to interrupt its path of movement.

Mass

The line and form of the individual plant is the basis for the planting group, which in turn creates the mass. Mass exists at different scales. The planting bed shown in Figure 5–27 depicts a massing of one plant species. Numerous plants of various forms and textures with an emphasis on one floral color are massed in Figure 5–28, and Figure 5–29 illustrates massing on a grand scale.

5-27 *(left) Repetition of one form, color, and texture creates mass.*

5-28 *(top right) Massing of variety in form and texture with emphasis on one floral color.*

5-29 *(bottom right) Plant massing on a grand scale.*

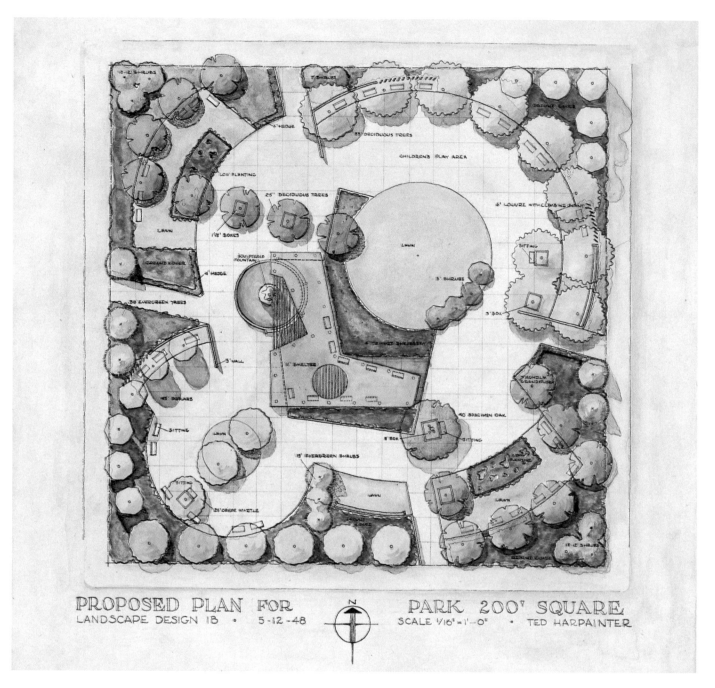

PROPOSED PLAN FOR   N   PARK 200' SQUARE

LANDSCAPE DESIGN 1B • 5-12-48   SCALE 1/16"=1'-0" • TED HARPAINTER

5-30 *Plan drawing of form and mass. (DRAWING BY TED HARPAINTER; COURTESY OF THE UNIVERSITY OF CALIFORNIA AT BERKELEY STUDENT ARCHIVES)[4]*

The following is one of my favorite examples of an initial plant study of form and mass sketched in the abstract. Examine the series of drawings in Figures 5–30, 5–31, and 5–32. The plan drawing depicts the composition in one dimension (Figure 5–30). Locate the plants on the plan based on their mature height and spread. Mark off the linear distance the planting will occupy; do not worry about the depth of the planting at this stage. Now, using a section drawn from the plan, think about the planting forms as proportional blocks or rectangles arranged according to the design (Figure 5–31). These two-dimensional forms can be represented in seasonal colors and the abstract rectangles eventually transformed to a desired form. Sketch your design from all four sides, if necessary, to obtain the desired view. Figure 5–32 represents the same design in a perspective view.

5-31 *Section drawing of form and mass.* (DRAWING BY TED HARPAINTER; COURTESY OF THE UNIVERSITY OF CALIFORNIA AT BERKELEY STUDENT ARCHIVES)

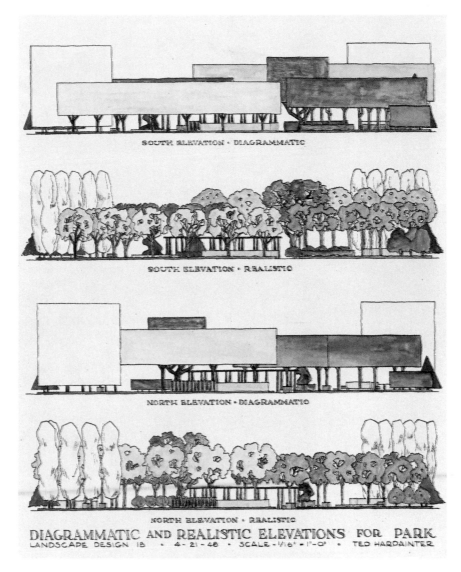

SOUTH ELEVATION · DIAGRAMMATIC

SOUTH ELEVATION · REALISTIC

NORTH ELEVATION · DIAGRAMMATIC

NORTH ELEVATION · REALISTIC

DIAGRAMMATIC AND REALISTIC ELEVATIONS FOR PARK
LANDSCAPE DESIGN 1B · 4-21-48 · SCALE-1/16"=1'-0" · TED HARPAINTER

5-32 *Perspective drawing of form and mass.* (DRAWING BY TED HARPAINTER; COURTESY OF THE UNIVERSITY OF CALIFORNIA AT BERKELEY STUDENT ARCHIVES)

BIRD'S EYE VIEW

PROPOSED CITY PARK 200' SQ.
L.D. 1B · 5-29-48 · 1/16"=1'-0" · TED HARPAINTER

5-33 *Mass and form create a point of transition.*

5-34 *Singular plants create variety and add shadows to plant massing.*

5-35 *Shadow, distance, and topography add depth and mystery to this mass planting.* (PHOTO: LAURA WEATHERALL)

This added dimension allows you to place yourself in the composition. Try to imagine walking around in the design. Composing in plan, section, and perspective affords an excellent study of plant massing.

Construction of a mass planting takes its cues from the layout of the plan. Plantings follow the guidelines of the spaces created. The goal is to emphasize the design decisions made thus far. If the axis is strong and accented by an allée leading to a focal point, then the plant massing needs to follow suit. Wavering lines and curves dissipate the power of a straight line. A row of trees, a low hedge, or a floral border—linear plant masses—all accent an axis. A point of transition in a plan may take the form of vertical emphasis defined by two fastigiate trees, cascading shrubs, or a change in the hedge configuration (Figure 5–33). If the lines of the plan are undulating and irregular, the insertion of a line of rigid planting may seem discordant.

Planting masses that are organic in form require special attention to open space, distance, variety, shadow, and topography. Organic forms derive their arrangement from nature or naturally occurring forms. As Gertrude Jekyll so aptly describes it in her book, *Wood and Garden,* "No artificial planting can ever equal that of nature, but one may learn from it. The great lesson is the importance of moderation and reserve, of simplicity of intention, of directness of purpose, and inestimable value of the quality called 'breadth' in painting. For planting ground is like painting a landscape with living things."[5]

Open space affects the scale and form of masses. Too much massing with too little open space can be suffocating. Too much open space with too little mass can make the viewer feel lost or unsettled. Mass should balance open areas, dark should balance light, sunlight and shadow should be proportional with climatic requirements. In a large-scale planting, specimen or singular plants break the monotony of the ground plane and add shadows to the landscape (Figure 5–34). Openings, hollows, and glades create light and shade that add depth and variety to the plant masses. Depth suggests mystery (Figure 5–35).

Variety in mass rhythmically varies the size and spacing of trees, shrubs, and ground cover. Small trees mingle with large trees and shrubs interweave with ground covers. Designers paint with living materials a picture in three dimensions. If topography is rolling or hilly its character must be observed and its silhouette retained.

Masses and plantings in the foreground become more important if the distant or borrowed view lacks appeal. If, from the initial analysis, a borrowed view is to be incorporated into a landscape scene, it is best to keep the foreground simple so that the eye will enjoy the scene beyond without distraction.

For example, the landscape architect Frederick Law Olmsted, working in 1889 on Mountain View Cemetery in northern California, employed a planting technique to enhance what he felt was a spectacular borrowed view but a chaotic middle ground. Mountain View Cemetery was one of Olmsted's first attempts to employ the principles of a regional style in the semi-arid American West.[6] His design concept illustrates two characteristics of the time. The first is Olmsted's belief in *communicativeness*—the cemetery was designed as a place where people of various faiths could share in their common grief. Secondly, his sensitivity to the environment led him to use California natives and Mediterranean plants in the design. Concerned with the lack of water and what he felt was the ragged look of the native grasses on the hillsides in the middle ground, he proposed a three-tiered planting concept. For the foreground he suggested a small soothing greensward that would be easy to maintain and water while offering serenity and repose for the grieving. He then proposed a middle ground of Mediterranean and native plants that were evergreen, drought tolerant, and appropriate to the planting concept of grief and death. Italian stone pine, *Pinus pinea*, Italian cypress, *Cupressus sempervirens*, Grecian laurel, *Laurus noblis*, Monterey Cypress, *Cupressus macrocarpa*, and coast Live Oak, *Quercus agrifolia* were planted. Plants were positioned in the landscape so that the eye traveled from the green ground plane to the taller evergreen planting and finally to the distant hillsides (Figures 5–36, 5–37).

When you work with line, form, and mass in planting design, examine each plant individually and in groupings. Think about the overall effect of a small scene as part of the larger landscape view. Look at the forms of plants that grow together naturally and

5-36 *Planting concept for Mountain View Cemetery in Oakland, California.*

5-37 *Mountain View Cemetery today.*

take your cues from nature. When it works the planting sings and soars, but when lines are weak or forms unrelated, the results are disagreeable and diffused.

TEXTURE

Texture is the most variable of all design characteristics. The tactile qualities of texture vary from fine to coarse, rough to smooth, hard to soft. Visually they can be expressed as light to dark. In textiles, texture is the result of the size and spacing of the threads that are woven together. In a landscape, texture is the result of the surface quality and size of a plant combined with the distance from which the plant is viewed. Through the exploitation of texture one may stimulate the imagination, symbolize strength and power, create an effect of personality, simulate distance, increase or decrease apparent space, produce a feeling of atmosphere, or refine landscapes. The use of texture can create harmony or discord.[7] Principles of balance, variety, and simplicity directly affect texture.

Texture must be in balance in a planting plan. The weight of texture on one side of the real or imaginary axis must balance the weight of texture on the other. If a coarse texture is used, medium and fine textures must be supplied in proportional quantity to balance it. Look at the planting in Figure 5–38. The pansies are light and airy in texture and cannot offset the coarse texture of the ornamental cabbages. In Figure 5–39, seemingly incompatible textures are balanced by proportion and color. If a large grouping of fine textures is used, medium or coarse textures may be added to hold or anchor the planting design. Sometimes people associate fine texture with softness and delicacy—lawns, hedges, some ferns—and coarse textures with feelings of harshness or roughness.

Texture is created by a variety of plant characteristics—size of plant leaves, spacing and surface of leaves and twigs, and, in certain seasons, the flowers and fruit. Coarse plants such as gunnera, *Gunnera manicata*, acanthus, *Acanthus mollis*, and verbascum, *Verbascum* spp., make a space appear smaller because the scale of the leaves is large in proportion to the space occupied (Figure 5–40). Fine-textured plants such as mayten tree, *Maytens boaria*, or honey locust, *Gleditisia triacanthos*, can make a space appear larger

5-38 *(left) Incompatible textures.*

5-39 *(right) Compatible textures.*

5-40 *(left) Coarse textured verbascum plants growing in gravel make the space appear smaller.*

5-41 and 5-42 *(bottom) Pruning affects texture and color.*

because the leaf size and surface is small in proportion to space. In mass the trees appear transparent due to their delicate texture.

The surface quality of leaves and their texture or appearance can be altered significantly through pruning. Look at the two hedges at Villa Gamberaia (Figure 5–41). The pruned hedge appears to be darker and more abstracted as a piece of mass and the unpruned hedge is softer and a lighter green in color. Figure 5–42 displays the effects of pruning on texture.

Texture can have seasonal effects, with deciduous plants appearing barren in winter and coarse-textured in summer. Flower and fruit size, shape, and color affect the seasonal texture of a composition. The deciduous witch hazel tree looks delicate when in flower but coarse when in leaf Figures 5–43, 5–44. It is important to keep these periodic changes in mind because they influence the success of the planting scheme.

Distance also affects the perception of texture. The massing of an entire plant creates one texture in the far view and a very different texture closer up. At the Bloedel Reserve in Washington State, a form in the distance (one of the boundaries of the Japanese garden) is first seen as a large, dark plant mass (Figure 5–45). On approaching the garden you see that the large mass becomes a fine mound of cotoneaster (Figure 5–46).

5-43 *(top left) Seasonal effects of texture; witch hazel in winter.* (PHOTO: CAROL BORNSTEIN)

5-44 *(top right) Witch hazel in late spring.*

5-45 *(bottom left) Texture from a distance.*

5-46 *(bottom right) The same plant up close.*

Figures 5–47 and 5–48 are texture studies of plants. The planting is reduced to four textures: fine, medium, coarse, and heavy. Fine and coarse lines abstract the textures in the image. This exercise can be done in the field. Select a scene that appeals to you and quickly sketch the textures at a distance of ten feet, a hundred feet, and two hundred feet. Study the effects of texture and distance.

COLOR[8]

Nature is the ultimate source of every palette. When asked to describe color we use terms such as moss green, indigo blue, saffron yellow, cherry red. As you establish your plant palette, the existing landscape can offer many simple clues to achieving color harmony. Here the subtleties of shape and texture create numerous gradations of color. The color of tree bark is a progression of warm browns and grays encircling the trunk. Color in nature does not depend solely on its inherent qualities; outside influences come into play. The rose-pink sunrise, the misty azure blue of twilight, and the clarity of sunlight on a winter afternoon all produce different effects on the same plant.

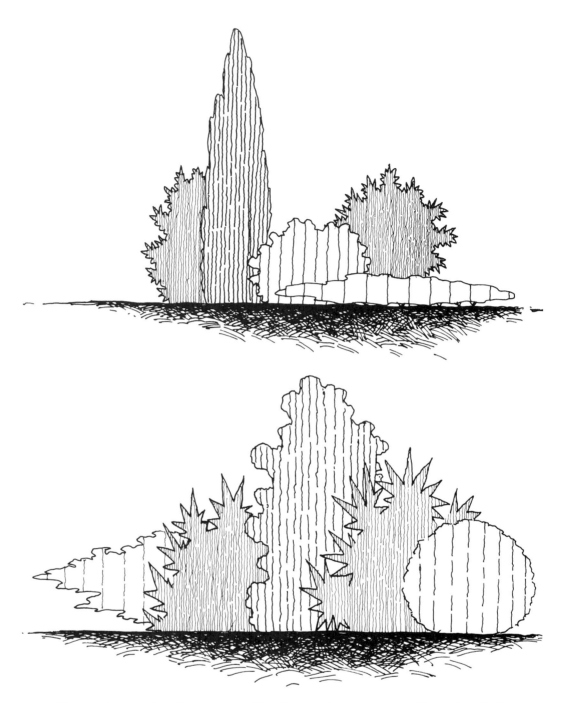

Nature gives us clues for color combinations with each season. Take a close look at the atmospheric color of a landscape in Virginia throughout the four seasons (Figures 5–49, 5–50, 5–51, 5–52). Spring color is tinged with white, a hint of yellow, or occasionally red. Summer appears to be the time of yellow-green or bright emerald-green color. Autumn is the season when warm colors dominate—red, yellow, and orange. These are vibrant colors that signal the last flourish of the season. Last, winter brings the grays and browns into dominance. The value in winter lies in the contrast of gray twigs against conifers or silvery olive trees against brown oak leaves. Each season has its own color effect.

The successful use of color in the landscape requires an understanding of color theory and color harmony. A designer needs to develop the ability to recognize hues, tints,

5-49 *(top left) Color in spring.*

5-50 *(top right) Color in summer.*

5-51 *(bottom left) Color in autumn.*

5-52 *(bottom right) Color in winter.*

and shades in plants. A *hue* is a variation of a color. For example, fire-engine red, blood red, tomato red—in plants, a red rose, red twig dogwood, or red autumn color. The degree of darkness in a color produces a *shade*. Adding white to a pure color creates a *tint*. Few colors exist in a pure state; nuance and variation are more the rule.

There are three basic characteristics of color that you will use:

1. physical color, or the fundamentals of color arrangement and color harmony

2. emotional effect of color on moods

3. color quality, or the artistic expression of life and nature through color choices

Physical Color

Color exists in objects because of their ability to reflect, absorb, or transmit different light. Light involves energy—sunlight, streetlight, moonlight—and the ultimate source of all light is the sun. Light is a series of spherical waves emanating from a source; as they hit the retina of the eye they produce a definite sensation called light. These waves move outward in every direction from the source and are subject to physical laws of reflection and refraction.

A light source generally produces a range of colors, not just one. *White* is a combination of all the waves capable of producing the sensations of light. *Black* is the absence

5-53 *The color of light through a prism.*

5-54 *Primary colors.*   **5-55** *Secondary colors.*   **5-56** *Tertiary colors.*

of such waves. You can see the components of white light by passing it through a glass prism, which sorts out the waves of different lengths by refraction. Each wave varies in length and bends at a different angle (Figure 5–53). The wavelengths of light vary from short to long—red is the longest, violet the shortest. This spectrum is the basis for the study of color and the key to color harmony.

The *primary colors* of the spectrum are red, yellow, and blue (Figure 5–54); these cannot be mixed or created from other colors. The blending of any two primary colors in equal amounts produces a secondary color; red and yellow make orange, yellow and blue create green, and blue and red create purple (Figure 5–55). Mix two secondary colors to form a tertiary color—citron, slate, or russet (Figure 5–56). The tertiary colors, when mixed, create quaternary colors—sage, plum, and buff. As this process proceeds the colors become more neutral until eventually gray is created. Work with a color wheel to choose the best sequence to achieve the desired effect. The study of the color wheel gives clues to color combinations that work in the garden.

Emotional Effect of Color

Color constitutes one of the deepest mysteries that confronts us when we investigate the relationship between the human mind and the greater world.[9] It has the power to enhance emotions or feelings. In Western cultures, red, yellow, orange, and their modifications are labeled *warm colors* and are associated emotionally with images of fire and heat. Red stimulates, excites, enlivens. It is often a symbol of danger, aggression, vitality, excitement, passion, war, and anarchy. The warmer the red the more it is influenced by yellow. The color of red deepens when paired with blues and brown, and are sometimes referred to as the "cold side of the reds and contain no warming yellows."[10] Yellow is the color of gold, the sun, and is a symbol of wisdom and power. Orange is the color of autumn and the flame. It is a sign of light and knowledge.

5-57 *(left) Primary colors are best in tropical climates.*
5-58 *(right) Pastel colors look washed out in brilliant sunshine.*

Similarly, blue, violet, and green are associated with water, ice, and shadows, and are referred to as *cool colors*. Blue is cool, reserved, distant, calm, retiring. Blue represents the enduring sky and constancy—"true blue." Blue can represent serenity and sadness. Green is soothing. It is the color of foliage, grass, and vigorous growth, a symbol of fertility and abundance. Green is restful to the eye. Violet is the color of shadows, serious and solemn. It provokes imagery of mourning, sorrow, and spirituality.

Color Quality

The color quality of any object is due to the selective absorption of the light waves; it is the ability of the object to absorb some waves and reflect others. To illustrate, if an object absorbs all wavelengths but reflects green, we see only the green light that escapes. If light from which all the red waves are eliminated falls on a red object, there is no reflection and the object appears black. If the object reflects all the waves and absorbs none, the object appears to be white. Thus the effect of light on a garden in sunlight changes in moonlight because the light of the moon is reflected from the sun. Colors are intense and true in sunlight but softened by blue in moonlight.

Colors change in sunshine—brighter colors are brilliant, cooler colors almost seem to disappear. For example, tropical and desert regions require bright colors to create effects because the light quality is so dazzling (Figure 5–57). Pastel colors are often washed out in brilliant sunshine. In Figure 5–58, the pale lavender blossom of Russian sage, *Perovskia atriplicifolia,* appears dull in contrast to the yellow flowers of the coreopsis, *Coreopsis grandiflora,* and the burgundy-leafed smoke tree, *Cotinus coggygria* 'Purpurea.' Temperate areas with overcast skies, such as the Pacific Northwest and England, require the use of warm colors against the gray skies. In Figure 5–59, the bright red flowers of the red border at Hidcote stand out, while the blue and purple flowers at Polesden Lacy tend to recede (Figure 5–60). White often leaps out at you in the landscape

5-59 *Warm colors stand out against overcast skies.*

5-60 *Cool colors recede against overcast skies.*

5-61 and 5-62 *White stands out in the garden.* (PHOTO, *5-61:* CAROL BORNSTEIN)

5-63 and 5-64 *Filoli Gardens on a sunny day and an overcast day.*

5-65 *(top left)*
Complementary colors of
yellow and blue.

5-66 *(top right) White roses*
and lavender catmint.

5-67 *(bottom left) Gray*
color displays the effects of
the colors around it.

5-68 *(bottom right)*
Different shades of green.

(Figures 5–61, 5–62). Figures 5–63 and 5–64 represent two views of Filoli Garden in California, one on a rainy winter day and one on a sunny summer day. Notice the effect of sunlight on the different shades of green.

Perception of color is influenced further by:

1. the *juxtaposition* of plants to each other

2. *color placement*

3. the *surface quality* of plants

Juxtaposition   How we perceive color is most often a relative perception. The way we see one color or several colors is strongly influenced by what is surrounding them. For example, complementary colors create the strongest color contrasts. Each color increases the apparent purity and brilliance of the other. Colors against their complements appear much more intense (Figure 5–65).

Color against white becomes deeper and more vivid (Figure 5–66). Light colors often look better with white as dark colors can create too great a contrast. White brightens an area in shadow, while color against black appears as if there were less color. Gray foliage colors appears lighter or darker when neighboring colors are lighter or darker. Gray accents the purity of brightness in near colors. With gray, pure hues glow and pale pastels brighten. Gray becomes tinged with a haze of other colors (Figure 5–67).

Green, the predominant color in gardens, has an enormous range of colors. Blue-green, gray-green, yellow-green, olive green, forest-green, and emerald-green plants create the framework, edges, boundaries, backdrops, and centerpieces of a garden (Figure 5–68).

5-69 (top left) Warm colors bring objects closer.

5-70 (top right) Cool colors recede and make a space appear larger.

5-71 (bottom) Color and texture of different plant leaves affect plant placement.

Color Placement The position of color is essential to the harmony and gradation of a landscape picture. Distance and space are modified with color. Warm colors lessen a distance and make a space appear smaller. Red carries across distance and affects the eye quickly, bringing objects closer (Figure 5–69). Cool colors create distance and make a space seem larger. Blue recedes, affecting the eye slowly; it makes objects appear further away (Figure 5–70).

A shadow over a color will dim the color. This is constantly occurring outdoors due to clouds, trees, shrubs, and structures. Intense light and shadow affect red, yellow, and orange less than blue, green, and violet because the cool colors tend to recede in sunlight and further recede in shadow. A dark shade or tint will appear darker in shadow and a light tint will appear weaker in sunlight

Surface Quality Texture affects color. Color appears much brighter when a surface is glossy than when it is dull. Coarse textures appear lighter in color. Small surfaces reflect light differently than large ones and their texture appears darker, richer, and stronger (Figure 5–71). In addition, scale influences color—a plant is sometimes chosen because of the size of the leaf, flower, or fruit that produces the color. Glossy leaves appear smaller because they are shiny. Fine-textured leaves appear dark and dense (Figure 5–42). Color influences emphasis on seasonal and sequential displays. At what time of year are the blossoms, leaves, or fruit displayed? Which part of the garden requires movement,

5-72 and 5-73 *Sections:*
Ellis-Mahoney garden.

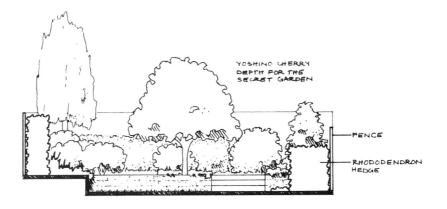

YOSHINO CHERRY
DEPTH FOR THE
SECRET GARDEN

FENCE

RHODODENDRON
HEDGE

ELLIS-MAHONEY GARDEN
SECTION — NORTH-SOUTH

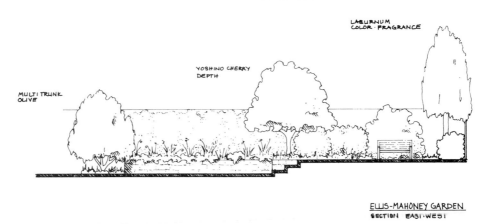

LABURNUM
COLOR · FRAGRANCE

YOSHINO CHERRY
DEPTH

MULTI TRUNK
OLIVE

ELLIS-MAHONEY GARDEN
SECTION EAST-WEST

transition, tranquillity? Color must be graded, molded, or focused to supplement texture and form. The colors must blend through all the seasons. The greater the number of colors used, the more difficult the interweaving.

SUMMARY

This chapter presents a lot of abstract information. It may seem overwhelming at first glance or with your first attempts at plant composition, but persevere. Remember that decisions made throughout the entire development of the planting design process necessitate interweaving related elements into a larger unity.

Let us turn once again to the Ellis-Mahoney garden to illustrate some of these concepts of planting composition. Beginning with form and mass, we draw two sections of the site and examine the evolution of the composition (Figures 5–72, 5–73). Tree forms, or the "bones," are chosen first. As mentioned in Chapter 4 (see Figures 4–61, 4–62), a specimen tree in the middle of the plan creates depth; it is required to be wide but not too tall. A small, multi-trunk tree is suggested as you enter the garden. This creates mystery, interest, and an unfolding effect so that the entire garden is not viewed in one sweep. Another small tree accents the secret garden. Hedges are required in the southern edge and secret garden and form a green mass or architectural walls. The perennial border is composed of a variety of forms and textures. Overall, the forms tend to be rounded, with horizontal lines keeping them in proportion to the size of the area. Variety is produced with texture and color.

Color and texture studies are combined to complete this step of the planting design process. From discussions with the client, the overall color scheme develops into a combination of white, blues, and yellows, with accents of peach and violet to keep the garden bright through the fog and keep the colors complementary. A green, fine-textured plant is needed as a backdrop to the perennial border. The specimen tree should be deciduous and light-textured, with a white flower, to produce an airy effect without making the garden feel dark or cramped. In contrast, the multi-trunk entrance tree should be evergreen for year-round entrance effect. Hedges are desired at approximately four to five feet in height for privacy without overwhelming the space. Their texture needs to be medium-coarse to provide an interesting view from the secret garden, yet not so coarse as to make the space feel small or chaotic. The textures in the perennial bed balance the textures of the hedges.

Designing a plant composition is not a simple task but a skill that must be developed over time with practice and experience. In a composition, every object is viewed in relation to every other object within the span of vision. No object in the composition can be viewed as an isolated element. You must keep the effects of the design components in mind as you work with each element of the composition. The plant composition choices—deciduous or evergreen, yellow or blue accents, coarse or fine textures—influence microclimate, define the quality of the allée or palisade, and affect architectural features. The process goes back and forth from the ecological, artistic, and functional plant associations to the effects of color, texture, form, mass, and line. The same artistic vision that chose a tapis vert or espalier as part of the design solution now begins to envision those garden elements as a coarse texture or covered with red berries. Therefore, to prevent a planting from becoming a jumble of unrelated elements, design principles must be consistently combined with the appropriate components.

ENDNOTES

[1] Calvin Tomkins, "The Garden Artist," *The New Yorker* (October 16, 1995), 147.

[2] John Brookes, *The Garden Book* (New York: Crown Publishers, 1984), 42.

[3] Florence Bell Robinson, *Planting Design* (Champaign, IL: Garrard Press, 1940), 61–62.

[4] These images are courtesy of the University of California at Berkeley student archives. The description of this exercise is a combination of Robinson's Application XIII in *Planting Design,* 202–203, and a planting design assignment from University of California at Berkeley done in 1948.

[5] Gertrude Jekyll, *Wood and Garden* (Salem New Hamphire: Ayer, 1983), 24.

[6] Ranney, Victoria Post, Gerard J. Rauluk and Carolyn Hoffman, *The Papers of Frederick Law Olmsted* Volume V: "The California Frontier." (Baltimore: John Hopkins University Press, 1990), 451.

[7] Robinson, *Planting Design,* 56–57.

[8] I have drawn upon two sources of inspiration for the majority of text on color. Florence Bell Robinson's superb section in her book *Planting Design,* and the text and imagery of Donald Kaufman's and Taffy Dahl's book, *Color* (New York: Clarkson Potter, 1992).

[9] Kaufman and Dahl, *Color,* 5.

[10] Penelope Hobhouse, *Color In Your Garden.* (Boston: Little, Brown and Company, 1985), 152.

CHAPTER 6

Developing a Plant Palette

I perhaps owe becoming a painter to flowers.

CLAUDE MONET[1]

Now it is time to choose the plants that will bring the planting composition to life. A landscape architect chooses a range of plants to create a garden in the same way that an artist chooses a range of colors with which to paint. Both develop a palette—one of plants, the other, paints. Landscape architects choose the right plants after sifting through their design requirements. A design concept, environmental analysis, clients' taste, and form and color studies help them narrow the choices. They all become criteria for selecting the plant palette. The selection criteria consist of the following:

1. functional requirements

2. horticultural requirements

3. maintenance requirements

Begin to research potential plant options. Seldom will a plant fulfill all the qualities desired; choose the best plant for the site while keeping the unity of the entire composition in mind. You must remember that planting design is not a formula. It is a concept based on plant combinations interwoven with twelve months of interest in texture, form, line, mass, and color. "Paradoxically, there are two approaches needed to improve our use of plant material. One is an ability to see each plant as a whole individual, with all its characteristics, and the other is to subordinate the individual plant to the picture as a whole."[2] You must appreciate each plant individually, but do not get myopic; look at each plant and envision it as part of the whole. In the words of the architect Eero Saarinen, "always design a thing by considering it in its larger context—a chair in a room, a room in a house, a house in an environment."[3]

In order to create a palette of plants you must first be able to identify them. The only way to use plants intelligently is to know their botanical and common names and their natural habit of growth. Be familiar with their native surroundings because this will enable you to choose a palette based on climatic associations. Observe individual plant qualities and structures, colors of leaf, flower, and fruit, and note aspects that change in various seasons. The best way to learn about plants is to work with them. Garden on your own or visit arboretums, botanical gardens, and estates open to the public. With a notebook in hand, sketch and jot down names of plant combinations (Figure 6–1).

6-1 *Taking notes at a botanical garden.*

Planting the Landscape

Frequent local retail plant nurseries in different seasons, making note of their displays. Join a horticultural society and attend its meetings, read its newsletters. Talk with local plants people to determine what plants grow well in an area. Read garden magazines. Keep your eyes open to planting design during travels and everyday life. Photograph plants and work with a botanist, horticulturist, or plant expert to help you identify unlabeled plants. An excellent method for learning about plants is to sit down in front of them, touch them, and look them over as carefully as possible. Know a plant intimately (Figure 6–2).

6-2 *Plant studies of the Mustard family. (Drawing by Barbara Giuffrida)*

You will develop favorites. For instance, envision the design as you read Jane Brown's description of a yew hedge, *Taxus* spp.: "The favorite material for enclosure was yew; with its omens of stability and eternity, it is the most symbolic of all garden plants. The patience to design in yew and to wait for the due time and season when the intention would be achieved, adds a sense of repose to the gardens."[4]

Learn your plants; love them. Become so familiar with plants that you can begin to write romantic literature about them, as Simone de Beauvior did in *When Things of the Spirit Come First:* "At home once more she gazed a long while at her face in the mirror: the skin beneath her soulful eyes was somewhat worn, transparent and flecked with reddish-brown, like the throat of a foxglove. This pathetic face deserved the love of a hero."[5]

Becoming a good designer demands rigor in understanding the art and science of plants. They are the foundation or building blocks of all our work. A good design can be ruined by the selection of the incorrect plants. Russell Page illustrates this point in his book, *The Education of a Gardener:*

> There is often in landscape gardening a special difficulty: that gap so hard to bridge between good design and good planting. I have known brilliant designers who were passionately keen on garden design but who had never pushed their study of plants far enough. They either used a very limited repertory of plants or left the planting to someone else. In the same way remarkable plant cultivators I have known, men with a vast knowledge of plants and their likes and dislikes, have rarely had any idea of how to use their plants to make a garden picture.[6]

Research your plant palette, become aware of new cultivars, plant introductions, and push the envelope—do not just round up the usual suspects but embrace plant choices as an ever-evolving artistic creation. Artistic development demands patience, skill, and vision.

No garden remains the same over time. The forms, texture, and colors are constantly changing as the plants move through the seasons. Planting design sometimes requires thinking in terms of succession and simultaneity. A sequential planting emphasizes spaces at different times of the year. For instance, planting spring-blooming bleeding heart, *Dicentra spectabilis,* followed by summer-blooming *hosta* and, lastly, Japanese anemone, *Anemone japonica,* which blooms all autumn long, creates a continuous succession of color. Simultaneous effects are contrasting mixes of color, form, and texture at the same time, such as *Yucca filamentosa* with *Sedum telephium 'Autumn Joy'.*[7] The flannel bush, *Fremontodendron californica 'California Glory,'* combined with California poppy, *Eschscholzia californica,* as seen in Figure 6–3, at the Santa Barbara Botanic Garden is composed of California native plants. Here, nature has been sensitively crafted to create a planting design that is colorful and drought-tolerant, and encourages the natural ecosystems of this plant community.

The thought process involved in planting design is a layering of pertinent information. At first the information may seem overwhelming, but do not give up! The rewards are bountiful. Nuances develop over time from close observation of what is aesthetically harmonious as well as what works on a difficult site. The expansion of your plant knowledge increases through careful concentration on species names as well as design interest. Determine the selection criteria and then begin to research the potential plant options. These choices may be drawn in a planting plan. Plant combinations are limitless paintings waiting to be created.

6-3 *California poppy, fre-*
montodenron, and salvia
blooming simultaneously
along the Porter Trail at the
Santa Barbara Botanic
Garden. (PHOTO: CAROL
BORNSTEIN)

FUNCTIONAL REQUIREMENTS

The goal is to translate form, mass, texture, and color into a tree, shrub, vine, perennial, or ground cover, including its ultimate height and spread. Aesthetic and microclimate effects determine whether deciduous, evergreen, flower, or fruiting characteristics are desired.

We continue examining the design process with the Ellis-Mahoney garden. Start to make a list of plant requirements. Our environmental analysis informed us that the garden is in a fog belt, USDA hardiness zone 9, and the more refined Western Garden zone 17. It contains acidic soil, with few existing plants for structure—a Japanese maple and a camellia. Sunlight varies from full sun to filtered sun to indirect sunlight throughout the year (Figure 6–4).

The Plants

First, the plants. Group plant requirements according to trees, shrubs, groundcover, and vines. Review the design plant by plant. Begin with the structural elements of trees and shrubs. They establish the bones of the garden, referred to in Chapter 5. This framework, generally the larger plants, anchors the garden or holds the design in place throughout all seasons. Create a chart that includes flower color and time, fruiting, deciduous, and evergreen characteristics (Figure 6–5). This chart enables you to think in terms of season and plant combinations.

The creation of a plant collage is another way of examining your plant combinations. Figure 6–6 shows a collage made from pictures cut from plant catalogues to illustrate the plants in the plan (Figure 6–7). The collage enables you to graphically compose your palette. If there are plants you cannot find images of, you can draw and color them by hand.

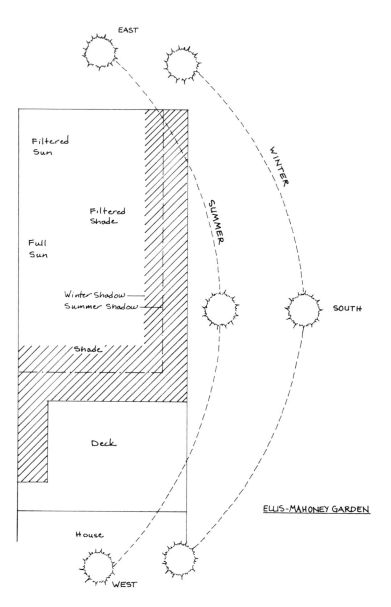

6-4 *Analysis of sun's movement throughout the seasons.*

Trees Trees are potentially the largest and tallest elements of the design and may take the longest time to grow. A tree is defined as a woody plant with a single or multi-trunk that is over twenty feet in height. It can grow in one place for centuries. Thus, the type of soil it is planted in and the room allowed for its growth are extremely important. It is necessary to plan for the ultimate height and spread of the tree as well as its growth rate. People are often impatient waiting for a tree or hedge to take shape; clients may demand a fast-growing plant for "instant effect." Keep in mind that, in general, fast-growing plants are short-lived plants and often have invasive root systems. Initial patience will pay off in the long term of the project.

Begin the chart, as shown in Figure 6–5, with tree ideas. As described in Chapter 5, the tree form requirements are a deciduous, airy tree that is wide but not too tall, to create depth in the garden. Perhaps a magnolia, cherry, redbud, or crabapple tree is entered into the chart. Another tree needed as you enter the garden is a multi-trunk evergreen; a laurel or olive tree is suggested. Last, in the secret garden a small flowering tree is desired: golden chain tree, *Laburnum watereri,* or the strawberry tree, *Arbutus unedo.*

				6-5 *Plant palette chart:*	

6-5 *Plant palette chart: functional requirements.*

Plant	Height	Spread	*Evergreen* E *Deciduous* D	*Flower* Color Time	*Fruit* Color Time
TREES					
Magnolia stellata	10'	20'	D	white early spring	N.S.
Malus 'Red Jade' Crabapple	15'	15'	D weeping form	white mid-spring	red autumn
Prunus yedoensis 'Yoshino' cherry	20'	20'–25'	D	white-pink early spring fragrant	N.S.
Olea europaea 'Swan Hill' Olive	20'	20'	E multi-trunk	N.S.	negligible
Laurus nobilis Grecian laurel	12–40'	10'–15'	E multi stem	N.S.	N.S.
Laburnum watereri Goldenchain tree	20'	10'–12'	D	yellow late spring	N.S.
SHRUBS ***Southern End of garden:***					
Azaleas spp. Azaleas	3'	3'	E	violet-blue late spring	NS
Mahonia lomariifolia Mahonia	6–10'	2'–3'	E multi-stem	yellow early spring	blue berry
Rhododendron spp. Rhododendrons	4'	3'–4'	E	periwinkle blue late spring	
Sarcococca humulis Sarcococca	18"	6'	E	white early spring fragrant	NS
Vaccinium ovatum Huckleberry	2'–3'	6'	E	white early spring	black berry
Secret garden:					
Azara microphylla Azara	12'–18'	8'–12'	E multi-stem	yellow February fragrant	
Hydrangea quercifolia	3'–6'	3'–6'	D	creamy white June	

(N.S. indicates "not significant")

(*continued on next page*)

Plant	Height	Spread	Evergreen E Deciduous D	Flower Color Time	Fruit Color Time
Oakleaf hydrangea					
Loropetalum chinense NCN	3'–5'	4'–6'	E Drooping	white	
Osmanthus fragrans Sweet olive	5'–10'	4'–6'	E	white all year fragrant	
Viburnum carlesii Korean spice Bush	4'–8'	4'–5'	D	white April–May	black berry
GROUNDCOVERS					
Asarum caudatum Wild ginger	7–10"	6"	E Dense	NS	NS
Galium odoratum Sweet woodruff	6"–12"	6"	E-D Spreading	white late spring	
Helainthemum nummularium Sunrose	6"–8"	3'	E Gray-green	many colors summer	
Lamium maculatum 'White Nancy'	12–18"	12"	E	white summer	
Phlox divaricata Sweet William	12"	12"	E creeping	blue-white spring fragrant	
CLIMBING PLANTS					
Clematis armandii Evergreen clematis	20'	—	E	white early spring fragrant	
Hardenbergia violacea NCN	10'–15'	—	E	lilac early spring	
Jasminum polyanthum Jasmine	20'	—	E fine texture	white/pink Feb.–July fragrant	

(N.S. indicates "not significant")

6-6 *Plant collage created from garden catalogs.*
(COLLAGE BY KIRSTEN MILLER)

6-7 *Planting plan.*
(DESIGN BY KIRSTEN MILLER)

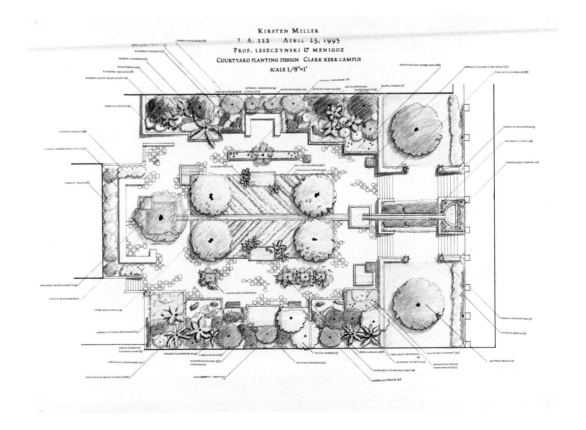

6-8 (left) Newly planted Yoshino cherry tree in the Ellis-Mahoney garden.

6-9 (top right) Hedges as green walls at the Walker Art Center, Minneapolis, Minnesota. (Photo: Carol Bornstein)

6-10 (bottom right) A newly planted hedge that provides a boundary but allows the view.

If you decide that your design requires a twenty-five-foot evergreen tree with white flowers that bloom in the late spring, find out what is available by looking up plant descriptions in horticultural manuals, or use a computer or CD-ROM program. Keep in mind that no list is all-inclusive and you should not rely on any one source for plant ideas. Expand the chart to include horticultural requirements of sun or shade, soil, and the amount of moisture the plant requires. What color green are the leaves? trunk characteristics? fruit color? All these distinguishing characteristics can be noted on the chart. Check the hardiness zone of the plant to determine its suitability for your site. Sensitivity to a plant's cultural needs and its proper placement make a good beginning for a harmonious result.

Plantings of small trees make small garden sites appear large—crabapple, *Malus* spp.; cherry, *Prunus* spp.; crape myrtle, *Lagerstroemia indica*; paperbark maple, *Acer griseum*; Japanese maple, *Acer palmatum*; redbud, *Cercis* spp.; and strawberry tree, *Arbutus unedo*, are good examples of small trees.

Large trees are useful in creating formality, anchoring a site, making a foreground and a shade pattern near a building or house, breaking a roof line, providing a canopy for an outdoor courtyard, and adding a grand scale to a street, neighborhood, park, or garden. These situations require trees with wonderful foliage, flowers, and fruit or picturesque branching, bark, or leaf arrangements. Think about trees such as Japanese pagoda tree, *Sophora japonica*; catalpa, *Catalpa speciosa*; the rugged, sculptural Kentucky coffeebean tree, *Gymnocladus diocus;* the ash, *Fraxinus* spp.; palm tree, *Phoenix dactylifera;* London plane, *Platanus* spp.; linden, *Tilia* spp.; white pine, *Pinus strobus;* and chestnut, *Aesculus* spp., for landscape planting on a large scale. Make a list of suggestions on or near the plan, put it aside for a while, and go back to it for further evaluation.

The trees chosen for the Ellis-Mahoney garden are the Yoshino cherry, for its white blossom, horizontal growth habit and open texture, although it is recommended to keep it pruned (Figure 6–8); the multi-trunk olive tree because of its evergreen, gray foliage (the Swan Hill variety is selected because it is not a prolific fruiter); and, in the secret garden, the golden chain tree, for its yellow floral color and fine texture. As a result of these choices, our design goals are satisfied; we have a sequence of bloom, in required colors, with pleasing textures and the right balance of deciduous and evergreen material.

Shrubs It is often easiest to classify and organize your shrub list by beginning with their function—green walls, outstanding specimen, or screen plant. Shrubs combined with trees complete the garden's bones or framework. When you classify shrubs according to parts of the garden for which you intend to use them, categorize your list according to height, spread, and horticultural characteristics. Shrubs as hedges create a framework or walls, provide protection, add color and texture, and serve as a backdrop for sculpture, a perennial border, or garden room. They can make a simple, quiet, reflective space or a complex maze of activity. As green architecture, the height and length of a hedge planting can anchor a building or house and extend the limits of the architecture into the garden. A tall hedge makes a garden room or enclosure in Figure 6–9. A medium-size hedge creates a boundary without blocking views in Figure 6–10. Hedges eight to twelve feet in height function as a frame to a picture or create an edge. Yew, holly, hornbeam, rhus, bay laurel, cypress, pittosporum, lavender, myrtle, escallonia, raphiolepis, and azalea make practical hedges.

Shrubs can be utilized as a shrub border, similar to the perennial border but of greater size and usually requiring less maintenance. A shrub border can provide year-round interest, attract wildlife, and supply cut flowers. In addition, shrubs planted under large trees form the understory planting and accent the garden.

If you specify a shrub whose ultimate height is much taller and wider than the design requirements, be certain to include the design requirements in your planting notes or maintenance manual so that your ultimate design intention is followed.

The following description of shrub design by Russell Page explains the use of his plant palette as a design solution:

> Even the most ordinary plants will take on new significance if you refuse the associations that spring to mind and try to see their form, texture, and color for the first time. In a garden near Chantilly I had to plant a rough bank some fifteen feet wide running down a path from a twenty-foot wall which faces due north and allows little sun to penetrate. The soil was bad—heavy, wet and limy—which meant I had to choose tough plant material which would stand these conditions.
>
> After some reflection I planted the hundred-foot length of the wall with quite ordinary ivy which after three years covered the entire surface. Next to the wall I planted groups of *Viburnum rhytidophyllum* alternating with *Aucuba japonica,* the plain green not the spotted variety, while still further to the front I put in bushes of the large-leafed Handsworth box. All these rise from a carpet of *Bergenia.* These are the most ordinary

6-11 *(top left) Newly planted specimen rhododendrons and azaleas in the Ellis-Mahoney garden.*

6-12 *(top right) Mass planting makes a space appear larger.*

6-13 *(bottom left) At the Lummis Garden in southern California, achillea,* Achillea millefolium, *is used as a substitute for a lawn. The Lummis Garden is maintained by the Historical Society of Southern California.* (PHOTO: CAROL BORNSTEIN)

6-14 *(bottom right) Parterre of annuals at Cranbrook Gardens. Bloomfield Hills, Michigan*

plants and the whole effect of this planting, all dark green, comes from the different way each species reflects or absorbs the light. The felty leaves of the viburnum make matte surfaces and contrast to the slight glow reflected by the smoothness of the aucubas. The box kept compact by careful pruning reflects light only in small points from their relatively tiny leaves, while under all these light catches all the complex and handsome modeling of the bergenias.[8]

The Ellis-Mahoney garden required four-foot hedges on the south side and accent shrubs for privacy and fragrance in the secret garden area. The suggestions are listed in Figure 6–5. In the end, specimen rhododendrons and azaleas[9] are chosen to merge with the texture of the camellia. They bloom after the camellia, peach and periwinkle blue, but at the same time as the cherry tree (Figure 6–11). Huckleberry was suggested near the lawn but was impossible to find and was replaced with sarcococca; with its rich, dark-green color, white, fragrant blossom, and fine texture, it is a good contrast to the rhodo-dendrons. Azara is the shrub choice for the secret garden because of its silhouette in the morning sun, its early, fragrant blossom, and its fastigiate form balances the design. It is perfect in combination with the osmanthus, which also has a fragrant flower blooming off and on year-round and a wonderful evergreen texture.

These plants are the bones of the garden. They form green walls that provide privacy, yet their ultimate height is in scale with the garden. The foliage—a combination of green colors and textures—adds variety and is a perfect backdrop for perennials, bulbs, and ground covers. For contrast, one oakleaf hydrangea is placed in front of the osmanthus hedge in the secret garden, its large leaves and blossoms a focal point to the serene composition.

Ground Covers   The term *ground cover* means permanent trailing or clump-forming plants, usually evergreen, that quickly join together to form a dense layer of leaves not more than sixteen inches tall. They can block out all light from the soil and thus prevent weeds from germinating. Ground-cover choices are critical because they are the fore-ground of the composition. Planted as a mass, they cause a space to appear larger (Figure 6–12) or are mixed to create a tapestry-like ground plane of different textures. Lawn can be categorized as a ground cover.

Keep in mind that a lawn requires mowing, watering, and fertilizers as well as pes-ticides; it is high-maintenance, expensive, and pollutes ground water. Try to work with the lawn organically; water it as needed in early mornings or late evenings when there is less wind and less water loss to transpiration. Locate the lawn near the house or building to minimize maintenance efforts and maximize the aesthetic effects. As Edith Wharton describes the commonsense approach to the lawn in Italy, "Italian gar-deners used the lawn sparingly knowing that it required great care and was not char-acteristic of the soil. These bits of sward [lawn] were always used near the house where their full value could be enjoyed and were set like jewels in the clipped hedges or statue-crowned walls."[10]

If you are working in a drought-prone region, lawn can be replaced with ground cov-ers, perennials, gravel, or mulch. Try different plant materials that can replace the lawn. In Figure 6–13, *Achillea millefolium* has been used in a southern California garden as a replacement for lawn.

Ground-cover requirements in the Ellis-Mahoney garden were numerous and varied, everything from sun to shade, flowering and evergreen, including a lawn. Suggestions are considered with the trees and shrubs in mind (see Figure 6–5).

In the final analysis, the sweet woodruff is chosen for both the secret garden and the southern side to tie both areas together visually at the ground plane. It creates a lush, del-icate foreground or base for azalea, rhododendron, azara, and sarcoccoca. In the full sun area, the helianthemum complements the olive tree because of its gray leaves. In a few places in the garden the helianthemum is planted right in the gravel. Phlox is planted under the existing Japanese maple, along with ferns and rhododendrons.

Annuals   An annual grows from seed, blooms, and goes to seed all in the same year. Annual flowers bloom quickly and are thought of as instant color, as in the sunken gar-den at Cranbrook (Figure 6–14). (Cranbrook is located in Bloomfield Hills, Michigan. The gardens were designed in 1904 by H. J. Corfield and by O. C. Simonds in 1910.)

6-15 *(left) The biennial hollyhock,* Alcea rosea.

6-16 (top right) Euphorbia *x* martinii, *a perennial, used as a shrub planting.*

6-17 *(bottom right) Peruvian lily,* Alstroemeria aurantiaca, *planted en masse.* (PHOTO: CAROL BORNSTEIN)

Here in the Sunken Garden the parterre is composed of carefully arranged annuals in the form of 19th-century carpet bedding. Annuals are best used in plantings where pattern and mass effect are desired. They can also be utilized to fill in areas newly planted with ground covers or perennials. They work well in containers and hanging baskets and are invaluable for keeping plantings colorful throughout the year, especially for edges or gaps left from early flowering bulbs. Their bloom span ranges from one to five months, longer than most perennials.

Annuals are of three basic types: warm-season, cool-season, and frost-hardy. Warm-weather annuals are frost-tender, which means they die in temperatures below 32°F, and are usually planted in warm soil in the late spring after the fear of frost has passed. This group includes zinnias, cosmos, celosia, impatiens, petunias, marigolds, and sweet peas, which are commonly grown all over the United States.

Cool-weather annuals include two classes: one that tolerates a few degrees of frost, and one that is killed by frosts. Cool-weather annuals do better in temperate coastal climates, high-altitude gardens, and in the northern United States. Among these plants are nierembergia, schizanthus, and snapdragons. Frost-hardy annuals withstand several degrees of frost. These are larkspur, stock, and pansies, and are planted in the fall in mild climates or in the winter for early spring bloom. They give a mass effect of color that few perennials can rival.

Biennials   Biennials are plants that usually take two years to complete their life cycle, such as foxglove, hollyhock, and sweet william (Figure 6–15). During the first season seeds germinate, but only leaves appear. The plants overwinter the first season, then flower and die in the second garden season. However, many reproduce from seed scattered every year after flowering, including hollyhock, cineraria, and foxglove, and reappear similar to perennials.

Perennials   Perennials can live for many years. There are short-lived perennials that flourish for three or four years, but their lives can be extended by dividing them each year. Other perennials can live longer than the person who planted them. Most perennials are herbaceous and can be deciduous or evergreen. *Herbaceous* describes plants with fleshy, soft, nonwoody stems. Perennials can be used in the traditional border or as low hedges (Figure 6–16), in a woodland planting, in island beds, for mass effect (Figure 6–17), or as part of a layered effect with trees, shrubs, and ground covers.

Creating a perennial border is one of the greatest challenges of planting design. The process is complex as you begin to think about evergreen and deciduous, form, color, texture, bloom sequence, and simultaneity. Begin by using one, two, or three colors, not more. Keep in mind light and shade, flower and foliage; try to emphasize the perennials for a certain time period or plant them to extend the season as long as possible, depending on the climate. Try starting with the selection of one choice plant; allow it to repeat to give it strength and proportion in the design. Study it and the other plants that will enhance its qualities. For example, achillea 'Moonshine,' with a pale lemon color and a height of twenty-four to thirty inches, often looks good in a summer border with lavender (yellow and blue are complementary colors) or blue salvia and perhaps a little gray foliage of artemesia or santolina. Together these plants comprise a drought-tolerant floral display.

The potential list of perennials for the Ellis-Mahoney garden is extensive, even though the space is small. A chart can be created to assess the choices, similar to the tree and shrub example. Because the clients wanted to collect perennial salvia plants, the following plants were suggested for the perennial border: fleabane, *Erigeron karvinskianus;* cranesbill, *Geranium macrorrhizum;* lavender, *Lavandula* spp.; catmint, *Nepeta mussinii;* Cleveland sage, *Salvia clevelandii;* Pineapple sage, *Salvia elegans;* Bog Sage *Salvia ulignosa;* blue-eyed grass, *Sisyrichium striatum;* lamb's ears, *Stachys lanata.* This combination of plants provides a sequence of bloom, a sensitive color palette, textures both similar and contrasting, and a variety of forms—spiky, clumping, and matting foliage.

Japanese anenome, *Anenome japonica;* Siberian bugloss, *Brunnera macrophylla;* maiden's wreath, *Francoa ramosa;* and hellebore, *Helleborus foetidus,* accent the shade garden. Their sequence of bloom, texture, and form complete the garden picture.

Bulbs   A true bulb is an enlarged and modified bud, always underground. It contains a vertical, foreshortened stem and has leaves crowded so closely together along the length of the stem that they form a dense mass. The leaves are scalelike and swollen with stored food material. Lilies, narcissus, alliums, and tulips are bulb plants. Bulbs and bulblike structures have distinct stages of growth, bloom, and dormancy in their annual life cycles, which vary according to bulb type, species, climate, and planting time.

Irises are the only bulb to be incorporated into the Ellis-Mahoney planting design. Their yellow blossoms and spiky form provide a wonderful accent to the olive tree, lavender, and helianthemum (Figure 6–18).

6-18 *(left) Yellow iris interplanted with helianthemum and lamb's ears accent the olive tree.*

6-19 *(right) Hardenbergia vine,* Hardenbergia violacea, *turns a trellis into a green wall. (PHOTO: MELANIE AUSTIN)*

Climbing Plants Climbing plants or vines create tremendous vertical effect while using very little horizontal space. If a garden is small, with a lot of wall space, this is an important element. Climbers can be a complement to architecture and an asset to a garden's color, texture, or form. Determine whether the plant will climb with or without support or a structure when choosing the climber (see Figure 6–5).

Hardenbergia vine is chosen for the trellis wall in the Ellis-Mahoney garden (Figure 6–19) because it blooms early, has a beautiful texture, and is located in a protected spot suitable for the plant. A jasmine vine supplies the evergreen backdrop for the perennial garden and is more suitable than a hedge because it takes up less space. Its fragrance is a bonus and it flowers when many of the perennials are dormant. Last, evergreen clematis winds its way around the fence in the shade garden; it adds texture and a fragrant early spring blossom to the design.

Seasonal Effects

Until you learn your plants well it is best to note seasonal characteristics. Enter into the chart special or unusual plant characteristics that affect the design: evergreen or deciduous, the color of green—glossy light green, gray-green, dark green—flower and fruit color, and the time of flowering and fruiting. A quick color study can be made to determine the effect of plants blooming simultaneously. Designers have a tendency to create a planting plan that emphasizes plants in bloom or autumn color at the time of the plan's creation, when plants are most noticeable. Do not fall into this trap! Keep seasonal color in mind and overall year-round interest as a goal.

HORTICULTURAL REQUIREMENTS

The horticultural requirements of plants are part of the plant palette creation. Now is the opportunity to combine the information from your environmental analysis with the plant choices. Refer to the environmental analysis drawing as you begin the palette. Break down the design into planting areas of similar horticultural requirements. This part of the process moves back and forth. Enter the plants chosen into the chart (Figure 6–20). You are creating a checklist. Each heading is a different horticultural requirement: light, soil type, moisture, hardiness. Edit the list, comparing your site conditions with plant requirements. Begin to list possibilities right on the plan drawing; sketch a small section next to the plant combination to test the effect. Figure 6–21 shows a planting plan in progress, where notes are made and plant ideas jotted down right on the plan.

Is the planting to be done in a city, along a street, in a public park, private garden, shopping center, corporate headquarters, or arboretum or botanical garden? Change your plant list according to site demands. Think about it over and over; continually evaluate and reevaluate your choices. For example, perhaps a plant you chose has the correct height, flower color, and hardiness for a particular location but it requires constant moisture and full sun, whereas the location offers dry conditions and filtered sun. Keep searching for the right plant in the right place. Check the microclimate requirements and characteristics of the planting site. Determine the direction and intensity of the winds, degrees of sun and shade, and make sure plants chosen match soil conditions. Little by little your plant palette will come together. The following is a brief explanation of the terminology often used in horticultural requirements.

Light Requirements

As you begin to research the plant palette you will discover a range of descriptions for soil, moisture, and light quality requirements. Light affects the look and health of garden plants as much as soil and water do. Each plant you choose has light requirements for optimum growth, which is also influenced by the light intensity of the local climate. Identifying the light requirements is essential to plant survival.

Numerous terms describe light in the garden:

- *Deep shade* generally falls under the canopy of trees or under the eaves of buildings. The sun is blocked and plants get only indirect light. Shade-tolerant plant species can photosynthesize in low light intensities. Shade tolerance is a well-established physiological characteristic of many species, so much so that their exposure to full sunlight can be fatal.[11] Some plants that tolerate deep shade are yews, hostas, clivia, ferns, ivy, and mosses.

- *Partial shade* means full sun for part of the day and shade for part of the day. Timing alters the effects of partial shade. If the full sunlight occurs in the middle of the day, some plants may suffer from the heat. Success depends on the right match of plant and climate.

- *Filtered sun* is a mix of sun and shade that occurs when sunlight passes between leaves and/or between openings in a lattice, pergola, or arbor. Many plants that like full sun can often grow in dappled shade and some shade plants can tolerate the higher light levels.

- *Full sun* is defined as at least six hours of direct sun per day between 9:00 AM and 4:00 PM, when the sun is stronger than it is in early morning or late afternoon. Full sun is required by many trees, shrubs, perennials, and annuals.

Plant	Light	Soil	Moisture	Plant Hardiness USDA	Comment
TREES					
Magnolia stellata Star Magnolia	full sun	rich	moist, well-drained deep, thorough H_2O	6	not good in arid regions
Malus 'Red Jade' Crabapple	full sun	good	regular	5	insect problems
Prunus yedoensis 'Yoshino' cherry	full sun	well aerated	moderate well-drained	5	no clay soils keep pruned
Olea europaea 'Swan Hill' Olive	full sun	poor	drought tolerant	9	keep pruned slow growing
Laurus nobilis Grecian laurel	fog to filtered sun to full sun	poor	drought tolerant	7	suckers
Laburnum watereri Goldenchain Tree	full to filtered sun	acidic-neutral	adequate well drained	5	keep pruned
SHRUBS					
Southern end of garden:					
Azaleas spp. Azaleas	filtered sun	acidic	adequate well-drained	5	feed 1/month
Mahonia lomariifolia Mahonia	filtered sun	acidic	drought tolerant	4	keep pruned
Rhododendron spp. Rhododendrons	filtered sun	acidic	adequate well-drained	5	feed 1/month
Sarcococca humulis Sarcococca	shade	acidic	adequate well-drained	6	slow growing
Vaccinium ovatum Huckleberry	partial shade	acidic	adequate	8	fruit for jams and jellies

(continued on facing page)

Plant	Light	Soil	Moisture	Plant Hardiness USDA	Comment
Secret garden:					
Azara microphylla Azara	filtered sun	rich	adequate fast draining	9	slow growing
Hydrangea quercifolia Oakleaf hydrangea	full sun to filtered sun	rich	well-watered	6	fast growing crimson autumn color
Loropetalum chinense NCN	full sun	rich	well-watered well-drained	8	good form
Osmanthus fragrans Sweet olive	east exposure	tolerant	adequate	8–9	slow growing
GROUNDCOVERS					
Asarum caudatum Wild ginger	shade-to filtered shade	average to rich	moist	8	fast growing
Galium odoratum Sweet woodruff	shade to filtered shade	acidic	moist	5	can be invasive
Helainthemum nummularium Sunrose	full sun	alkaline sandy	well-drained drought toletant	6	grow in gravel
Lamium maculatum 'White Nancy'	shade	rich	moist	4	
Phlox divaricata Sweet William	shade to filtered shade	rich	moist	4	slow growing
CLIMBING PLANTS					
Clematis armandii Evergreen clematis	filtered sun to full sun	rich fast draining	adequate	8	needs support
Hardenbergia violacea NCN	sun to partial shade	light well-drained	adequate	9	needs support
Jasminum polyanthum Jasmine	sun	average	adequate	9	keep pruned

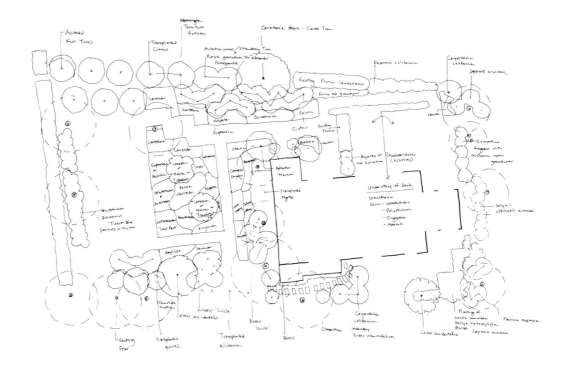

Another way to assess a plant's light needs is to study its growing habits. Plants that require full sun often have small or narrow leaves to minimize the leaf surface exposed to the sun. Many shade-loving plants have large, coarse leaves. Numerous gray-leafed plants or succulents are adapted to intense sunlight by their color, waxy coating, or pubescence. A plant that is not receiving enough light often displays symptoms: branches stretching out for more light, too few branches, few flowers or fruits, or an overall weak and spindly look. A plant receiving too much light also suffers; symptoms include stunted leaves or bleached or sunburned foliage.[12]

Keep in mind that the planting will change as it grows. What begins as a ground cover in full sun under a young tree will over time become shaded ground cover under a mature tree. The design must allow for growth and change. If possible, use a plant that tolerates sun-to-shade conditions. Many plants withstand a variety of light conditions from shade to full sun. Another suggestion is to propose to the client that the ground cover or perennials be evaluated and possibly replaced with another choice in future years if light conditions change.

As you refine the plant palette, it is important to keep in mind another effect of sunlight on the design. The changing angle of the sun on plants during the different seasons produces a dramatic effect—shadows. As the sun moves through the sky throughout the day the shadows change and fall; different objects in the planting design emerge or are in shadow. These shadows are longer in winter, when the sun is low on the horizon, and shorter in summer, when the sun is directly overhead. Long shadows in the morning and evening add interest to a planting composition. They modify colors, textures, and mass in the landscape. Gradations of rolling lawns or distant landscapes are enhanced by shadow; they allow you to judge depth in the landscape.

In addition to aesthetic affects, the functional use of shadow is important. People appreciate sunlight in winter when the temperature is cool. In summer shadows are a tremendous respite from the intense sun. Plants should be placed so that the shadows will fall pleasantly for comfort in living as well as for patterns to delight the eye.[13]

Soil and Moisture Requirements

Test the soil following the directions in Chapter 3. Check each plant choice to determine its soil and moisture requirements. The soil conditions are directly related to water requirements. Soils are loose, loamy, sandy, acidic, calcerous, rich, or poor. The moisture requirements are for dry, well-drained, well-aerated, moist or moist but not wet soil; plants may require frequent or regular watering, allow the soil to dry out between waterings, or may be drought tolerant. These terms may seem vague or confusing but are used repeatedly in the profession. Familiarize yourself with the terminology and be observant of your growing environment.

Some native plants, such as ceanothus and artemesia, are drought tolerant and will die with too much water. Other plants, such as willow trees and yews, require moist conditions and well-drained soils. Check each requisite to make sure plants with different water needs are not planted together. Think about water requirements in conjunction with soil conditions. A plant requiring supplemental water planted in sandy conditions will have a difficult time surviving. Likewise, a plant that needs well-drained soil will struggle in a clay environment. Does your plant palette contain numerous plants that require ericaceous or acid soil but your site feature calcerous soil? This is not easily amended and alternative plant choices should be made.

- Plants that thrive under *dry conditions* and require little water to survive—desert species—are plants that need the soil to dry out completely in between waterings to ensure root growth. Some plants are adapted to a dry environment and, once established, need little supplemental water to survive. (Cactus, Agaves, Dudleyas, and Echevarias).

- *Drought-tolerant* plants survive because adaptations allow them to conserve water. Extensive root systems, dormancy in dry periods, or reduced leaf size or gray leaf color allow plants to use less water. These plants require less water and can die if overwatered (cistus, raphiolepis, santolina, lavender).

- The descriptive term *regular watering* indicates plants that prefer to be watered regularly on a permanent basis. Depending on weather conditions, these plants respond well to supplemental water (lilacs, mock orange).

- The expression *frequent watering, but well-drained* refers to plants that prefer moisture but require the soil to drain rapidly; they resent excessive moisture retained around their root crown (rhododendrons and azaleas).

- The *moist but not wet soil* requirement is a challenge. This indicates plants that like their roots wet but will not survive sitting in water (primroses, cyclamen).

- *Moist soil* describes the preference of plants that will grow in shallow water at the edge of ponds and streams or plants that are suitable for damp soils (bald cypress, globe flowers).

Keep in mind that water and soil needs change with the use of mulch and with climate conditions. Think your choices over carefully. If you feel doubtful about your palette, speak to a professional nursery person or horticulturist in the area.

Let us evaluate our plant choices for the Ellis-Mahoney design from a cultural standpoint (Figure 6–20). Many of the plants in the secret garden and on the southern side have similar cultural requirements that agree with our site needs; rhododendrons, azaleas, hydrangea, sweet woodruff, francoa, sarcococcoa, phlox, hellebores, Japanese anenome, brunnera, azara, and ferns all require shade to partial sun and like rich, acidic soil that is well drained, with adequate moisture. In the sunny area of the garden the multi-trunk olive tree, lavender, helianthemum, and bearded iris need sun, are drought tolerant, and grow well in average to poor soils. All the plants chosen for the perennial border enjoy sun and well-drained soil and do well with regular to drought-tolerant watering.

MAINTENANCE REQUIREMENTS

Special maintenance requirements are another aspect of the checklist or chart. These should be assessed for three stages in the garden development process: the design phase, discussed here; the initial planting phase, discussed in Chapter 7; and the long-term program, discussed in Chapter 8.

Maintenance is considered in the design phase by assessing its projected cost, the capabilities of the client, and practicality issues. No garden or landscape is maintenance-free! Some gardens require less maintenance than others, but all gardens require some degree of attention. Once your plant list is completed, examine it for maintenance requirements. Should any special conditions be indicated in the planting notes? A tree to be trained for espalier or pruned regularly to a certain height? Try to choose plants that grow to an appropriate size for the area planted. Envision the design in ten years, fifty years, a hundred years. Do not create unnecessary maintenance by using plants that constantly require topping, shearing, and pruning to reach the desired effect. If the design calls for a four-foot hedge, choose a plant that ultimately grows to four feet in height. If this is impossible, be judicious in the number of plants in the design that require constant maintenance. Is the design of such detailed maintenance demands that it is impractical for a public institution to undertake? Are the overall requirements too great for the homeowner to afford? Try to estimate the average weekly number of hours you think it would take to maintain the garden. It is possible to send the design to a landscape maintenance company that can estimate by week or month the number of hours of maintenance required.

Be aware of potential litter (picking up fallen leaves or fruit can be a nuisance or potentially dangerous), insect, or disease problems. Have you chosen any plants that could create a litter problem due to their location over a sidewalk or in a parking lot, such as fruit dropping on a public sidewalk or leaf drop that occurs year round? Review your list with maintenance needs in mind.

THE PLANTING PLAN

Plan Drawing

Once the plant palette is chosen, it is time to create a working drawing or planting plan for the design. Thus far in the process we have produced a schematic drawing (Figure 6–22) depicting the design concept, and a design development drawing representing the

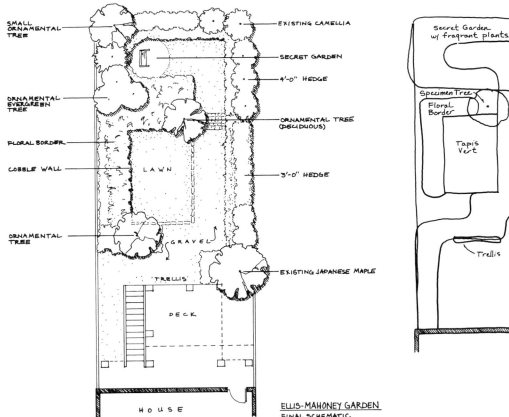

6-22 *Schematic drawing of the Ellis-Mahoney garden.* (DRAWING: ARCADIA)

6-23 *Design development drawing of the Ellis-Mahoney garden.*

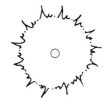

6-24 *Planting plan drawing evergreen plant symbol.*

6-25 *Planting plan drawing deciduous plant symbol.*

plants in a massing or large scale forms (Figure 6–23). The principal purpose of the planting plan is to instruct the contractor on how to plant the garden. The drawing includes a plan drawing, planting notes, plant list, and drawings of planting details, along with specifications that are part of the contract document for the project.

The planting plan should be created at a large scale, one-eighth inch or one-quarter inch = 1 foot, so that details are accurate. All drawings should be made on vellum, or Mylar, which will withstand a lot of handling and erasing and from which diazo prints or copies can be made. Different graphic symbols are used to illustrate a variety of plants. It is best to choose a simple format and be consistent. The best method is one that is clear, concise, and communicates the information easily. The following examples are standard for a simple planting plan.

Often the basic graphic symbol for a tree or shrub is a circle drawn at a circumference that represents the size of a plant at approximately seven years of age. This may seem odd but it is an accepted rule of thumb and aids in determining plant spacing. Evergreen trees and shrubs are often represented by the symbol shown in Figure 6–24 and deciduous trees and shrubs by that in Figure 6–25. Ground covers are represented by cross-hatching or other delineation. The exact location of each plant is shown. Note existing trees or shrubs with a plus and new plants with a circle. The name of the plant can be written out, as shown in Figure 6–26. Avoid using keys that list plants elsewhere—they can be confusing and difficult to follow.

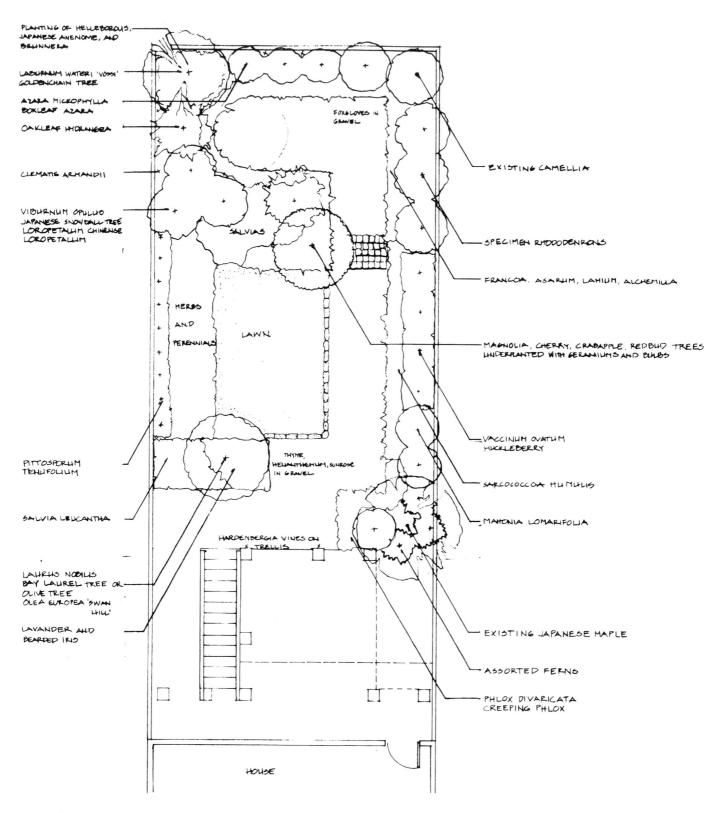

PLANTING OF HELLEBOROUS, JAPANESE ANENOME, AND BRUNNERA

LABURNUM WATERI 'VOSSI' GOLDENCHAIN TREE

AZARA MICROPHYLLA BOXLEAF AZARA

OAKLEAF HYDRANGEA

CLEMATIS ARMANDII

VIBURNUM OPULLO JAPANESE SNOWBALL TREE LOROPETALLM CHINENSE LOROPETALLM

PITTOSPORUM TENUIFOLIUM

SALVIA LEUCANTHA

LAURUS NOBILIS BAY LAUREL TREE OR OLIVE TREE OLEA EUROPEA 'SWAN HILL'

LAVANDER AND BEARDED IRIS

FOXGLOVES IN GRAVEL

SALVIAS

HERBS AND PERENNIALS

LAWN

THYME, HELIANTHEMUM, SUNROSE IN GRAVEL

HARDENBERGIA VINES ON TRELLIS

HOUSE

EXISTING CAMELLIA

SPECIMEN RHODODENRONS

FRANCOA, ASARUM, LAMIUM, ALCHEMILLA

MAGNOLIA, CHERRY, CRABAPPLE, REDBUD TREES UNDERPLANTED WITH GERANIUMS AND BULBS

VACCINUM OVATUM HUCKLEBERRY

SARCOCOCCOA HUMULIS

MAHONIA LOMARIFOLIA

EXISTING JAPANESE MAPLE

ASSORTED FERNS

PHLOX DIVARICATA CREEPING PHLOX

6-26 *Planting plan for the Ellis-Mahoney garden.*

Plant spacing is an integral part of the working drawing. Species, mature density, height and spread, and growth rate determine each plant's placement in the landscape. For example, if a slow-growing ground-cover plant has a spread of eighteen inches, the density of the planting may be increased to twelve inches to achieve cover in a reasonable time. Vice versa, if a plant is fast growing and has a broad spread, less density of planting is required. The ultimate plant form also influences spacing. A shrub may have a spread of thirty to thirty-six inches; however, if its ultimate intended form is an impenetrable hedge, the density of the planting may be increased. Last, a project with minimum maintenance after planting requires tighter plant spacing to ensure successful establishment and to provide weed or erosion control. Knowledge of plant growth rate and habit is essential for precise spacing of plants. Remember, the space between plants is as important as the plants themselves!

Plant List

The plant list is part of the drawing that lists the botanical name, common name, total quantity of plants, size, spacing, and condition or form of the plant in chart form. Plants are listed in alphabetical order by botanical name, the genus name is capitalized, and the species name is in lower case, followed by the cultivar name if required (Figure 6–27). Common names, which vary region to region, country to country, can be included, but do not depend on common names to indicate a plant choice.

6-27 *Plant list for Ellis-Mahoney garden.*

Botanical Name	Common Name	Quantity	Size	Comments
Trees				
Laburnum watereri	Goldenchain Tree	1	15 gal.	
Olea europaea 'Swan Hill'	Olive Tree	1	24" Box	multi-trunk
Prunus yedoensis	Yoshino Cherry	1	24" Box	keep pruned
Shrubs				
Azalea sp.	Azaleas	5	specimen	nursery select
Azara microphylla	Azara	3	15 gal.	multi-stem
Hydrangea quercifolia	Oakleaf hydrangea	1	15 gal.	
Mahonia lomariifolia	Mahonia	1	15 gal.	multi-stem
Osmanthus fragrans	Sweet Olive	3	15 gal.	
Rhododendron spp.	Rhododendrons	3	Specimen	nursey select
Sarcococca humulis	Sarcococca	5	5 gal.	
Groundcovers				
Galium odoratum	Sweet woodruff	17	1 gal.	
Helainthemum nummularium	Sunrose	7	1 gal.	plant in gravel
Phlox divaricata	Creeping Phlox	9	1 gal.	
Climbing Plants				
Clematis armandii	Evergreen clematis	3	5 gal.	
Hardenbergia violacea	NCN	3	5 gal.	train on trellis
Jasminum polyanthum	Jasmine	3	5 gal.	

6-28 *(left) Plants container-grown in a nursery. (*PHOTO: DARREN PRINCIPE*)*

6-29 *(right) Plants balled and burlapped. (*PHOTO: DARREN PRINCIPE*)*

Planting Notes

Planting notes indicate special planting conditions. For example, if a plant has special transplant requirements or requires particularly careful handling, this can be explained in the notes column.

Plant Details

Planting details clarify specifics about the planting process. These drawings detail the staking, mulching, and unique or unusual planting requirements.

Specifying Plant Size

Plant size is indicated on the plant list, but the subject demands special attention. First, what is meant by *plant size?* Plant size is specified by the type of container or method of nursery growing conditions. Plants are generally referred to as container grown, balled and burlapped, or bareroot. The size at which plants are commonly grown and sold varies according to climate. Plants are grown in containers in California and Florida because there is little fear of frost and it is economical (Figure 6–28). Balled-and-burlapped and bareroot are the nursery growing methods used in the colder climates so that roots will not freeze from exposure (Figure 6–29). The size of container chosen for a plant also depends on whether the plant is a ground cover, tree, shrub, or perennial.

There are three common categories of plant sizes:

1. *Container sizes*

   • flats are rectangular or square plastic containers in which ground cover or herbaceous plants are grown. There are approximately 24–36 plants in a flat.

   • 4-inch pots

   • 1-, 5-, 7-, 10-, or 15-gallon containers

   • 24-, 36-, 48-, 72-, 96-inch boxes

   Container planting makes year-round planting possible. Plants tend to have greater uniformity to each other. Container plants sometimes have root defects and should be thoroughly inspected for kinked roots, circling roots, girdling root surfaces, and outer circling roots (matted roots). (This is explained in Chapter 7.)

2. *Balled-and-burlapped,* often called B & B, refers to deciduous and coniferous plants that are field grown and dug out of the ground with a ball of soil around the roots, which is then wrapped in burlap. B & B plants have a longer planting season than bareroot plants but should be planted before warm spring weather occurs.

3. Many deciduous plants, especially fruit trees, are dug out of the ground and shipped to nurseries *bareroot* during the autumn and winter months. Bareroot plants are best planted in the autumn and are generally less expensive than container and B & B plants. They should be inspected upon delivery to make certain the main roots are free from breaks, desiccation, and disease.

A number of factors need to be considered when determining the plant size to recommend:

1. the plant species and its rate of growth

2. the location of the planting

3. the project budget

Opinions diverge concerning the appropriate size of nursery stock to recommend. As living things, plants vary in size according to age. It is best to study all the relevant factors and make an informed decision. Trees are customarily specified in a large size because most are slow growing and represent major forms of the planting design. A 15-gallon or 24-inch box tree, if grown in a container, or a two- or two-and-a-half-inch caliper tree, if sold balled and burlapped or bareroot, are common size recommendations for trees. A tree caliper is the measurement of the thickness of the tree trunk at about chest height. Shrubs and vines are typically specified at 1-, 5-, or 15-gallon containers. Perennials are purchased in 4-inch pots or 1-quart or 1-gallon containers, if necessary, and ground cover in flats.

Sometimes a plant species is better planted at a small size because it can withstand the shock of transplant more easily. If a plant is fast growing, a smaller container size may be more economical. If the location of the planting bed is in a remote or hard-to-reach area of the site, smaller plant material is often used to save unnecessary expense.

The project budget may immediately determine the size of plant materials used. If the budget is adequate, it is best to work proportionately with the plant species and its function in the landscape. For example, rhododendrons, azaleas, and many trees are slow growing and look better in the design if purchased at a larger size.

This presents a challenge for the designer. Some clients want a landscape that looks mature as soon as it has been installed, but cannot afford it. When a garden is first installed, it is unfinished. Virtually all plants require a maturation period before the garden is complete. Patience and vision are necessary elements of the planting design process.

NURSERY SOURCING AND CONTRACT GROWING

The last items to discuss are nursery sourcing and contract growing. *Nursery sourcing* is researching your plant choices to ensure that you can find them through the wholesale nursery trade. This means calling, writing, faxing, or e-mailing nurseries to find out if they have the sizes and quantities you need. This step is often overlooked and is essential for the success of the project. How can you estimate a planting budget or implement the design if the plants cannot be found? Try to develop a good working relationship with several plant growers. They are a tremendous source of vital information for your work. These skilled professionals are aware of the best plant material available, know about problems a specific plant species may be having in the field, and can often recommend new varieties and cultivars unknown to many designers.

Some wholesale nurseries are available for *contract growing*, wherein a contractual agreement is made for a specific number of plants to be grown for a project. This is usually done for unusual plants or large quantities. For instance, if a project requires 1,200 four-inch Spanish lavender plants, *Lavandula stoechas*, you or your client may want to set up a nursery contract to ensure their availability. This process is invaluable because it can keep you from having to settle for what is available. It is a good idea to secure the contract once the project has reached the design development or working drawing stage to ensure the project is viable and will proceed as planned. Depending on the plant species, a slow-growing plant may not be possible to obtain due to a fast-moving project schedule. Often a partial down payment is required and tempers will flare if a contract is canceled or money is lost.

SUMMARY

The development of a plant palette is a critical step in the planting design process. Realities of the environment—soil and sunlight, spacing of the plants, and the necessity for pruning—are combined with artistic desires—color, texture, rhythm, sequence. Decisions are made as the tapis vert becomes a lawn, the hedge is composed of rhododendrons or azaleas, and the masses of color have become irises, salvias, and geraniums. A succession of drawings have taken the design from an abstract concept to a formalized plant composition and finally to a palette or list of plants ready for planting.

ENDNOTES

[1]   Claude Monet speaking to guests at Giverney in 1924 and quoted, but not footnoted, in *Monet at Giverney* by Claire Joyes (New York: Mayflower Books, 1975), 37.

[2]   Sylvia Crowe, *Garden Design,* (Woodbridge, UK: Garden Art Press, 1958), 151.

[3]   Eero Saarinen, *Eero Saarinen on His Work.* (New Haven and London: Yale University Press, 1962).

[4]   Jane Brown, *Gardens of a Golden Afternoon* (Middlesex England: Penguin, 1982), 126.

[5]   Simone de Beauvoir, *When Things of the Spirit Come First.*

[6]   Russell Page, *The Education of a Gardener* (London: Collins Clear-Type Press, 1962), 144.

[7]   Wolfgang Oehme and James Van Sweden with Susan R. Fry, *Bold Romantic Gardens* (Herndon, VA: Acropolis Books, 1991), 263.

[8]   Page, *Education of a Gardener*, 194–195.

[9]   Specimen rhododendrons are field-grown plants that are hand-picked at a nursery and dug at the time of transplant. They are generally larger than container-grown plants.

[10] Edith Wharton, *Italian Villas and Their Gardens* (New York: Century, 1903), 47–48.

[11] Brian Capon, *Botany for Gardeners* (Portland, OR: Timber Press, 1992), 100.

[12] Lee Hallgren, "The Kinds Of Sun And Shade," *Fine Gardening* (May/June 1993), 62–63.

[13] Florence Bell Robinson, *Planting Design* (Champaign, IL: Garrard Press, 1940), 81–83.

Planting the Garden

I have always liked horticulturists, people who make their living from orchards and gardens, whose hands are familiar with the feel of bark, whose eyes are trained to distinguish the different varieties, who have a form memory. Their brains are not forever dealing with vague abstractions; they are satisfied with the romance the seasons bring them, and have the patience and fortitude to gamble their lives and fortunes in an industry which requires infinite patience, which raises hopes each spring and too often dashes them to pieces in the fall. They are conscious of the sun and wind and rain.

DAVID FAIRCHILD, *THE WORLD WAS MY GARDEN*[1]

Planting a garden brings the design into reality. It is the rewarding culmination of all the prior stages of the design process—site analysis, design development, plant selection (Figure 7–1). The following sections discuss suggested practices for planting. Observe the results and learn from your successes and mistakes.

Successful planting depends on several factors:

1. site preparation

2. quality of planting stock

3. time of year planting takes place

4. on-site plant placement

5. planting method

6. initial maintenance

SITE PREPARATION

Existing vegetation that is to remain on a site may require protection before construction begins. Enclose the plants or tree root zones with fencing or bright orange construction tape, tie up low branches, and prune susceptible branches to aid plant survival.

If the soil level is graded or an irrigation system installed, existing plants may suffer if their roots become exposed, buried, or cut. These plants should be carefully transplanted or protected while grading takes place. If plants are too large to be transplanted, maintenance of the original soil level is essential for survival of existing plants; these areas can be protected with six to eight inches of mulch. If the soil is regraded and its level raised or lowered around a plant, the plant can suffocate or, if its root structure is

7-1 *Newly planted palm trees along the Embarcadero in San Francisco.*

exposed, be killed. Communicate to the construction crew the significance of maintaining soil levels for plant survival. Show protection measures on construction drawings and observe soil levels on site inspections.

Landscaping and other construction can severely compact, erode, or deplete soil during installation, particularly if a building is being built at the same time as the garden. Soil compaction greatly reduces water infiltration, drainage, and aeration because it compresses pore space in soil and, as a result, plant roots suffocate or rot. It is essential to cultivate or loosen compacted soil. After loosening compacted soil, irrigate the ground thoroughly and delay planting for two weeks to allow the soil to settle. Eroded and depleted soils require an addition of topsoil after construction. Keep in mind that new soil generally compacts approximately 15–20 percent after application.

The choice of amendment and the amount used depends on the soil test, plant type, and location. For native plants, soil amendment is less important because the plant is adapted to its native soil.[2] If a native plant is planted into an unusually barren, depleted, or congested soil, amendment is an aid to plant growth because it provides a lighter soil with greater pore space for the new, young roots to develop. The key is to amend the entire planting area rather than just the planting hole. Amendments are generally recommended for vegetable gardens, flower beds, new lawn, and any intensively cultivated landscape. Well-decomposed manure, shredded bark, leaf mulch, and peat moss are good soil amendments and should be incorporated with the existing soil to a depth of six inches for new lawn, twelve to sixteen inches for vegetable and flower beds, and, if possible, twenty-four inches or more for shrub beds and new trees.

QUALITY OF PLANTING STOCK

Hand-selecting and tagging the planting stock ensures the quality of plant material you are getting. This entails visiting different nurseries to physically examine each and every plant to be used on the project. Some designers and landscape architects develop good relationships with nursery growers and some growers have a reputation for supplying high-quality plant stock so a personal visit is not always necessary. If in doubt, make the nursery visit. It gives you a chance to see additional new plants that are on the market or identify plants for another project.

The plant material must be inspected and evaluated for quality at the nursery or when it arrives at the project site. Examine the overall vigor of the plant. Look at the foliage color, bark texture, and for healthy, white root color. A tree should also display healthy taper, a proportional crown, and proper branching habit. *Taper* refers to the trunk decreasing in caliper as the height of the plant increases; it prevents wind damage and breakage. The *crown* of the tree should have 50 percent or less of its foliage on the upper third of the plant and 50 percent or more on the lower two thirds of the tree. This allows the lower limbs to nourish and shade the trunk to increase caliper and taper. Trees should possess a healthy central leader or branch without touching or crossing branches. Examine the tree from all sides because the initial form indicates its growth habit in the future. Check carefully for insect or disease problems.

All plants should be carefully inspected for girdling, kinked, or pot-bound roots, especially if the plants have been container grown. Lift the plant up out of the pot to visually inspect the roots. A kinked root has a sharp bend in the main root of 90 degrees

or more, with the majority of the root system developed below the kink. This causes the plant to be unstable and to have difficulty anchoring itself in the soil. Circling roots occur when 80 percent or more of the root system encircles and eventually girdles the plant. It is difficult for the roots to straighten and grow downward, and consequently only 20 percent of the roots remain to anchor the plant. The only way to examine a plant for circling and girdling root is to take it out of the container and wash the soil off the rootball. Outer circling roots or roots matted at the exterior of the rootball are not as serious, as the condition can generally be corrected by scoring the roots before planting. If large masses of roots are at the bottom of the plant it could be pot-bound and the plant's overall vigor should be examined. Roots damaged in these ways can eventually weaken or kill the plant. If the plants do not meet specifications or standards they can be rejected at the site and new plants ordered at the contractor's expense.

PLANTING TIME

In many areas the best conditions for planting are often in the autumn when the temperature of the soil is warm, moisture is available for root growth, and the temperature of the air is too cool for top growth. This gives the plant a good chance to anchor its roots in the soil. In the northwestern and southern United States or the Mediterranean climate of California the autumn is the best time for planting because the region is subject to winter rains, spring and fall growing seasons, and dry summers. Planting or transplanting at this time requires the minimum of care and allows nature to take its course. Because the ground does not generally freeze in this climate the roots continue to grow during the winter, preparing the plant for the onslaught of spring growth. In colder regions plant and transplant trees and shrubs in late winter to early spring, when the plant is dormant.[3]

The budgets and time constraints of some projects may necessitate planting under less than ideal conditions. If this occurs take every precaution to guard against plant loss. Do not plant when it is too hot or too cold for normal plant development; 45–80°F is optimum. If planting must be done when it is extremely warm, plant early in the morning and water plants in before the heat of the day or they can become scorched from water loss. When there is fear of a frost during the planting time, cover the plants with a thick layer of mulch, six to eight inches deep, and do not water too heavily so that water will not freeze in the plant.

PLANT PLACEMENT

Plant placement is the physical act of working with the contractor and crew to place the plants on the ground at the exact spot where they will be planted; this is sometimes referred to as *bedding out*. The twist of a certain branch or the angle of a specific plant can only be addressed if you are on the site for plant placement (Figure 7–2). This step, often overlooked, guarantees successful execution of the design and is best included in an estimate of design fees.

PLANTING METHOD

There are numerous methods for planting plants and it is best to choose the procedure that is appropriate for the specific plant, the soil conditions, and location of the planting.

The Planting Hole

Plant a young tree, shrub, or herbaceous plant "high," whether it is bareroot, balled and burlapped, or container grown. Dig the hole no deeper than necessary—approximately two inches less than the depth of the soil in the container or the depth of the root ball. If soil is of reasonable tilth, the hole for trees or shrubs should be at least twice the diameter of the container or rootball and one half the diameter of the rootball for herbaceous plants. In compacted soils the hole for trees or shrubs should be three to four times the diameter of the rootball, and for herbaceous plants two times the diameter of the root ball. In either case the sides of the hole should be almost vertical and roughened to produce easier root penetration. Planting deeper or in loose soil can lead to future crown rot problems. Loose soil in the bottom of the hole will settle, causing the plant to drop deeper than intended. Add a mixture of soil amendment to the planting hole in 1:1 proportion to the existing soil. This gives the plant roots a transitional soil to grow through and strengthen in as they permeate the original soil layer.

To plant bareroot plants, make the hole large enough to contain the roots without crowding. Backfill the hole with soil dug from the hole or a 1:1 proportion amendment.

Hold the plant "high" as you backfill the soil so it will be at the same ground level as it was in the nursery. A color difference on the stem indicates this level.

Balled-and-burlapped trees and shrubs should be planted on an undisturbed base with the top of the ball even with the surrounding ground level if the soil is sandy or average and two to four inches above the ground if the soil is heavy and does not drain well. Remove wire ropes, twine, pins, or nails that have been used to hold the ball together, but not the burlap, because the rootball could become damaged or fall apart.

Watering plants in after planting is most important. This is done to establish the initial root-to-soil association. Mulching with wood chips, bark chunks, pine needles, oak leaves, etc., after planting reduces both the need for frequent watering and competition from weeds.

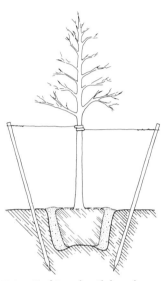

7-3 *Staking detail for planting a tree.*

Staking Trees

Staking requirements depend on the ability of a tree to stand upright and the particular landscape situation. The more freedom the top of the tree has to move, the better it is able to develop the structure to stand upright and withstand storms. Stakes are not necessary for many trees that can stand upright by themselves or plants that have branches to the ground or are planted where little protection is needed from strong winds. Most conifers, trees with upright growth habits, or multiple trunks usually do not need support. This is better for the development of the plant because unstaked trees develop thicker, more uniform trunks due to the additional movement they experience. If you must stake, make certain there is a little give in the staking and that the plant will not become chafed or broken at the stake locations (Figure 7–3).

Protective stakes are needed for trees that can stand without support but that need protection from equipment, vehicles, or animals. To protect trees from equipment and vehicles stakes need only be high enough to be seen to avoid tripping. Three tall stakes with wire mesh encircling them may be needed to prevent animal damage.

Anchor stakes are needed for trees whose trunks are in good shape but whose roots may not be able to support the trunks upright, particularly in wind when the soil is muddy.

Support stakes are required for trees unable to stand by themselves. Top support for these trees should be as low on the trunk as possible but high enough to return the tree upright after deflection. Use two or three support stakes and, if possible, tie the trunk to them at only one height to allow the trunk above the tie to bend in the wind. Tie material should contact the trunk with a broad, smooth surface and elasticity to minimize trunk abrasion and girdling.

Mulch

Mulching is one of gardening's oldest techniques for creating a healthy environment for plant growth. The difference between soil amendment and mulch is not the material but the method of application: a soil amendment is incorporated into the soil to improve soil texture and structure, whereas a mulch is applied to the top of the soil. Mulch is extremely beneficial in the following ways:

• reduces soil temperature

• preserves moisture

- limits light reflection and consequential water loss from the plant
- builds up the soil as it decomposes and adds essential organic matter
- controls erosion
- controls weeds

The depth of mulch needed depends on the material chosen. Fine-grained organic mulches, such as well-composted sawdust, should be applied at a thickness of one to two inches. Coarse or fluffy materials can be applied three to four inches thick. Too thick a layer of mulch, especially in humid parts of the country, may reduce oxygen and water penetration into the soil, which can kill shallow-rooted plants such as azaleas, rhododendrons, and camellias. Too shallow a layer, two inches or less, especially in arid areas of the country, may allow sunlight to penetrate the soil through the mulch. In these locations you may want to increase your mulch layer to four inches. Apply mulch evenly and maintain its usual thickness. As it thins down, add new material because as the mulch decomposes into the soil, it improves soil structure. Guidelines for specific mulches and mulch depth are taken from the book *Xeriscape Gardening* and are as follows: One cubic yard of mulch (twenty-seven cubic feet) covers:

- 80 square feet   when four inches deep
- 100 square feet   when three inches deep
- 160 square feet   when two inches deep
- 325 square feet   when one inch deep[4]

The best time to mulch for water conservation is in the late spring, after the soil has absorbed water from the spring rains but before summer heat has started to build up and pull the moisture out of the soil. Mulches to enhance the appearance of the garden and to control weeds can be applied at any time. Those applied to protect fall transplants from freezing should be put in place soon after transplanting. Remove the mulch in early spring to allow young perennials to grow and flourish.

Mulching Materials   I recommend only organic mulching materials—that is, those materials made from animal or plant sources such as manures, plant trimmings, or decaying vegetation. They are part of the life-death-decay cycle that occurs in nature and themselves break down in the soil eventually and need to be replenished. In the process of breaking down they enrich the soil. (Earthworms also assist the breakdown of mulches.)

The most appropriate mulch for each plant is the leaf and twig litter from the plant itself; pine trees do best with pine needles, oak trees with oak leaves. You can take a cue from nature and not rake up dead leaves from trees and shrubs but let them mulch themselves. If this is not possible, be judicious in your handling of mulch; a little bit, applied at the right time in the correct quantity, greatly enhances plant life.

The following are examples of organic mulches:

- *Chipper debris* is often available from city or private tree pruning crews or can be created from your own garden refuse. The rate of decomposition depends on the original material chipped: hardwoods take longer to decompose than softwoods.

Chipper debris allows water to penetrate. It can look rough in appearance and should be used when this is not a concern.

- *Evergreen boughs* are available from judicious pruning or recycled Christmas tree branches. They are easily applied but can be a fire hazard and should be placed in beds located away from wooden structures including houses, fences, and decks.

- *Fir bark* is available in a wide variety of sizes for use as a mulch or soil amendment. When used as a mulch fir bark will weather to an attractive gray color. It allows water to percolate, holds the soil in place, and the smaller material is less prone to wash away than coarse mulch.

- *Lawn clippings* are best used when applied dry and spread loosely on the surface of the soil. Extremely fresh grass clippings may draw nitrogen out of the soil as the material breaks down and cause a temporary nitrogen deficiency in it. Yellowing of the lowest plant leaves can be a sign of this. Do not use clippings if the lawn has been treated with chemicals. Be aware that weed seeds may be present in grass.

- *Leaf mold* is made from leaves that are composted in the autumn of the year and ready for use in the spring. This is an excellent mulch for acid-loving plants such as azaleas and rhododendrons. It can be a fire hazard in the western United States and should be placed in beds located away from wooden structures including houses, fences, and decks.

- *Pine needles* make a light, porous, attractive mulch that can increase the water-holding capacity of the soil. This mulch is moderately acidic and therefore beneficial to acid-loving plants (rhododendrons, azaleas, camellias).

Keep in mind that some organic mulches encourage insect pests such as slugs, snails, sowbugs, and earwigs by creating dark, moist environments. In addition, mice and other small rodents may tunnel under thick layers of mulch.

INITIAL MAINTENANCE

Initial maintenance is the upkeep of the landscape that occurs immediately after planting. It is a sensitive and critical time of transition that, when properly handled, advances the future success of the garden.

Watering

Correct watering after the initial planting is crucial for plant survival and one of the most difficult and challenging aspects of planting to master. Drought-tolerant or not, all plants need similar care at this point (unless you are in a Mediterranean climate and have timed your planting to coincide directly with winter rains). The exact watering frequency of newly installed plants depends on the plant species, the size of the rootball, weather conditions, planting time, and soil conditions. It is best to monitor the planting for signs of stress or overwatering to determine the best course of action.

Do not stick to a scheduled time frame or irrigation clock as your rule of thumb for watering but look at the plant itself.

Try to envision the roots as you water. If you are uncertain of the amount of water a plant is receiving, try this procedure: About an hour after you have watered, dig a hole next to the newly planted plant and look at how deeply the water has infiltrated the soil. Scratch the soil surface for moisture content. Or, an hour after watering, dig up a small plant very carefully and look at the root development. Are the roots moist, white, fibrous, and in healthy condition? Remember, shallow watering produces shallow roots because the roots remain near the soil surface. Overwatering can produce waterlogged roots, root rot, and, eventually, death of the plant. It is best to water early in the morning or late in the day to avoid water loss through transpiration.

Insect and Disease Problems

How will disease and pest control be handled? New plants are often susceptible to insect and disease damage. Careful monitoring of a new planting can help to avoid plant loss. Become familiar with potential plant problems associated with the chosen plant palette. Keep an eye out for changes in plant vigor and respond immediately. Newly transplanted young plants are especially vulnerable to attack.

The best way to control insect and disease problems is to prevent them in the first place. By purchasing healthy plants and giving them the appropriate care, many potential problems can be avoided. Keep planting beds weed free to discourage insects and diseases. Prune away any infested or diseased plant parts and do not add this material to your compost pile. Spray plants with a regular garden hose to dislodge insects. Do not spray foliage that appears to have mold or fungal problems. It is best to water these plants at the root zone and to avoid watering them right before nightfall in order to allow their leaves to dry. Tolerance is also a key element of prevention. Many insects and diseases are seasonal and will not ultimately injure the plant.

If you cannot identify a cause, clip a piece of the infected plant, seal it in a plastic bag, and take it to a reputable nursery or to the Cooperative Extension Service in your area for identification and advice.

Pruning

The current recommendation for pruning newly planted trees and shrubs favors trimming damaged or broken branches only and saving more extensive shaping for the next growing season. Preserving all possible leaves gives the plant a better chance to generate food and overcome transplant shock sooner.

Fertilizing

As a rule of thumb, most plants do *not* need to be fed immediately after planting. Nursery growers tend to fertilize plants with a slow timed-release fertilizer that often lasts three to five months after planting. Talk to the nursery people to determine the food requirements of your new plants.

SUMMARY

The planting segment of the planting design process is described in detail, from working with a landscape contractor to installing the garden and beginning the initial maintenance tasks, as generally required by contract. The project is not finished when the last plant is planted. Actually, the physical work is just beginning. Chapter 8 discusses the all-important process of ongoing maintenance that assures the success of the design.

ENDNOTES

[1]   David Fairchild, *The World Was My Garden* (New York: Scribner's & Sons, 1939).

[2]   This is assuming native soil is present at the job site, which is becoming less and less common.

[3]   This is a guideline for planting. The dates of the first and last frosts in your area are the best indicators for correct planting time.

[4]   Connie Ellefson, Tom Stephens, and Doug Welsh, *Xeriscape Gardening: Water Conservation for the American Landscape* (New York: MacMillan, 1992), 119–123.

Maintaining the Garden

I have done a good deal of work in my way, but it is constantly and everywhere arrested, wrenched, mangled, and misused and it is not easy to get above intense disappointment.

FREDERICK LAW OLMSTED, *THE CALIFORNIA FRONTIER*[1]

Good design, good installation, and good maintenance: the three practices are completely interrelated. One will not succeed without the other. The final step in the planting design process is to ensure proper maintenance of the new garden. Proper maintenance provides the key to the success of any planting design. Standards of maintenance differ greatly from the residential scale to corporate park or public open space. In planting design, where one of the primary interests of the garden is the intrinsic qualities of the plants, it is important to control the desired plant results through continual maintenance.

When working with a landscape contractor on a large-scale project, the contractor will often have a 30-60 or 90–day maintenance contract to oversee and maintain the landscape as part of the construction agreement. This means the firm checks for any problems with the irrigation system (if there is one), mows the lawn, and replaces dead plants if necessary. No matter how engaging the original concept, it will rapidly be lost without skilled maintenance (Figure 8–1). In order to prevent problems work directly with the client to secure a competent landscape gardener and make certain he or she thoroughly understands the design concept and the maintenance procedures necessary to control the plantings in the form and size required by the design.

One way to help guarantee the appropriate maintenance of a landscape is to develop a maintenance manual to serve as a reference guide for your design intentions. Such a document enables garden and plant preservation and is a guide for upkeep and development of the future landscape. The manual highlights maintenance issues of scale (how large a plant grows), anticipates potential problems, addresses plant replacement issues, and contains a yearly calendar of maintenance practices. A good example of a maintenance manual is *Beatrix Farrand's Plant Book for Dumbarton Oaks*. Written in 1941, this manual continues to provide a relevant, detailed description of the designer's plans and objectives for the present and future of the Dumbarton Oaks garden. For example, Farrand describes the maintenance requirements for the north vista of the house: "On the north walls of the house, in the north court, a few plants of *Ampelopis englemannii* may

8-1 *Is this planting maintained as the designer intended?* (PHOTO: CAROL BORNSTEIN)

P l a n t i n g   t h e   L a n d s c a p e

be used, but probably not more than two. The ivy should be restricted to cover approximately one-third of the walls, and not be allowed to cover more than half at most."[2] Although this description may seem painstaking, it can help save you and your project from the future mistakes and disappointments that Olmsted describes in the opening quote of this chapter.

It is essential that the manual include a maintenance schedule. This is a guide for the maintenance contractor or gardener to ensure that all maintenance tasks are carried out at the correct time of year and in proper sequence. A monthly calendar describing the seasonal tasks of pruning, transplanting, fertilizing, and bed preparation can be spelled out in this document.

Excessive maintenance can be avoided through careful planning and design, appropriate installation, and frequent monitoring of the new stock, bed conditions, and irrigation systems. Figure 8–1 shows a garden in Williamsburg, Virginia, where the boxwood hedge has been allowed to grow both tall and wide, obscuring the view to and from the house and making the walkway virtually impassable. These are the types of errors that can be avoided through explicit maintenance instructions. It is important to review the garden over the next few months, even years, to guarantee adequate maintenance.

Whether giving instructions for the maintenance of a garden or maintaining your own garden, there are five maintenance tasks to accomplish:

1. watering

2. fertilizing

3. pruning

4. weeding

5. monitoring and controlling insects and disease

WATERING

Foremost in the matter of maintenance is proper and accurate watering. Less weeding and pruning is needed if water is kept to a minimum. Overwatering contributes to the presence of insects and diseases. In general, the higher the water requirement of the landscape, the higher the maintenance needs. Water thoroughly and deeply to encourage adequate root development. If soil is dry, apply water slowly and directly to the rootball area. Give the soil an initial watering and then wait a few minutes and go back and thoroughly soak the soil. Container watering is a good example of this practice. When a container-grown plant is dry, the initial application of water tends to run through the soil. It is only the second, third, and even fourth application of water that begins to be absorbed by the soil and consequently by plant roots.

Automatic irrigation systems facilitate watering and are a necessity in many areas of the United States. It is prudent to approach the use of an irrigation system with water efficiency in mind. Irrigation equipment is available for every type of application: overhead spray, drip, misting, soaker hoses, and agricultural operations. By working with an irrigation specialist, the correct system can be designed for your project needs. An irrigation system allows you to apply the water directly to the plant by choosing the correct equipment for a plant's needs—rhododendrons, azaleas, and camellias enjoy overhead watering; roses and drought-tolerant plants generally prefer drip irrigation. The timing and duration of watering can be adjusted to climatic conditions so that little water is wasted.

FEEDING AND FERTILIZING

The simplest way to feed plants is through a healthy soil rich in nutrients. Compost, organic mulches, and manures add to the vigor of soil.

Composting is the art and science of mixing organic materials in a pile and controlling the conditions so that the original materials are transformed by means of microorganisms into humus (Figure 8–2). The best compost is rotated or mixed every two weeks until it is four to six months in age. A mature compost contains abundant nutrients for plants. Recycling residential or commercial organic matter (grass clippings, leaves, vegetable wastes, etc.) makes compost cost-effective and readily available.

- *Organic mulches* decompose, adding nutrients to the soil. They are described in detail in Chapter 7.

- *Green manures* are plants often referred to as cover crops. These plants are sown from seed and then, upon maturity (generally three to six months, depending upon the plant), tilled into the soil to increase soil fertility. They can also be an important source of biodiversity, crucial for ecological pest control systems.[3] Green manures are extremely useful on newly constructed sites where erosion and weed control are necessary. Many plants can be utilized as green manure crops—for example, buckwheat, *Polygonum fagopyrum*, for poor soils; trefoil, *Medicago lupulina*, for light soils; and spring vetch, *Vicia faba*, for heavy soils.[4]

8-2 *A mature compost pile.*

Planting the Landscape

The most important considerations are appropriate selection and timing of application.

- *Animal manures* are another rich source of organic matter. Cow and horse manures tend to be rich in potassium. Sheep manure is good for alkaline soils. Goat and rabbit manures are nitrogen rich and chicken, pigeon, and guano manures contain phosphorus, calcium, and trace elements that are good for alkaline soils. Fresh or raw manure that has not been allowed to age for at least six months should not be applied just before planting because it will burn plants. The best time to spread manure is when it can be incorporated readily into the soil.

A note on the difference between fertilizers and soil amendment: Fertilizers are applied primarily to provide nutrients to plants; soil amendments, which might contain the same nutrients as fertilizers, are materials used primarily to improve soil tilth.

PRUNING AND MOWING

The simplest way to avoid a lot of unnecessary pruning is to be conscientious about your plant choices. If a four-foot-high shrub is required to create a desired effect, choose a shrub that will eventually grow to a maximum of four feet. Do *not* choose a shrub that is four feet high at the time of planting or one that eventually reaches eighteen feet in height Although this sounds extremely simple, it is a step often overlooked in the plant palette creation. Figure 8–3 shows the elaborate maintenance procedures required to maintain the green walls of the garden at Hidcote.

Pruning objectives are many; it is essential to coordinate design intentions with maintenance pruning.

8-3 *Scaffolding assembled for pruning at Hidcote garden.*

Objectives for trees and shrubs:

1. Improving plant vigor by pruning crossing and touching branches, broken limbs, and insect- and disease-ridden boughs.

2. Thinning out a tree canopy to allow sunlight and air to penetrate and to enhance its health and beauty.

3. Training a young plant into a desired form, correcting poor growth habits, or compensating for root loss during transplanting to benefit plant performance.

4. Controlling rampant growth in vines and ground covers.

5. Increasing flower production and enhancing fruit production by strengthening fruiting wood.

6. Stimulating stagnant plants by initiating new growth or dwarfing overgrown plants by the severity of the pruning.

7. Creating special effects with plants by applying techniques of pollarding, pleaching, espalier, topiary, and bonsai.

The subject of pruning is complex and books devoted solely to the subject are numerous; further reading is suggested.

WEEDING

Remember, a weed is just a plant in the wrong place. OK, this is a simplistic view of the situation. However, if you have a landscape with healthy soil that is mulched sufficiently and watered economically, the amount of weeds generated can be minimal. If a new garden has been cultivated with the addition of manure or compost, there will be weeds. The best way to remove the weeds is to pull them by hand or nudge them out with a soil cultivator, taking care to remove *all* the root and stem, or the weed will return. Replace the disturbed mulch and throw the weeds on the regularly rotated compost pile.

INSECT AND DISEASE CONTROL

Prevention is the best way of handling insect and disease problems. Healthy and correct plant choices, watering at the proper time of day, monitoring for the first sign of problems, and tolerance are practices that prolong the life of plants.

Monitoring plants creates awareness of weather and soil conditions in addition to the natural cycles in the garden. It is critical to make weekly or biweekly checks during the growing season, especially in the vegetable garden. If a problem is identified, *tolerance* is a sound practice. This means learning to tolerate a few insects in the garden, a few spots or holes in leaves, and to cut out or remove any devastated plant or plant part. If you find you must do something more aggressive to control the situation, visit a local retail nursery. Take a sample of the infestation or disease problem in a plastic bag and stress that you would like to use an environmentally safe product for eradication. Numerous biological controls are available on the market today.

Maintenance is the continuous assessment of a garden's health and design progress. Timing of new planting or proper pruning is essential. Knowledge of the design goals, annual or semiannual visits to a garden, use of proper tools, and routine inspection of irrigation systems maintain the integrity of the design. Remember, good design, installation, and maintenance together are the key to the success of any garden.

ENDNOTES

1 Victoria Post Ranney, Gerard J. Rauluk, and Carolyn Hoffman, eds., *The Papers of Frederick Law Olmsted,* Vol. 5: *The California Frontier* (Baltimore: Johns Hopkins University Press, 1990), p. 378.

2 Beatrix Farrand, *Beatrix Farrand's Plant Book for Dumbarton Oaks,* ed. Diane Kostial McGuire (Washington, D.C.: Dumbarton Oaks, 1980), 38.

3 Grace Gershuny and Joseph Smillie, *The Soul of Soil* (Davis California: Agricultural Access, 1995), 106.

4 Heidi Gildemeister, *Mediterranean Gardening* (Palma de Mallorca, Spain: Editorial Moll, 1995), 76.

Glossary

acropolis   The pinnacle of a Greek city containing the chief temples and public buildings.

allée   A walk or road bordered by trees or shrubs.

arbor   A leafy, shady recess formed by tree branches, shrubs, or vines often intertwined on a latticework or architectural structure.

atrium   An inner court open to the sky and surrounded by a roof.

axis   An imaginary line about which a form, area, or plane is organized.

barco   An Italian term for hunting park.

border   A planting bed, usually linear in form, made up of layers of plant materials that one walks beside.

borrowed view   A feature of gardens where external views form an integral part of the design. The background is described as *borrowed* or brought into the garden as part of the composition although it lies far beyond the reach of one's own land or project site. In Chinese gardens it is described as *jie jing,* in Japanese landscapes as *shakkei,* and in Italian design as *integrazione scenica.*

bosco   An Italian term for a grove of evergreen oaks or formal woods that is an element of villa design.

bosquet   A French term for a formal grove of trees planted in geometrical arrangements, often using the same plant species.

carpet bedding   The practice of forming beds of low-growing foliage plants, all of an even height, in patterns that resemble a carpet both in intricacy of design and in uniformity of surface. Designs can vary from geometrical shapes to images and lettered inscriptions.

colonnade   A series of columns, set at regular intervals, that supports a base or roof.

conservatory   A glass house for protecting tender plants.

courtyard   A space, usually square in shape, open to the sky but enclosed by walls or buildings.

drift   An irregular mass of plants characterized by bold sweeps of mass plantings featuring perennials and ornamental grasses.

ecosystem   The interrelationship of plants and animals in a given community.

environmental relationship   A plant's natural affinities that evolve from interaction with the physical characteristics of a site—light, soil, moisture, and wind.

espalier   From the Italian word *spalle* meaning *shoulder* or *to lean on,* a line of fruit trees whose branches are pruned and trained into formal patterns against a wall or fence in order to make the most of sunshine and space.

eyecatcher   A feature placed on a distant, prominent point integral to the overall design of the landscape. It is most commonly found in eighteenth-century English gardens and can take on various forms.

flowery mead   An expression for a carpet of turf or meadow bejewelled with flowers.

folly   A species of garden structure characterized by a certain excess in terms of eccentricity, cost, or conspicuous inutility.

genius loci   The special qualities of a place or the inherent spiritual character of a site that gives a landscape its own intrinsic potential or emotional appeal.

giardino segreto   Meaning *secret garden,* a feature found in many Italian Renaissance gardens of the fifteenth century. It is often a small enclosed garden for private use or a space one comes upon by surprise.

giocchi d'acqua   Meaning *water games,* a fountain device conceived of in fifteenth-century Italy and consisting of water jets located in strategic places throughout a garden that surprise and delight the visitor.

golden section   A rectangle whose sides are proportioned according to the golden section, a mathematical system of proportion that originates with the Pythagorean concept of "all is number" and the belief that certain numerical relationships manifest the harmonic structure of the universe. The ratio is approximately 5:8.

glade   A clearing in a wood.

green theater   An invention of the Italian Renaissance, a stage constructed of plant material for play and concert performances, ritual enactments, storytelling, or the creation of illusions.

grotto   A cavelike chamber, natural or manmade, often decorated with minerals, shells, or pebbles. It has evolved throughout history as different cultures interpret the space and adapted its use. Its usually subterranean location provides a cool place to sit or a shelter from wind.

grove   A grouping of trees either planted or occuring naturally, usually of the same plant species and organic in form. Groves form an enclosure or connection between earth and sky and were often considered by the ancients to be places of mystical and intellectual power, a sacred grove.

ha-ha   A ditch wide and deep enough to serve as a barrier to animals.

hedgerow   A type of plant grouping that protects agricultural fields or open space from wind, snow, rain, and erosion. It is often composed of a combination of numerous trees and shrubs, either pruned or unpruned.

hortus conclusus   An enclosed garden consisting of a variety of garden elements. Encircled by walls, it is often square or oblong within trellised fences and consists largely of a lawn. It is intersected by paths, punctuated by a pool or fountain, and surrounded by flowers and raised seats made of turf.

humus   The dark brown residue that results from decaying organic matter.

loggia   A roofed porch or gallery with an open colonnade on one or more sides.

maze   An intricate, usually confusing network of walled or hedged pathways. The maze is a very ancient form that has appeared in many shapes and sizes; all mazes have a deliberate design containing twists and turns.

meadow   A richly grassed area for mowing or pasture. It can be composed of open and undulating grasses, wildflowers, or wild prairie plants.

microclimate   The study of a climate of a very small area which directly effects the plants and animals living there.

moon-viewing pavilion   A structure built and located specifically for the purpose and pleasure of admiring the moon's progress over the garden.

mount   A small hill in Medieval pleasure gardens, either square or round in shape, used as a vantage point from which the attractions of the garden might be seen.

orangery   A structure for cultivating oranges or exotic plants that are normally placed outside in the warm months and kept in the orangery in winter.

orchard   An area for the cultivation of fruit trees.

palisade   A row of trees or shrubs forming a hedge clipped into a green wall for bordering an allée, concealing walls, or terraces.

parterre   Originally from the Italian verb *partire,* to divide; later the French term *parterre* evolved, literally translated as *on the ground.* It is a flat terrace usually adjacent to or near a building on which foliage patterns are created from plants, flowers, or gravel. Parterres emphasize the ground plane or serve as a picture for viewing, especially from above.

parterre en broderie   A French term denoting a flat terrace on which the design of the foliage patterns mimics the fine embroidery historically worn by patrons of the garden.

patio   In Spanish architecture, an inner court open to the sky.

pergola   An Italian term meaning arbor, bower, or close wall of boughs. It is often constructed of substantial columns supporting cross-beams.

peristyle   A roofed porch, generally supported by Doric or Ionic columns, surrounding a courtyard.

pH   The measure of alkalinity or acidity in soil. pH values range from 0 to 14. A pH of less than 7 indicates an acid soil, greater than 7 alkaline, and 7 itself a neutral soil.

photosynthesis   The chemical process of the energy in sunlight being trapped by plant leaves in order to convert carbon dioxide from the air and water transported by plant roots into sugars which feed the plant. Oxygen is a by-product of the process.

plant community   A group of plants which are similarly adapted to a local climate and soil type and consequently grow together successfully as a group.

pleached walkway   A row of closely planted trees trained to form a continuous narrow wall or hedge. This is accomplished by interlacing the branches of the trees and keeping their sides tightly pruned.

quincunx   A grouping of trees planted in a formation of five, with four trees at the corners and one tree in the middle of the square.

rill   A small channel, originally a simple irrigation ditch, through which water flows to a garden. It can cool the air on a warm day and relax garden visitors with the sound of the running water. Rills are often associated with dry climates and a need for irrigation.

sculpture   A multifaceted and diverse art form used to adorn gardens since the Egyptians. It can take myriad forms in the landscape. In some instances, landforms themselves become sculptures.

shelterbelt   A type of plant grouping that protects agricultural fields or open space from wind, snow, rain, and erosion. It consists of a row of trees and shrubs in three distinct layers of tree, small tree, and shrub.

soil profile   A grouping of distinctly visible layers of soil called soil horizons that develop over a long period of time.

specimen plant   A singular tree or shrub that is significant enough in its form, color, or size to stand alone as a design device—as a piece of sculpture, to emphasize a point of transition, or as a focal point. A specimen plant possesses enough interesting characteristics to attract attention.

tapis vert   Literally translated, "green cloth." It is a swath of lawn, usually rectilinear in shape, used to strengthen a visual axis or focus attention on an object.

terrace   A raised level of earth, sometimes retained by stone or concrete, with a surface of stone, brick, turf, pea gravel, or a combination thereof.

topiary   The art of clipping, trimming, and training trees and shrubs into specific shapes. Topiary hedges can be architecturally clipped to define an edge or playful green living sculptures that decorate and amuse.

treillage   A French term meaning trelliswork, a traditional garden craft. The term generally implies a sophisticated lattice that is architecturally significant.

windbreak   A type of plant grouping that protects agricultural fields or open space from wind, snow, rain, and erosion. A windbreak is a single row of trees, generally of the same species.

Bibliography

GENERAL

Carpenter, Phillip L., Theodore D. Walker, and Frederick O. Lanphear. *Plants in the Landscape*. San Francisco: W.H. Freeman, 1975.

Crowe, Sylvia. *Garden Design*. Woodbridge U.K.: Garden Art Press, 1958.

Ranney, Victoria Post, Gerard J. Rauluk, and Carolyn Hoffman, eds. *The Papers of Frederick Law Olmsted*. Vol. 5, *The California Frontier*. Baltimore: Johns Hopkins University Press, 1990.

Robinette, Gary O. *Plants, People, and Environmental Quality*. Washington D.C.: U.S. Department of the Interior, 1972.

Robinson, Florence Bell. *Planting Design*. Champaign, IL: Garrard Press, 1940.

Wharton, Edith, *Italian Villas and Their Gardens*. New York: Century, 1904.

PREFACE

Beardsley, John. *Gardens of Revelation*. New York: Abbeville Press, 1995.

Spirn, Anne, Martha Schwartz, and Diane Balmori. "Perspectives." *Progressive Architecture* (August 1991).

CHAPTER 1: HISTORICAL PRECEDENT FOR PLANTING DESIGN

Allan, Mea, *William Robinson, 1838–1935*. London: Faber and Faber, 1982.

Baumann, Helmut. *The Greek Plant World in Myth, Art and Literature*. Translated by William T. Stearn and Eldwyth Ruth Stearn. Portland, OR: Timber Press, 1993.

Blomfield, Reginald, and F. Inigo Thomas. *The Formal Garden in England.* London: Waterstone, 1892.

Carpiceci, A.C., and L. Pennino. *Paestum and Velia Today and 2500 Years Ago.* Salerno: Mantonti, 1992.

Cunningham, Lawrence, and John Reich. *Culture and Values: A Survey of the Western Humanities,* Vol. 1. Orlando: Harcourt Brace, 1994.

Eckbo, Garrett. *Landscape for Living.* New York: F.W. Dodge, 1950.

Frankel, Felice, and Jory Johnson. *Modern Landscape Architecture: Redefining the Garden.* New York: Abbeville Press, 1991.

Hazelhurst, F. Hamilton. *Gardens of Illusion: The Genius of André Le Nôtre.* Nashville: Vanderbilt University Press, 1986.

Highstone, John. *Victorian Gardens.* (New York: Harper & Row Publishers, San Francisco, 1982).

Hobhouse, Penelope. *Gardening Through the Ages.* New York: Simon & Schuster, 1992.

Hubbard, Henry V., and Theodora Kimball. *An Introduction to the Study of Landscape Design.* New York: Macmillan, 1917.

Hunt, John Dixon, and Peter Willis. *The Genius of the Place: The English Landscape Garden, 1620–1820.* Cambridge: MIT Press, 1975.

Jashemski, Wilhelmina. "The Campanian Peristyle Garden." In *Ancient Roman Gardens,* edited by Wilhelmina Jashemski. Washington, D.C.: Dumbarton Oaks, Vol. 7, 1981.

Jellicoe, G.A. *Studies in Landscape Design.* London: Oxford University Press, 1960.

Keswick, Maggie. *The Chinese Garden.* New York: Rizzoli, 1978.

Klare, Michael T. "The Architecture of Imperial America." *Science and Society* 33 (Summer/Fall 1969).

Kostof, Spiro. *A History of Architecture.* New York: Oxford University Press, 1985.

Lazzaro, Claudia. *The Italian Renaissance Garden.* New Haven: Yale University Press, 1990.

McHarg, Ian. *Design with Nature.* Garden City, NY: Doubleday/Natural History Press 1969.

Meyvaert, Paul. "The Medieval Monastic Garden," in *Medieval Gardens,* edited by Elizabeth MacDougal, Washington, D.C.: Dumbarton Oaks, Vol. 9, 1983.

Newton, Norman T. *Design on the Land.* Cambridge: Harvard University Press, Belknap Press, 1971.

Ottewill, David. *The Edwardian Garden.* New Haven: Yale University Press, 1989.

Prest, John. *The Garden of Eden: The Botanic Garden and the Re-Creation of Paradise.* New Haven: Yale University Press, 1981.

Smith, Stevenson W., with additions by William Kelly Simpson. *The Art and Architecture of Ancient Egypt*. London: Penguin, 1988.

Thacker, Christopher. *The History of Gardens*. Berkeley: University of California Press, 1979.

Treib, Marc, ed. *Modern Landscape Architecture: A Critical Review*. Cambridge: MIT Press, 1993.

Treib, Marc, and Ron Herman. *A Guide to the Gardens of Kyoto*. Tokyo: Shufunotomo, 1980.

Tunnard, Christopher. *Gardens in the Modern Landscape*. London: Architectural Press, 1938.

Wharton, Edith, and Ogden Codman Jr. *The Decoration of Houses*. New York: Norton, 1902.

Wilson, Richard Guy. "The Great Civilization," in *The American Renaissance: 1876–1917*. New York: Brooklyn Museum, 1979.

CHAPTER 2: ENVIRONMENTAL ANALYSIS

Armitage, Allan M. *Herbaceous Perennials*. Athens, GA: Varsity Press, 1989.

Druse, Ken. *The Natural Habitat Garden*. New York: Clarkson Potter, 1994.

Fairchild, David. *The World Was My Garden*. New York: Scribner's & Sons. 1939.

Farrand, Beatrix. "The Garden as a Picture," in *Scribner's* 43 (July 1907).

Foth, F.D., and L.M. Turk. *Fundamentals of Soil Science*. 5th ed. New York: John Wiley & Sons, 1965.

Gershuny, Grace, and Joseph Smillie. *The Soul of Soil*. Davis, CA: Agricultural Access, 1995.

Harris, Richard W. *Arboriculture: Integrated Management of Landscape Trees, Shrubs, and Vines*. Englewood Cliffs, NJ: Prentice Hall, 1992.

Perry, Bob. *Landscape Plants for Western Regions*. Claremont, GA: Land Design Publishing, 1992.

Sullivan, Chip. *Drawing the Landscape*. New York: Van Nostrand Reinhold, 1995.

CHAPTER 3: DESIGN EXPLORATION

Brown, Jane. *Gardens of a Golden Afternoon*. Middlesex England: Penguin Books, 1982.

Ching, Francis D.K. *Architecture: Form, Space, and Order*. New York: Van Nostrand Reinhold, 1976.

Clark, Roger H., and Michael Pause. *Precedents in Architecture*. New York: Van Nostrand Reinhold, 1985.

Francis, Mark, and Randolph T. Hester, eds. *The Meaning of Gardens: Idea, Place and Action*. Cambridge: MIT Press, 1990.

Inskip, Peter. "Lutyens' Houses," in *Edwin Lutyens: Architectural Monographs*. London: St. Martin's Press, 1979.

Moore, Charles W., William J. Mitchell, and William Turnbull, Jr. *The Poetics of the Garden*. Cambridge: MIT Press, 1988.

Norberg-Schulz, Christian. *Existence, Space and Architecture*. New York: Praeger, 1971.

CHAPTER 4: DESIGN VOCABULARY: ELEMENTS OF THE GARDEN

Higgins, Adrian Thomas. "Off the Beaten Path." *Garden Design* (Autumn 1990).

Jellicoe, Geoffrey, Susan Jellicoe, Patrick Goode, and Michael Lancaster. *The Oxford Companion to Gardens*. Oxford: Oxford University Press, 1986.

Lyndon, Donlyn, and Charles W. Moore. *Chambers for a Memory Palace*. Cambridge: MIT Press, 1994.

Nelson, William R. *Planting Design: A Manual of Theory and Practice*. Champaign, IL: Stipes, 1979.

Robinson, Nick. *The Planting Design Handbook*. London: Gower Publishing, 1992.

Index

Absolute scale, 115–117

Acanthus, 129

Acanthus leaves, 2, 5

Achillea "Moonshine," 155

Acid soils, 52

Adam's needle, 37

Aeration, 51

Aesthetic consciousness, 33

Aesthetic effects, 95–98

Agricultural Research Service (USDA), 43–44

Alberti, Leon Battista, 19

Allées, 2, 22–23, 83, 93

Almond orchard, xiii

American gardens, early, 31–35

American Indians, planting traditions of, 57

American landscape architecture, modern, 36–37

American wilderness, preservation of, 34

Animal manures, 185

Annuals, 27

  functional requirements for, 153–154

Arboriculture (Harris), 105

Arbors, 88, 92, 102

Arches, as garden openings, 92

"Architect's Plants," 37

Architectural framework, plants as, 84–95

Artistic expression, via gardens, 12

Ash trees, 101

Asymmetry, as a design component, 116–117

Atrium, 6–7

"Autumn Joy," 144

Axial conditions, 63–65

Axis, role in design, 63–65

Azaleas, 11–12, 14

Balance, as a design component, 114–115

Bald cypress, 51

Balled and burlapped plants, 166–167, 175–176

Bamboo, 11, 14

Barco, 19

Bareroot plants, 167, 175

Barragan, Luis, 55

Base plan, 47–48

Basil, 15

Beardsley, John, x

Beaux-Arts design tradition, 34

Bedding out, 175

Beech trees, 101, 119

Behavior, effect of plants on, 95–97

Benedictine cloister (Switzerland), 14

Biennials, functional requirements for, 155

Biltmore estate, 34

Birch trees, 34, 119

Blake, Edward, 38

Bleeding heart, 144

Bloedel Reserve, 68–69, 75, 130
  Zen Garden at, 31

Blomfield, Reginald, 28–29

Blue cornflower, 4

Blue-eyed grass, 155

Blue Steps, 34

Bog sage, 155

Borders, 93. *See also* Planting beds
  perennial, 155

Borrowed view, 12, 61, 77, 127

Bosco, 19

Bosquet, 23, 102

Botanical gardens, 20–21

Botany, creation of, 19

Boxwood, 8

Boxwood hedges, 91

Broad-leafed trees, 102

Brookes, John, 118

Brown, Jane, 144

Brown, Lancelot "Capability," 25

Building/landscape connection, 84

Bulbs, 155

Cacti, 51

Calcareous soils, 49

Calciferous soils, 52

California Frontier, The (Olmsted), 181

"California Glory," 144

California oak, 42

California poppy, 144–145

Camellias, 11–12, 34

Camperdown elm, 119

Carob, 4

Carpet bedding, 27, 86

Catmint, 15, 155

Central Park, 32

Cherries, flowering, 12

Chestnut trees, 151

Chinese gardens, ancient, 9–11

Chinese witch hazel, 37

Chipper debris, 177

Chrysanthemum, 11

Church, Thomas, 36

Circulation, 65–69

Circulation pathways, 11

Citrus trees, 16–17

Classical forms, 33

Clay soils, 50

Clients, discussions with, 140

Climate, 42–49. *See also* Microclimate
  environmental analysis drawings and, 47–49
  light and, 45–46
  moisture conditions and, 44–45
  plant modification of, 98
  temperature and, 43–44
  wind and, 46–47

Climate information, 44

Climbing plants, 156

Clipped box, 8

Cloister gardens, 14

Color, 131–139. *See also* Light
  defined, 112–113
  emotional effect of, 134–135
  juxtaposition of, 137–138
  physical, 133–134
  placement of, 138
  quality of, 135–139

Color harmony, 131

Columnar plant forms, 120–121

Communicativeness, 127

Composition. *See also* Plant composition
  command of, xiv
  of the planting design, 111–140

Composting, 184–185

Coniferous evergreens, 100

Conifers, 37, 102

Conservatories, 28

Construction, effect on soil, 172–173

Container-grown plants, 166–167

Container watering, 183

Contextual regionalism, 37

Contract growing, 167–168

Cool colors, 135-136
Cool-weather annuals, 154
Coral bells, 121
Coreopsis, 135
Corinthian columns, 5
Country Place Era, 34
Courtyard gardens, 16
Courtyards, 2
Crabapples, flowering, 12
Cranbrook gardens, 152–153
Cranesbill, 155
Crosby Arboretum, 38
Crowe, Sylvia, 2, 83
Crown of a tree, 173
Cultural design modes, 2
Cypress trees, 17

Daisies, 19
Daisy chrysanthemum, 8
Date palm, 3, 17
de Beauvoir, Simone, 144
Deciduous trees, 100
Deep shade, 157
de Forest, Elizabeth, 57
de Forest, Lockwood, 57
Desert regions, 45
Design. *See also* Garden design;
    Landscape design
  artistic aspects of, 56
  components of, 112–118
  creating, 59-61
  criteria for, 61
  developing, 106–109
  evolution of forms in, xiv
  principles of, 118–139
  vocabulary of, xiv, 2, 36, 81–110
Design analysis, xiv
  of Folly Farm, 61–78
Design concept, xiv
  Chinese, 9
  establishing, 56–58
Design ideas
  exploring, xiv, 55–79
  transforming to reality, 61
Design program, xiv

determining, 59
Design with Nature (McHarg), 37
Discordant plant forms, 121
Disease control, 179, 186–187
Distance
  effect on scale, 117
  effect on texture, 130
Distant scenes, incorporating, 77
Donahue, Marcia, 96
Donnell Garden, 36
Downing, Andrew Jackson, 32
Drifts, 28, 106
Drought-prone regions, lawns in, 153
Drought-tolerant plants, 161
Dry conditions, plants for, 161
Dry garden, 12–13
Dumbarton Oaks, 33, 69–70

Eckbo, Garrett, 1, 36
Eclectic garden design, 27
Ecological communities, 42
Ecosystems, 42
  preserving, 37
Education of a Gardener, The (Page), 144
Edwardian gardens, 28–30
Egyptian gardens, ancient, 3–4
Ellis-Mahoney garden, 49, 53, 106–109,
    139, 145
  final design solution for, 108
  ground cover in, 152–153
  perennials in, 155
  plant choices for, 158–159
  plant list for, 165
  schematic drawing of, 107
  shrubs chosen for, 151
  trees chosen for, 146–147
Embarcadero (San Francisco), 172
Emotional effect, of color, 134–135
Emphasis, as a design component, 114–115
Engineering problems, plants as solutions
    to, 104–106
English gardens
  Edwardian, 28–30
  landscape, 24–27
  Victorian, 27–28

Environment
   analyzing, xiv, 41–53
   climate and, 42–48
   public awareness of, 32–33
   soil and, 48–53
Environmental analysis, 156–157
Environmental analysis drawings
   climate and, 47–49
   soil and, 53
Environmental movement, 37–38
Environmental relationships, xiv, 42
Environmental science, 37
Ericaceous plant community, 52
Erosion control, 104
Espalier, 89–90
Estate planting, American, 34
European gardens, medieval, 14–16
Evergreen boughs, 178
Evergreen clematis, 156
Evergreen oak, 19
Evergreen trees, 11–12, 100
Eyecatchers, 97

Fairchild, David, 171
Farrand, Beatrix, 33, 35, 53, 182
Feeding, 184–185
Ferns, 12, 101, 121
Fertilization, 177, 184–185
Field poppies, 4
Fig trees, 4
Figure-and-ground diagrams, 77–78
Filoli Garden, 75–76, 136–137
Filtered sun, 157
Fir bark, 178
Flannel bush, 144
Fleabane, 155
Flower gardens, Moorish, 16–17
Flowers
   in Chinese gardens, 11
   scented, 15
Flowery mede, 15
Fog, 102
   as a moisture source, 45
Foliage plants, beds of, 86
Follies, 97

Folly Farm
   axial conditions at, 63–64
   circulation at, 65–69
   design analysis of, 61–78
   diagrams of, 82
   figure and ground diagram of, 78
   garden plan at, 62
   geometric forms at, 69
   hierarchy of space at, 71–72
   points of transition at, 71–75
   primary axis at, 82
   public and private spaces at, 76–77
   rose garden at, 71–72
   structuring elements at, 75-76
Form, plant, 118–123
Formal Garden in England, The
      (Blomfield), 28
Francis, Mark, 63
French, Daniel Chester, 98
French gardens, formal, 21–23
Frequent watering, 161
Frost-hardy annuals, 154
Fruit trees, 89
   medieval, 15
Full sun, 157
Function, role in garden forms, 2

Garden architecture, 83
Garden ceiling, 88–89
Garden design, 2. *See also* Design;
      Landscape design
   art/nature concepts in, 17–20
   eclectic, 27
   hierarchy in, 71
Garden Design (Crowe), 2
Garden elements, structuring, 75
Garden figurals, 6
Garden floor, 85–87
Garden forms, cultural factors in, 2
Garden framework, 84
Garden hallways, 93–95
Gardening culture, Egyptian, 3
Garden magazines, 143
Garden of Hesperides, 57, 77
Garden openings, 91–92

Garden planning, American, 31
Garden rooms, 85
Gardens
    Chinese, 9–11
    circulation through, 65–68
    as cultural reflections, 2
    Egyptian, 3–4
    elements of, 81–110
    Greek, 4–6
    maintaining, xiv, 181–187
    medieval, 14–16
    microclimate elements of, 102–104
    planning, xiii
    planting, xiv, 171–179
    public versus private spaces in, 76–77
    Roman, 6–9
Gardens in the Modern Landscape
    (Tunnard), 37
Garden styles, 2
Garden walls, 89–91
Gates, as garden openings, 92
Gateway Garden of New World Plants, 57
Gazing ball, 95–96
Genius loci, 25, 57
Geometric gardens, 19, 34
Geometric plant forms, 19
Geometry, as a design tool, 69
Georgics (Virgil), 9
Germander, 121
Giardino segreto, 97
Ginger, wild, 101
Ginkgos, 106
Giocchi d'acqua, 97
Glades, 34
Golden Age of Landscape Architecture,
    36, 75
Golden chain tree, 147
Golden chain tree palisade (Folly Farm),
    73
Golden oleaster, 37
Golden section, 69
Grade, changes in, 23
"Grand tour" tradition, 25
Grapes, 19
Grass, 85

Gray foliage, 137, 151
Grecian laurel, 128
Greek classical ideal, 5
Greek gardens, ancient, 4–6
Green, range of colors in, 139
Greene, Isabelle, 111
Green manures, 184–185
Green-on-green plants, 23
Green theater, 97
Grid system, 69–71
Grottoes, 10–11, 102–103
Ground cover, functional requirements for,
    153
Groves, 34, 89, 102
Growing seasons, 46
Guilin River area, 10
Gunnera, 129

Ha-ha, 26
Hardenbergia, 156
Hardiness zones, 43–44
Harmonious plant forms, 121
Harris, Richard, 105
Hedgerous plant forms, 47
Hedgerows, 102–103
Hedges, 15, 93, 152
    as garden walls, 89–91
    Laurustinus, 19
    as structuring elements, 75
Hellebore, 52, 155
Herbaceous perennials, 34, 155
Herbaceous plants, 27
Herbals, medieval, 14
Herb gardens, 15
Hester, Randy, 63
Hestercombe, 29–30, 98–99
Hidcote garden, 135, 185
Hierarchy, in garden design, 71
Historical precedent, examining, xiv, 1–40
History of the Modern Taste in Gardening
    (Walpole), 24
Honey locust trees, 101, 129
Honeysuckle, 19
Horseradish tree, 4
Horticultural manuals, 150

Horticultural requirements, 156–162
Horticultural societies, 143
Hortus, 9
Hortus conclusus, 15
Hosta, 144
House lines, projection of, 29
House sitings, Roman, 8
Hue, defined, 133
Humanism, 17
Human scale, 115–117
Humidity, influence of, 45. *See also*
    Moisture
Humus, 50
Hunt, John Dixon, 2

Ideas, sketching, 58
Insect control, 179, 186–187
Inspirations, for the design concept,
    56–57
Integrazione scenica, 77
Irises, 12, 155–156
Irish yews, 75
Irrigation systems, 183–184
Italian cypress, 128
Italian gardens, Renaissance, 17–21
Italian stone pine, 128
Italian Villas and Their Gardens
    (Wharton), 28, 79
I Tatti, 122
Ivy, 9

Japanese anemone, 142, 155
Japanese Black Pine, 15
Japanese gardens, 13–15
Japanese maple, 15, 150
Japanese pagoda tree, 150
Japanese Red Pine, 15
Jashemski, Wilhelmina, 8
Jasmine vine, 156–159
Jekyll, Gertrude, 28–30, 34, 61, 124
Jie jing, 77
Jones, Fay, 38

Kawana, Koichi, 31
Kent, William, 25

Kentucky coffeebean tree, 150
Kiley, Dan, 36, 111
Koranic teaching, influence of, 16
Kostoff, Spiro, 3

La Foce, 87
Lamb's ears, 155
Land, stewardship of, 37
Landscape
    at Folly Farm, 66–68
    formal composition in, 33–34
    "reading," 43
Landscape architects
    as artists, 95
    plant choices by, 140
Landscape architectural history, 2
Landscape architecture
    axis in, 63
    design vocabulary of, 81
    modern American, 36–37
    seventeenth-century French, 21–23
Landscape/building connection, 84
Landscape contractors, working with,
    182
Landscape design. *See also* Design;
    Garden design
    American, 31–38
    Moorish, 16
Landscape for Living (Eckbo), 1
Landscape gardens, English, 24–27
Landscape Plants for Western Regions
    (Perry), 42
Laurel trees, 6, 8
Laurustinus, 52
Lavender, 19, 155
Lawn, 86. *See also* Ground cover; *Tapis
    vert*
Lawn clippings, 178
Leaf abscission (fall), 46
Leaf mold, 178
Leaves, surface quality of, 129
Le Nôtre, André, 22–23
Levi Plaza, 68
Light. *See also* Color; Sunlight
    color and, 131–132

conditions of, 45–46
requirements for, 157–161
Lin, Maya, 95, 97
Linden trees, 151
Line, 118–119
defined, 112
Litter, avoiding, 162
Live oak, 128
Local climate, 44
Loggias, 8, 19, 102–103
London plane trees, 151
Lorrain, Claude, 25
Lotus blossoms, 11
Loudon, John Claudius, 32
Louis XIV, 23
Lummis Garden, 152
Lutyens, Edwin, 29, 61

Madonna lily, 8, 15
Maiden's wreath, 155
Maintenance, 181–187
initial, 178–180
requirements for, 162
schedule for, 183
Maintenance manuals, 182
Mallow, 19
Man/nature relationship, 19
Manures, 184–185
Maple trees, 119
Mass
defined, 112
plant, 122–129
Matilija poppy, 91
Mayten tree, 129
Mazes, 34, 83, 97
McHarg, Ian, 37
Meadows, 83, 87
Meaning of Gardens, The (Francis and
Hester), 63
Medieval European gardens, 14–15
Mediterranean plants, 45, 127
Microclimate, 37. See also Climate
observing, 44
plant modification of, 98–102
Microclimatic requirements, 157

Mint, 15
Modern landscape architecture,
American, 36–37
Moist soil, 161
Moisture. See also Humidity; Water
changes in, 102
importance to soil, 51
requirements for, 161–162
Moisture conditions, 44–45
Monastery gardens, 14
Monastic libraries, 14
Monet, Claude, 141
Monkey Puzzle Tree, 37
Monterey cypress, 128
Monticello, 26, 77
Moon viewing pavilions, 10–11
Moorish gardens, 16–17
Moss, 12
Moss Garden (Bloedel Reserve), 75
Mountain View Cemetery, 32, 127–128
Mounts, 15
Movement, plant sequence and, 117
Mowing, 185–186
Mughal gardens, 16
Mulch, 51, 104, 176–178
organic, 184
Mulching materials, 177–178
Mustard plants, 143
Myrtle, 8, 17, 19

Native plants, 38, 42, 128, 161
Native soil configurations, 50
Natural landscape scenery, 33
Nature
English philosophy of, 26
mathematical interpretation of, 19
Naumkeag, 34–35
rose garden at, 68–69
New Zealand flax, 37
Noise control, 104–105
Nursery growers, relationships with, 173
Nursery sourcing, 167–168

Oak/savannah landscape, 42–43
Oak trees, 101

Oleander, 8, 106
Olive trees, 101, 146–147, 151
Olmsted, Frederick Law, 26, 32–33, 127, 181
Opium poppies, 4
Opluntis, villa of, 8
Orangery, 23
Organic plant forms, 127
Organ Pipe National Monument, 41
Ornamental grasses, 121
Ornamental shrubs, 34

Padua Botanical Garden, 20–21
Page, Russell, 144, 151–152
Palisades, 2, 91, 103
Palm trees, 151
Papyrus plants, 4
Parterre, 2, 22–23, 34, 71, 73, 86–87, 106
Parterre beds, 19
Parterre en broderie, 23
Partial shade, 157
Pastel colors, 135
Pastoral gardens, English, 24–27
Path. *See* Axis
Pathways, 87
Patios, 16
Pavilions, 10–11
Paving. *See also* Allées; Walkways
  material for, 85
  patterns of, 67–68
Pedestrian traffic, controlling, 105
Peonies, 34
People, role in garden forms, 2
Perennial borders, 29, 34, 155
Perennials, 106
  functional requirements for, 155
  herbaceous, 34
Pergolas, 18–19, 88–89, 95, 101, 103
Peristyle gardens, 7–8
Periwinkle, variegated, 37
Perry, Bob, 42
Persian garden carpets, 16
Photosynthesis, 45
Physical color, 133–134

Physical environment, role in garden forms, 2
Pineapple sage, 155
Pinecote Pavilion, 38
Pine needles, 178
Pine savanna landscape, 38
Pine trees, 11, 106
Pin oaks, 106
Plan drawing, 162–165
  of form and mass, 122–123
Plane trees, 5–6
Planning stage, xiii
Plant alliances, 42
Plant Book for Dumbarton Oaks (Farrand), 182
Plant choices, hierarchy of space and, 71
Plant collage, 145, 149
Plant collecting, 24, 27–28
Plant combination, harmonious, 118
Plant communities, 42–43
  effect of wind on, 46–47
Plant composition. *See also* Composition
  design principles of, x
  developing skill in, 140
  elements of, 112–118
Plant details, 166
Plant explorations, 26, 33
Plant growers, working relationships with, 168
Plant hardiness zones, 43–44
Plant identification, 53, 142
Planting
  naturalistic, 28
  sequential, 144
  visual connections and, 77
Planting beds, quadrangle, 17
Planting design, 83. *See also* Design; Landscape design
  American, 33
  as an art and a science, xiii
  complexity of, 42
  composing, xiv, 111–140
  historic precedent in, 2
  importance of, ix
  Japanese, 12

lack of proficiency in, x
modern, 36
planning stage of, xiii
process of, x, xiv–xv
Planting Design (Robinson), x
Planting hole, 175-176
Planting methods, 175–178
Planting notes, 160, 166
Planting plan, 145, 149, 162–167
Planting stock, quality of, 173–174
Planting time, 174–175
Plant list, 165
Plant massing, 26, 123–128
Plant options, researching, 142
Plant origins
  learning, xiv
  understanding, 2
Plant palette, 131
  criteria for choosing, 142
  developing, xiv, 141–168
  researching, 144
Plant palette chart, 146–148, 158–159
Plant placement, 175
Plant requirements, 145–156
  grouping, 145
Plants. *See also* Vegetation
  aesthetic effects of, 95–98
  architectural framework of, 84–95
  climate modification by, 98
  as a design device, 11
  dominant line of, 118
  form and function of, 84–106, 121–123
  hardiness of, 43
  monitoring, 186
  photographing, 143
  role in Greek architecture, 5
  role in modifying microclimate,
    102–104
  sketching, 118
  as solutions to engineering problems,
    104–106
  sound mitigation by, 104–105
  stimulating effect of, 95
  use in announcing transitions, 71–75
  as visual regulation, 104

Plant selection, x, 142
Plant size, specifying, 166–167
Plant spacing, 165
Plant symbolism, 6
Plant uses, historical, 2
Pleached walkways, 93–94, 100–101
Plum tree, flowering, 12
Polesden Lacy, 135
Pollution control, 105–106
Pomegranate, 4, 6, 19
Pompeiian gardens, 6–7
Pools, as a design device, 10–11
Pope, Alexander, 58
Poppies, 4
Pore space, 51
Poussin, Gaspard, 25
Primary colors, 134–135
Privacy, creating, 104
Private gardens, medieval, 14–15
Private space, 76–77
Proportion, as a design component,
  114–115
Prospect Park, 32
Pruning, 179, 185–186
  effect of, 130
Public space, 76–77

Quaternary colors, 134
Quince, 12
Quincunx, 19

Rainfall, 102
Redwood trees, 101, 121
Reef Point, 34
Reflection Garden (Bloedel Reserve), 75
Regular watering, 161
Relative proportion, as a design compo-
  nent, 114–115
Relative scale, 115, 117
Renaissance, influence of, 17
Renaissance Italian gardens, 17–21
Repetition, as a design component,
  114–115
Repton, Humphrey, 25, 32
Research. *See* Nursery sourcing

Rhododendrons, 34, 106
Rhythm, as a design component,
    114–115
Riggs, Lutah Marie, 57
Rills, 16, 98–99
Robinson, Florence Bell, x, 41, 49–50
Robinson, William, 28
Rocks, as a design device, 11
Roman gardens, ancient, 6–9
Roots
  examining, 173–175
  growth of, 50
Rose, James, 36
Rosemary, 21
Roses, 15
Rue, 15
Russian sage, 134

Saarinen, Eero, 142
Sage, 15, 134, 155
Salvia, 108, 155
Sandy soils, 50
Santa Barbara Botanic Garden, 144–145
Scale, as a design component, 115–117
Schematic drawings, 59–60
Sculptural plants, 37
Sculpture, garden, 98–99
Seasonal color combinations, 132–133
Seasonal effects, 156
Seasons
  effect on light, 46
  effect on texture, 130
Secondary colors, 134
Secret gardens, 97
Sequence, as a design component,
    116–117
Serpentine wall, 91
Shades of color, 133
Shadows. *See also* Light
  as color dimmers, 138
  functional use of, 160
Shakkei, 12, 77
Shaw Arboretum, 98–99
Shelterbelts, 46, 102–103
Shrub borders, 151

Shrubs
  deciduous, 100
  functional requirements for, 151–153
Siberian bugloss, 155
Simplicity, as a design component,
    116–117
Site planning, Greek, 5
Sites
  analyzing, 47–48
  character of, 57
  inventory of, 59–60
  preparing, 172–173
Sketchbooks, 58, 118–119
Smoke tree, 135
Snow, as an insulator, 102
Soil, 49–53
  chemical structure of, 52–53
  composition of, 42
  determining the pH of, 52
  environmental analysis drawings and,
    53
  mineral content of, 52–53
  moist but not wet, 161
  physical structure of, 49–51
  requirements for, 161–162
Soil aggregation, 50
Soil amendment, 173, 185
Soil analysis, 52–53
Soil configurations, native, 50
Soil density, 50
Soil erosion, 104
Soil horizons, 50
Soil profile, 50
Soil-testing kits, 52
Soil-testing labs, 53
Sound mitigation, role of plants in,
    104–105
Space
  determining hierarchy of, 71
  plant massing and, 127
  public versus private, 76–77
Spanish gardens, 16
Specimen plants, 26, 98
Specimen trees, 108
Spirn, Anne, ix

Spraying, 179
Square grid, 70
Steele, Fletcher, 34
Stourhead, 25
Strawberry trees, 21, 52
Style, defined, 2
Succulents, 51
Sullivan, Chip, 58
Summer Palace (Beijing), 10
Sun, seasonal movement of, 143
Sunken Garden, 152, 153–154
Sunlight, 45–46. *See also* Color; Light
  effect on design, 160
  plant modification of, 100–102
Sunshine, color changes in, 135
Survey drawings, 47
Swan Hill foliage, 151
Sycamore trees, 5, 17, 23
Symmetry, as a design component,
  116–117

Taoism, influence on garden forms, 9
Taper, 173
Tapis vert, 23, 86–87, 106
Temperature, plant selection and,
  43–44
Terraces, 19, 87
Tertiary colors, 134
Texture
  defined, 112
  as a design characteristic, 129–131
  effect on color, 138
  studies in, 131–132
Three-tiered planting concept, 127
Tints, defined, 133
Tomb architecture, 3
Topiary, 19, 23–24, 33, 98
  Roman, 8
Topography, effect on climate, 46
Traffic control, 105
Transition points, 71–75, 91
  plant forms and, 122
*Treatise on the Theory and Practice of
  Landscape Gardening Adapted to
  North America* (Downing), 32

Tree peony, 11
Trees
  allées of, 3
  colonnade structure of, 76
  functional requirements for, 147–148
  grafting of, 15
  grid of, 69
  size of, 150
  staking, 176
  as structuring elements, 75
Treib, Mark, 36
Treilliage, 91, 108
Trelliswork, 91–92, 104
Tunnard, Christopher, 37

United States Department of Agriculture
  (USDA), 43–44

Val Verde, 31
Variegata, 37
Variegated plants, 37
Variety
  as a design component, 116–118
  in plant masses, 127
Vaux, Calvert, 32
Vegetable gardens, medieval, 14–15
Vegetation. *See also* Plants
  light intensity and, 46
  pollution control by, 106
Vehicular traffic, controlling, 105
Verbascum plants, 129
Versailles Palace, 21–23
Viburnum, 8
Victorian gardens, English, 27–28
Villa Bozzolo, 65
Villa Farnese, 18
Villa Gamberaia, 130
Villa gardens, 18–21
Villa Lante, 97
Villa Medici, 18–19
Villa Ruspoli, 18–19, 84
Villas, English, 30
Villa suburbana, 8
Villa Uzzano, 19
Vines, 156

Violets, 15
Visual regulation, plants as, 104

Wakehurst Place, 26
Walker Art Center, 150
Walkways, pleached, 94, 100, 103. *See also* Allées
Walpole, Horace, 24
Warm colors, 134–135
Warm-season annuals, 154
Water. *See also* Moisture; Watering
  in English gardens, 26
  in French gardens, 23
  in Moorish gardens, 16
  movement of, 12
Water erosion, 104
Watering, 159, 178–179, 183–184
  after planting, 173
"Water game," 95–97
Water mirrors, 23
Wave Field (Lin), 95
Weeding, 186
Weeping cherry trees, 76
Weeping European spruce, 37

West Lake, 98
Wharton, Edith, 28, 81
When Things of the Spirit Come First (de Beauvoir), 144
Wild Garden, The (Robinson), 28
Windbreaks, 47, 102–103
Wind conditions, 46
Wind control, 100
Windmill palm, 37
Witch hazel tree, 131
Wood and Garden (Jekyll), 127
Woods, geometric, 24
World Was My Garden, The (Fairchild), 171

Xeriscape Gardening, 177

Yellowstone National Park, 35
Yosemite National Park, 35
Yoshino cherry tree, 151

Zen Buddhism, influence of, 12
Zen Garden (Bloedel Reserve), 31